Jonath... Swift: An Introductory Essay

Jonathan Swift
An Introductory Essay

DAVID WARD

METHUEN & CO LTD
11 New Fetter Lane, London EC4

First published 1973
by Methuen & Co Ltd
11 New Fetter Lane London EC4P 4EE
© *1973 David Ward*
Printed in Great Britain by
Richard Clay (The Chaucer Press), Ltd
Bungay, Suffolk

SBN 416 76470 3 Hardback
SBN 416 76480 0 Paperback

Distributed in the U.S.A. by
Harper & Row Publishers, Inc.
Barnes & Noble Import Division

For C. J. Rawson

Detur Dignissimo

Contents

Passages of Swift's prose are quoted from Herbert Davis's edition of *The Prose Works of Jonathan Swift*, 14 vols., Oxford, 1939–64. Verse is quoted from *Poems of Jonathan Swift*, edited by Harold Williams, Oxford, 1958.

I
Introduction

George Saintsbury wrote of the peace of the Augustans; another well-worn phrase describes the period as the Age of Reason. But the age of the Augustans was a muddled, insecure and unhappy one, and its greatest writers wrote some of their finest works out of a deep sense of the insufficiency of reason alone as a guide to man. The idea of order was of the first importance to Swift and his contemporaries, but (and this is the real reason why they were so insistently explicit about the need for it), order seemed far more distant and unattainable to them than it did to the writers of either the preceding or succeeding ages. There is a far more achieved sense of order (though no less a consciousness of terror in chaos) in Shakespeare, Donne or Jonson than there is in Swift or Pope. There is a great deal in common between the Romantic idea of Imagination and the Augustan concept of Wit: perhaps the most important difference is the trust of a Blake, a Coleridge or a Wordsworth that the Imagination is itself the principle of order, a force which is capable of harmonizing the universe.

It is as if the Augustan age, by giving such prominence to order as a virtue, forced its imaginative writers on to the defensive. They are not, as Shakespeare, Donne, Blake or Wordsworth might be, called upon to define the peace which lies on the other side of chaos – society believed, with too much confidence, that it had the definitions at its fingertips already. Instead, the writer has to fight the barbarians at the gates – or rather wage the war street by street, house by house right through the city itself. In the hugger-mugger of hand-to-hand fighting we can forget what the battle is for, and sometimes, in for instance the *Dunciad* or *A Tale of a Tub*, the modern reader (and perhaps many of Swift's contemporaries) can become so caught up in the bewildering detail of contemporary controversy that he loses sight of the total aim.

It is impossible to understand Swift fully without some knowledge of the world he lived in. In all his works Swift took a controversial stand, arguing for or against a religious or political viewpoint, a partisan attitude in literary or philosophical quarrels, or for immediately practical causes such as the campaign to get Ireland to boycott Wood's debased coinage. However, it is also possible to lose sight of Swift's work by immersing oneself too deeply in the background to it. In this book there will be no attempt to give a detailed account of any of the topical issues to which Swift refers. Nor will we be concerned with biographical puzzles such as the medical history of Swift or whether a marriage with Esther Johnson was ever contracted – there's quite enough of this kind of thing cluttering library book-shelves already. Some reference to the background will be necessary: on one very important level even *Gulliver's Travels* is a commentary on a particular historical situation. However, *Gulliver* and the other great satires go far beyond the immediate subject, unlike Swift's non-ironic prose writings, which have very little application outside his own time.

His greatest satires are frequently those in which it is most difficult to determine precisely what his controversial stand is. They go beyond the immediate target, and question in the most profound way the disorders and insecurities of the social world and the human animal. In these cases the satire is so thorough that the writer himself is not excepted from the questioning process: if all humanity is under attack it is not legitimate for the satirist to exempt himself. Sometimes, therefore, it is difficult to find anything positive to hold on to in Swift's most thoroughly questioning moments, and one is tempted to react too hastily in one of two ways: either to condemn Swift for being entirely negative or to search too anxiously for a positive moral, on the grounds that one cannot allow as great a writer as Swift to be so condemned. Both reactions, I think, hinder us from understanding Swift. The vast majority of his writings are the work of a man of action, positive, practical and immediately purposeful, as are the Drapier's letters. The works in which he comes closest to a positive statement of his faith, like 'The Sentiments of a Church of England Man', are deliberately unadventurous, confined to ways and means of tackling superficial symptoms rather than the disease itself. In most of his writings Swift, like his great contemporary Defoe, was concerned with the problem of survival in a hostile world. But whereas Defoe's heroes and heroines struggle to survive against nearly overwhelming external and material odds, Swift finds the real enemy within, in Man's nearly endless capacity to deceive himself. Therefore he distrusted and satirized mercilessly those who were always ready with great plans for a settlement of the world's ills. He was very energetic in campaign for piecemeal reform – beyond that, the only way he could see was a steady, continuous and thorough self-questioning. The ultimate source of the world's evils is in man, therefore man must be cured first.

The attitude is, of course, native to the Christian tradition; and even when Swift spills over from disgust at man's spiritual depravity to horror of the body, he cannot be accused of straying quite outside the Christian tradition, or at least one aspect of it. But he brings a quite unusual personal intensity to the horror, something which cannot be explained entirely by referring to the Pauline and Augustinian tradition, or excused by pointing out that in eighteenth-century England standards of hygiene were so low that the dirt and filth really were horrifying. Poems like 'The Lady's Dressing Room', 'A Beautiful Young Nymph Going to Bed' and 'Cassinus and Peter' display an aspect of Swift's personality which most of us would rather forget, a horrified obsession with natural physical processes which would be symptomatic of some dangerous problems in a child of six, but in a grown man and an ordained priest is evidence of a terrible and pathetic sickness. However, D. H.

Lawrence is slightly off target in his comment on this aspect of Swift:

> The mind has an old and grovelling fear of the body and the body's potencies. It is the mind we have to liberate, to civilize on these points. The mind's terror of the body has probably driven more men mad than ever could be counted. The insanity of a great mind like Swift's is at least partly traceable to this cause. In the poem to his mistress Celia which has the maddened refrain 'But – Celia, Celia, Celia s∗∗∗s' (the word rhymes with spits), we see what can happen to a great mind when it falls into panic. A great wit like Swift could not see how ridiculous he made himself. Of course Celia s∗∗∗s! Who doesn't? And how much worse if she didn't. It is hopeless. And then think of poor Celia, made to feel iniquitous about her proper natural functions, by her 'lover'. It is monstrous. And it comes from having taboo words, and from not keeping the mind sufficiently developed in physical and sexual consciousness.
>
> (D. H. Lawrence, 'A Propos of Lady Chatterley's Lover')

In fact Swift is not addressing his mistress in either 'The Lady's Dressing Room' or in 'Cassinus and Peter', in both of which poems the offending line occurs. Both are concerned with the ridiculousness of trusting in superficial appearances. In both poems the lovers, Strephon and Cassinus, are shocked out of their conventionally romantic amorousness by discovering that the unreal visionary mistresses whom they worship are like every other animal, human or otherwise. Swift ridicules the conventional love poem and the conventional literary lover by bringing them to that shocked realization. There can't be any doubt at all that Cassinus' extravagant dismay is the subject of the satire here, rather than Celia's animality (the very name Cassinus seems to be a diminutive formation from the Latin *cassus*, empty, null or void):

Think, *Peter*, how my Soul is rack'd.
These Eyes, these Eyes beheld the Fact.
Now, bend thine Ear; since out it must:
But when thou seest me laid in Dust,
The Secret thou shalt ne'er impart;
Not to the Nymph that keeps thy Heart:
(How would her Virgin Soul bemoan,
A Crime to all her Sex unknown!)
Nor whisper to the tattling Reeds,
The blackest of all Female Deeds.
Nor blab it on the lonely Rocks,
Where *Echo* sits, and list'ning, mocks.
Nor let the Zephyr's treach'rous Gale
Through *Cambridge* waft the direful Tale.
Nor to the chatt'ring feather'd Race
Discover Cælia's foul Disgrace.

'Cassinus and Peter', like 'Strephon and Chloe', is a plea that love and marriage should be built on firmer ground than romantic imaginings, that the lover should accept that his mistress is human in every way; sentiments which are worthy enough as far as they go, and of which we must all approve. But nevertheless there is a sickness underneath it all, which comes out more clearly in 'The Lady's Dressing Room' and 'A Beautiful Young Nymph' with their repetitive, anguished dwelling upon dirt and stink, presented with a furious insistence which quite drowns out the pedestrian moral:

On Sense and Wit your Passion found,
By Decency cemented round,
Let Prudence with Good Nature strive,
To keep Esteem and Love alive.
('Strephon and Chloe')

Here, Passion is merely something to be curbed and checked by Decency, Wit and Sense; Love is reduced to the chill temperature of Esteem. There is no sense at all that real decency, prudence and the rest are the products of love, and that passionate love is capable of the kind of sensitive responsiveness which is its own control, far more purposeful and constructive than simple Good Nature. The sickness goes far beyond an excessive interest in excrement; it is really a blindness to some of the possibilities of human life and emotion.

Swift was an emotional cripple, then, and his deficiencies disabled him from doing certain things. But it is quite idle to complain that he was incapable of some of the moral insights which make, say, Shakespeare, Blake and Lawrence great. None of these other writers was a perfect human being but they all, in their different ways, worked from the perception that humanity does not reach its proper fulfilment in simple obedience to the social codes of decency and moderation, and Swift was liable on occasion, perhaps when his mind was not fully engaged by what he was writing, to stop short at the socially acceptable ethical code. Shakespeare, Blake, Lawrence all, in their different ways, sought out a more passionate understanding of life as a whole; Swift's effort was always to secure freedom from passion, or at least a submission of passion to good sense. But if he had succeeded in eradicating passion, he would not have been capable of the satire (and would no longer have been capable of being human; something of the sort is recognized in the fable of the Houyhnhnms). The leading passion of his satire is, in his own phrase, *saeva indignatio*, savage indignation; but the thing which distinguishes *saeva indignatio* from wild and irresponsible contempt is compassion. When compassion is wilfully absent, as it is in 'A Beautiful Young Nymph', Swift can be despicable. He can also be wrong-headed, short-sighted or narrow-minded, and often is in his ephemeral writings on long-forgotten issues. But when he lashes the world most brutally for its depravity and destructiveness, the moral energy is indistinguishable from the compassion which informs it, and it is this compassionate satirical wrath which makes Swift live still for us.

In his satires Swift rarely makes this compassion explicit; it is implied most of all in the demands he makes of his readers. In the Preface to *The Battle of the Books* he satirically defines satire: 'Satyr is a sort of Glass, wherein Beholders do generally discover every body's Face but their Own; which is the chief Reason for that kind of Reception it meets in the World, and that so very few are offended with it.' This is not the only place where he pretends that his only wish is to hurt: in a famous letter to Pope (29 September 1725) he declares that 'the chief end I propose to my self in all my labors is to vex the world rather than divert it'. But satire simply to vex or offend would be the 'Timons manner' which he rejects in the same letter; a much graver kind of irresponsibility than merely to amuse the world. In the same letter he writes to Pope of his mock project for a treatise 'proving the falsity of that Definition *animal rationale*; and to show that it should only be *rationis capax*'. The real significance of this isn't in the denial that man is a rational animal, but in the assertion of faith that he is capable of choosing reason. We ought to qualify 'vex' and 'offend' with 'amend': in August 1725 he wrote exultantly to his friend Charles Ford, in a much more spontaneous and non-ironic vein, 'I have finished my Travells, and am now transcribing them; they are admirable Things, and will wonderfully mend the World'.

In short, Swift's satire is designed to shock the reader into a new awareness of himself, and of the follies and vices which he shares with the rest of mankind. In Swift, as in Franz Kafka, the reader is often the most important character in the book: in the third book of the *Travels* the reader follows Gulliver in his fantasies of the power and joy offered by immortality; like Gulliver he is allowed to enter into a state of vain illusion, and then suddenly is confronted with the reality of the Struldbrugs. As in, for instance, Kafka's *The Castle* it is the reader's habit of mind that is the real point of the experiment rather than the adventures of the protagonist.

Swift adopts many different strategies in his satire, but all of them have something in common. He dramatizes a human vice or folly in such a way that the reader can perceive the degree to which he himself may share it, but also gives the reader the opportunity to see the vice or folly for what it is. This involves the need to persuade the reader into a very special relationship with the writer on the one hand and what is written on the other hand. In his satires Swift usually affects to retire into the background and hand over responsibility to a *persona*. Many modern writers on Swift, perceiving this, have tended to exaggerate the consistency of his narrative technique in this respect; as Denis Donoghue says, Swift 'is not Flaubert or James'. Gulliver, for instance, shifts in his role many times in *Gulliver's Travels*: sometimes he is the sensible, moderate, even wise observer, sometimes the vicious and feeble figure who carries with him, everywhere he goes, all the follies and inadequacies of mankind. He is never important in himself, never the subject but the vehicle for moral questioning. He is never simply or completely a representative of reader, author or mankind in general, but always the means by which Swift manoeuvres the reader into a way of seeing the fiction, seeing himself and seeing humanity. Unlike Flaubert or James, Swift doesn't set out to make his *personae* human beings, more often than not he deliberately creates something less than human, to turn us back to look at our own humanity.

Let me take one example of this: *A Modest Proposal*. It cannot be said that this work will display the whole range of Swift's satirical method, but in many ways it shows Swift at his most characteristic. In particular, the note of compassion is inescapable in this brief, tightly organized and powerful satirical discourse. The note of compassion is so clear that it is tempting to stress it too much; but pity is so closely bound in with anger, and in so complex a way, that it is as well to begin by a note of warning. Swift is angry and irritated by the whole of Irish society for its apathy; he is also angry, perhaps out of embarrassment, perhaps out of a frustrated sense of order, with the beggars for being beggars. Swift is too closely involved in the problems he satirizes to be quite as detached about them as, perhaps, we would like him to be. In reading him we tend to universalize the occasion of the satire: there is no need, we might say, for footnotes about the condition of the Irish peasantry in 1729. The satire might equally well refer to the sufferings of the Biafran peoples at the time of their secession, or the misery of Bengal in the midst of famine, flood and war. But in such a reaction we are likely, unconsciously, to pick situations which we can do little or nothing about, and situations about which it is relatively easy for us to have simple and straightforward reactions. This is not the case with Swift's reactions to the sufferings of the Irish people. He was closely, passionately involved, and part of his involvement is his conviction that something real, something practical, *can* be done.

He chooses, therefore, a *persona* who is almost, but not quite, Everyman then or now: intelligent and rational, public spirited, and even, in certain ways, unusually far-sighted. More to the point, he chooses someone very like Swift, in that he is certain that something can be done about the situation.

But the *persona* is not quite Everyman, and not quite Swift; he is not entirely human. In his concern for the starving poor he has what looks at first like pity; but if it is pity, it is pity of the kind which a practical and unemotional man would feel for a suffering domestic animal, concern of the kind that a Houyhnhnm might have for a Yahoo – and even this breaks down at certain points in the argument. He lacks completely that instinctive respect for the value of human life which is an essential part of humanity.

There is no hint of this inhumanity in the first few paragraphs; until the beginning of the fourth paragraph there is no hint that this is not anything more than the opening of a forceful, non-ironic account of the distresses of an unhappy country, the preface to a worthy, perhaps rather unrealistic plan for the amelioration of distress. The first hint that there is something amiss is in the slightly pompous sentence:

> As to my own part, having turned my Thoughts for many Years, upon this important Subject, and maturely weighed the several *Schemes of other Projectors*, I have always found them grosly mistaken in their Computation.

One already has the sense here that the supposed author of the *Proposal* is claiming a little too much virtue and intelligence for himself, preening himself on his practicalness, but at the same time trying to use the detached, unemotional tools of calculation where they are entirely inappropriate. The phrase 'Schemes of other Projectors' helps to confirm the impression: anyone who has read the third book of *Gulliver's Travels* will know how Swift detested 'Projectors' and their 'Schemes', the solemn vanity with which men advance ill-founded plans for the reformation of the world, and the *persona* here is claiming that he has gone one better than all his rival projectors. Finally the word 'computation' suggests altogether too chilly an attitude towards what should, after all, be treated as a moral as well as an economic disgrace.

> It is true a Child, *just dropt from its Dam*, may be supported by her Milk, for a Solar Year with little other Nourishment; at most not above the Value of two Shillings; which the Mother may certainly get, or the Value in *Scraps*, by her lawful Occupation of *Begging*: And it is exactly at one Year old, that I propose to provide for them in such a Manner, as, instead of being a Charge upon their *Parents*, or the *Parish*, or *wanting Food and Raiment* for the rest of their Lives, they shall, on the contrary, contribute to the Feeding, and partly to the Cloathing, of many Thousands.

And yet, inhuman as the attitude is, Swift contrives to use only the simplest and most ordinary language: 'A Child, just dropt from its Dam' mimics the language of the farmer exactly. The only thing which sets it apart from the everyday speech of the country man is the word 'child' used instead of foal, kid, calf or whelp; the slight shock that this gives us (and we are quick to realize that it is neither a slip of the tongue nor a slighting jocularity) is fully exploited by what follows: we begin to understand why the word 'Computation' disturbed us.

At this point the *persona* makes bold claims for his own humanity and tenderness by saying how his scheme will prevent abortion and infanticide 'which would move Tears and Pity in the most Savage and inhuman Breast'. The effect

of this is to force us to wonder how such mutually contradictory attitudes can exist in one person, for it is still the
persona speaking; this is not an intervention of the author.
But, contradictory as the attitudes seem to be, it isn't un-
believable that one person could express both of them without
realizing the clash; on the contrary, it seems only too likely.
'It will prevent those *voluntary Abortions*, and that horrid
Practice of *Women murdering their Bastard Children*; alas! too
frequent among us; sacrificing the poor innocent Babes' –
the tone is no longer that of the prosperous farmer or tradesman, the amateur economist calculating the costs and the
profits of a new trading venture. It is instead that of the same
prosperous farmer, tradesman, amateur economist determined to show that he, too, has a social conscience, a respect
for human life, as society demands (even though he cannot
see how the claim is subverted by everything else he says).
The passage throws us back into an examination of our own
attitudes: the moral indignation which we ourselves show
over this issue or that; our own moral indignation at the plan
to turn children into meat for rich men's tables; the words
we ourselves use when we express our indignation. Are these
things really of a piece with our actions, our private system
of values, our whole way of life – or are they ways in which
we dress up our real motives to win public approbation and
self-respect?

We must not allow ourselves to think that it is the attitudes of the *persona* that are the prime object of the satire.
His postures are irreconcilable in the extreme. But it is only
because they are extreme that their irreconcilability seems
absurd. All that Swift has done is to take a way of thinking
that is, in general, perfectly acceptable in society, and to
push it to a logical conclusion, while at the same time
allowing the virtuous protestations which commonly accompany this way of thinking to remain more or less as they
usually are. This is one of Swift's most important devices:
we might call it the polarization of attitudes. The reader
is persuaded to look at the world from a strange new angle,
an angle which rapidly becomes intolerably uncomfortable.
The discomfort forces him to readjust by seeking to see the

same facts from a much more sane point of view at the same time: a kind of moral squint which one is forced to correct by making as clear choices as one can about how we are to see reality – what values one should give priority to, what habits of language and of understanding blur one's vision, what sympathies and insights one suppresses because they disturb our peace of mind too much. This is both to vex *and* to mend the world; to mend by vexing.

The language of the sixth paragraph mimics the language of the economist or political scientist of Swift's day; detached, logical, precise and uninvolved. It will not have escaped the reader's attention that the pamphlet attacks certain aspects of what we should today call colonialism – Swift got into trouble with the colonizing authorities several times for his subversive activities, though ironically he himself was a *colon*, a Tory, an ardent champion of the limited Monarchy, and one of the stoutest defenders of the Established Church in the whole of Irish and English history. The paragraph satirizes the lordly detachment with which the Englishman or even the assimilated Irishman views the situation of Ireland from his comfortable armchair, even if he is in Ireland in the midst of all the distress and poverty, reducing individual pain and degradation to figures which can be added, subtracted and multiplied. But the attitudes satirized are not peculiar to the colonialist. Statistics, like any other method of sociological generalization, may help us to make judgements and decisions which could not so surely be made on the basis of immediate personal experience; but they can equally be a refuge for those who wish to escape from the emotional and moral demands of personal experience.

Swift pushes the logic of computation to the extreme, and at last submits it to the test which has been hinted at ever since the beginning of the third paragraph. We may just possibly be able to accept the split in consciousness implied in 'The Number of Souls in *Ireland* being usually reckoned one Million and a half; of these I calculate there may be about Two hundred Thousand Couple whose Wives are Breeders'. 'Soul' is after all a conventional figure of speech (synec-doche) for a human unit, and so the clash with wives merely as 'breeders' is slightly muted. But even the most insensitive will be shocked into attention by this:

> I have been assured by a very knowing *American* of my Acquaintance in *London*; that a young healthy Child, well nursed, is, at a Year old, a most delicious, nourishing, and wholesome Food; whether *Stewed*, *Roasted*, *Baked*, or *Boiled*; and, I make no doubt, that it will equally serve in a *Fricasie*, or *Ragoust*.

It is the calm, yet busy industry of the *persona* which affects us so deeply, I think: the way he refuses to leave us at the word 'Food', but presses on, apparently oblivious to the terror, all the way through the cookery book to fricassee and ragout. It goes without saying that Swift *is* aware of the terror and the evil, and takes the most powerful possible means of making us aware of it too; but if it is true that he is a pessimist in his habit of stressing what is worst in human attitudes, it is also true that his insistence that we should become aware of the evil arises out of his own passionate commitment to the good. In 1709 he wrote to Archbishop King:

> I very much applaud your Grace's sanguine Temper, as you call it, and your Comparison of Religion to paternal Affection, but the World is divided into two Sects, those that hope the best, and those that fear the worst; your Grace is of the former, which is the wiser, the nobler, and the most pious Principle; and although I endeavour to avoid being of the other, yet upon this Article I have sometimes strange Weaknesses.

There is a note of irony even here, of course; not so much, I think, in the suggestion that optimism is the nobler principle – if Swift had not something of the optimist in him he would not have hoped that his *Travels* would 'wonderfully mend the World' – but in the idea that pessimism is necessarily a weakness. Swift employs pessimism as a weapon to scourge away the smug credulity of most optimists, just as he employs the language of evil – and the *persona* of *A Modest Proposal* is as evil as Adolf Eichmann – to make us fear the worst within ourselves. In *A Modest Proposal* the *persona* is wholly an optimist, albeit with a defective idea of what is best, and, as optimists will, habitually ignores the debit side of the account sheet in his scurrying haste to list the credits. The result is many painfully exact parodies of a certain kind of tortured reasoning, for instance:

> Men would become as *fond* of their Wives, during the Time of their Pregnancy, as they are now of their *Mares* in Foal, their *Cows* in Calf, or *Sows* when they are ready to farrow; nor offer to beat or kick them, (as it is too frequent a Practice) for fear of a Miscarriage.

But here the irony has other directions too, suggesting that in some ways the *persona*'s standards might even be the right ones from which to judge other men.

I suggested earlier that the *persona*'s attitude towards human kind is like the attitude a rational man might have for a suffering domestic animal – one which has a potential cash value, of course – but that even this measure of frigid pity breaks down from time to time. The most striking instance of this, perhaps, is a passage which begins with a dismissal of pessimists and pessimism, before going on to express attitudes so brutally insensitive that a rational man could not take them towards a domestic animal – though the implication is that many of us, in our daily actions, tolerate such attitudes towards human beings, and we must do to remain optimists:

> Some persons of a desponding Spirit are in great Concern about the vast Number of poor People, who are Aged, Diseased, or Maimed; and I have been desired to employ my Thoughts what Course may be taken, to ease the Nation of so grievous an Incumbrance. But I am not in the least Pain upon that Matter; because it is very well known that they are every Day *dying*, and *rotting*, by *Cold* and *Famine*, and *Filth*, and *Vermin*, as fast as can be reasonably expected. And as to the younger Labourers, they are now in almost as hopeful a Condition: They cannot get Work, and consequently pine

away for Want of Nourishment, to a Degree, that if at
any Time they are accidentally hired to common
Labour, they have not Strength to perform it; and thus
the Country, and themselves, are in a fair Way of
being soon delivered from the Evils to come.

It could be objected that Swift makes the *persona* speak
inconsistently here; after all, for the most part he is a
rational man, and a rational man would certainly shoot a
horse or a dog that was too old or too weak for its work,
rather than allow it to rot to death. But we should never
look for complete consistency in Swift's *personae*. They are,
as I have said, the vehicles by which Swift manoeuvres the
reader into a new way of seeing. When the vehicle abruptly
shifts the viewpoint as it does here the moral squint is
aggravated, and we are forced to begin work again to clear
our vision. It is, after all, true that more men are deliberately
brutal and destructive towards other men than they are to
animals, and that, for all of us, compassion for animals
is sometimes easier than compassion for other humans.
Swift throws the challenge at our feet, pretending to be the
optimist confounding the arguments of the pessimists, but in
fact demanding to know what possible grounds for optimism
there are if the old die like this and the young live like this.

Implicitly Swift gives some very practical partial solutions
in listing the plans which the *persona* rejects – taxing absentee
landlords, using home manufactures and so forth: the busy
practical man in Swift was never entirely extinguished, nor
was the optimist. But a far more ambitious solution can be
discerned in the whole strategy and habit of his satire – that
people should learn to see through their own lies. It would
seem to me that Swift's satires can all stand or fall by one
criterion only – whether or not they will help to achieve this
end.

II
A Tale of a Tub

Swift addresses *A Tale of a Tub* 'only to the Men of Wit
and Taste'. The phrase has a special ring about it; it be-
longs very much to its time; we have to ask what it
means.

'Wit' is a strange word, one of those words which shift
in value from age to age, multiplying the possibilities of
confusion of understanding between the ages. The *Oxford
English Dictionary* devotes more than fourteen tightly packed
columns to its various definitions, beginning with the very
comprehensive set of meanings it had in Anglo-Saxon usage,
when it could mean the faculty of thinking, the understanding, the intellect or reason. The word gave ground to its
competitors over the centuries, surrendering parts of its
meaning to French and Latin importations like 'reason' and
'intellect', or newer English formations, like 'learning' and
'understanding'. Its meaning in popular usage today has
become very specialized indeed; now, for most people, it
means simply a sharp and humorous play with words. In
Swift's time it had not yet reached this narrow limitation of
function. The core of its meaning was, to quote the *O.E.D.*,
'that quality of speech or writing which consists in the apt
association of thought and expression, calculated to surprise
and delight by its unexpectedness'. But the word still
retained all sorts of overtones from its past that it now, for the
most part, lacks. And it acquired, for a brief period, a very
special significance, a resonance of meaning which made the
definition of the word almost as complex and difficult as a
definition of the culture of which it was part; the word had

become extremely closely identified with a cultural attitude, almost coterminous with it.

For this brief period 'Men of Wit' would suggest those gifted individuals who are quick to perceive the relationships between things and ideas which others would think to be unrelated; shrewd enough to cut their way through hypo- crisy, cant, irrelevant conventions, and see reality with a fresh, clear and amused eye. For a few decades in the seventeenth century the word carried with it rich overtones of the creativeness, playfulness, energy and deep seriousness of the human mind as adventurer and discoverer; at the same time it implied a demand for detachment and critical poise, wariness of the deceptions of the world (and of the mind's adventurous imagination too). But already, before the seventeenth century had ended, the view of life and the system of values which went with 'Wit' began to be challenged by an alternative view. This alternative view continued to gain ground, and has become the dominant view of life in our own twentieth-century world: it is the view of life which lies behind the scientific method. Locke, its great champion and theorist, develops a contrast between 'Wit' and ·'Judg- ment' in *An Essay Concerning Human Understanding* (1690):

> And hence perhaps may be given some reason of that common observation, that men who have a great deal of wit, and prompt memories, have not always the clearest judgment or deepest reason. For wit lying most in the assemblage of ideas, and putting those together with quickness and variety, wherein can be found any resemblance or congruity, thereby to make up pleasant pictures and agreeable visions in the fancy: judgment, on the contrary, lies quite on the other side, in separating carefully, one from another, ideas wherein can be found the least difference, thereby to avoid being misled by similitude, and by affinity to take one thing for another. This is a way of proceeding quite contrary to metaphor and allusion, wherein for the most part lies that entertainment and pleasantry of wit, which strikes so lively on the fancy, and therefore is

so acceptable to all people: because its beauty appears
at first sight, and there is required no labour of thought
to examine what truth or reason there is in it.

From the time of Locke onwards the concept of Wit
acquired more and more the air of rakishness and irresponsibility (though in truth it had never *entirely* lacked this
reputation, even in the days of Jonson or Donne). Locke
compares himself with 'an under-labourer . . . clearing the
ground a little, and removing some of the rubbish that lies
in the way of knowledge' so that the master builders,
scientists like Boyle and Newton, can work more easily.
But for some, like Swift and Pope, the 'rubbish' was worth
fighting for. Experiment, observation, measurement and
systematization of thought, though in one way not a jot less
creative than the free play of wit, encouraged scepticism of
traditional values. The great Wits of the age, among them
Swift and Pope, believed that Wit (which was the means by
which *true* judgement could be reached and enforced most
powerfully) depended upon tradition; and that Wit, dependent as it was upon the securities of tradition, stimulated
precisely that 'labour of thought to examine what truth or
reason there is in it' which is the essence of Locke's 'judgment'.

A Tale of a Tub is a work of Wit, then, written at a time
when men who valued Wit were beginning to feel insecure
about the meaning of the word, and what it represented, and
perhaps for this reason the defence of Wit became even more
challenging and assertive. *A Tale of a Tub* is certainly full
of challenge and reckless energy, but with a serious purpose:
to satirize 'the numerous and gross Corruptions in Religion
and Learning', and by doing so to direct his readers back to
what Swift felt were the real foundations of religion, of
learning and (what seems at this insecure time of the world's
experience almost to comprehend both religion and learning)
of civilized life.

The reckless energy of the work has impressed more of its
readers than are impressed by its serious purpose – and
sometimes this is true of readers who are in the fullest sense

of the words 'Men of Wit and Taste' like Samuel Johnson and F. R. Leavis. Leavis, for instance, believes that the only real positive in *A Tale of a Tub* is Swift's *superbia*, his insolent and savage egotistical self-assertion:

> Swift's intensities are intensities of rejection and negation; his poetic juxtapositions are, characteristically, destructive in intention, and when they seem most creative of energy are most successful in spoiling, reducing, and destroying.

For Leavis, the 'destructiveness' of the energy is inseparable from the personal animus against life in general: *A Tale of a Tub* is 'probably the most remarkable expression of negative feelings and attitudes that literature can offer – the spectacle of creative powers (the paradoxical description seems right) exhibited consistently in negation and rejection'. Samuel Johnson is a little less explicit in his hostility and puzzlement, but he speaks of 'this wild work', and remarks with obvious distaste: 'of this book charity may be persuaded to think that it might be written by a man of peculiar character, without ill intention; but it is certainly a dangerous example'. Like Leavis, Johnson doesn't attempt to deny the unique fertility, power and *energy* of the book; indeed, it is these qualities which make it so 'dangerous' an example:

> It exhibits a vehemence and rapidity of mind, a copiousness of images, and vivacity of diction, such as he afterwards never possessed or ever exerted. It is of a mode so distinct and peculiar, that it must be considered by itself; what is true of that, is not true of anything else which he has written.

Indeed, *A Tale of a Tub* is like a ride on a wild horse; one has neither rein nor saddle to give one the feeling of security or control: exhilarating, intense, absorbing and frightening, and one has to use every skill one has to keep one's balance. But it is neither egotistical nor insane; nor is it empty. Like Shakespeare, for whom, in one of his *dramatic* moods 'Life's but a walking shadow', Swift knew how to exploit fear of emptiness; he *knew* fear of emptiness, the terror of madness and despair. He *uses* the language of insanity, but consciously as a test of soundness of mind and heart, just as he deliberately uses the language of hypocrisy and cant to throw back the reader into re-considering the reality of things and his own attitudes towards them. The wild ride is to challenge one's security so profoundly that some means of control, some way of finding stability must be found. 'Never trust the artist, trust the tale,' said Lawrence; and though trust is hardly the thing one would think of bringing to *this* tale, trust in certain established and profound realities is at the centre of Swift's purpose. At first sight, in its copious energy and apparently chaotic arrangement, it's difficult to find a centre, but at last we find everything cohering around stability, sanity, intellectual integrity, poise and control; virtues associated in Swift's mind with continuity and tradition. At all times Swift's formidable satirical artillery is directed at the fashionable, the love of novelty for its own sake and delight in irrelevance and distraction; the vanity and self-centredness of fops, the conceit of pedantic scholars, Grub Street hacks, the silliness of passing religious follies, man's desperate inability to be serious about serious things.

Poise, sanity, self control and intellectual integrity do not exhaust the list of virtues – they are not even, perhaps, the most necessary to human completeness. I have already argued that there are ways in which Swift very strikingly lacks completeness; there are ranges of human feeling which he seems incapable of exploring; and perhaps his commitment to order and tradition are in some sort a consequence of his distrust of human emotions, his passion for balance evidence of imbalance in his passionate life. Nevertheless the implied virtues of *A Tale of a Tub* are real and substantial. The reader (the real subject of the book) is taken through a series of tests and challenges, and emerges (if he is not wholly thrown by the roughness of the ride) with a new awareness of folly, vice and madness, a new clarity of vision and a re-inforced desire for order and harmony.

The form of *A Tale of a Tub*, with all its elaborate machinery, is part of the satirical pattern, suggesting as it does the self-absorbed and scatterbrained energy of the author's *persona*; his inability (characteristic, as Swift would imply, of contemporary society) to hold straight to the point. But the apparently loose shape also gives an enviable freedom of manoeuvre; not that it allows Swift to digress – strictly speaking he never digresses from the essential point of attention, whether in dedication, preface, introduction, tale or 'digression'. However, it does allow him to speak with a variety of satirical voices. Just as the satirical form is in some ways loose, in other, more important ways, tight, so the shape, as it were, of the *persona* is in some ways loose and in some ways tight. At times Swift affects to be the nonpareil of dullness and stupidity; at other times a voice which is recognizably his own breaks through the disguise with dry, sharp ironic effectiveness. There's no telling which voice will follow which and when; one has to remain on one's guard all the time. Perhaps the only rule is to look for the fickle, the ephemeral, the proud, self-preening and the lie, and to distrust the voice which recommends it or accepts it; to test every word by a standard of permanence, authority, stability and order.

Swift is so changeable in his guises that it is often difficult to tell where he stands precisely; Swift enjoys creating this kind of uncertainty, and exploits it to ambush the reader from time to time, as Leavis shows so well, choosing the Digression on Madness to illustrate the anarchy of values towards which, in his view, all the rest of the satire tends irresistibly. Certainly it's true that the Digression on Madness is the ultimate point of the satire; the focusing point of the total experience of the book, and it's also true that its ambush appears to leave us with the choice of being fools or villains, to damn sanity and praise the insane, and in all the restless movement of the irony to leave nothing for faith, hope or charity to feed upon. But it is part of a larger context: the whole tendency of the *Tale* is not to preach sanity at us but to cauterize silliness, and it is in this context that one must enter into the very strange but deliberate ambiguities of the Digression on Madness. Let us, then, trace the progression of the satire as it leads towards that point.

But Satyr being leveled at all, is never resented for an offence by any, since every individual Person makes bold to understand it of others, and very wisely removes his particular Part of the Burthen upon the shoulders of the World, which are broad enough, and able to bear it.

This, from the Preface, is a kind of declaration of war upon the reader in much the same vein as the more famous 'Satyr is a sort of Glass' which prefaces *The Battle of the Books*; forbidding the reader the most ready and natural form of escape. Like much, or most satire, it depends upon a calculated distortion. Of course the reader excepts himself from the satire in one sense, but in doing so he may be adopting the position of critical detachment towards the world (and towards himself) which is necessary if he is to co-operate with the satirist; detachment of *that* kind does not mean that the reader excuses himself from the processes of satirical surgery – indeed the surgery can't be effective without some measure of anaesthesia. And, if the satire is to be successful, something like this must also be true of the satirist: if Swift were to exclude *himself* from the satire, that would be egotism indeed; but if he were to accept too intimate an involvement, he would lose control. Most critics of the *Tale* accuse Swift of one or other of these two errors; either he is the insane egotist lashing others for his own unrecognized diseases of mind and spirit, or he is so overwhelmed with the experience of sickness that he loses the capacity for articulate communication, and collapses into chaos and madness.

I would contend that Swift avoids both these dangers; that in leading the reader into such a dangerous state of doubt and discomfort he is recording and expressing his own deepest self-questionings; while appearing to condemn curiosity and praise credulity he is in his least credulous, his most probing and questioning mood; pushing himself and his reader to the point where a comprehensive revaluation of experience and understanding becomes urgently necessary. And while he is doing this he remains critically aware of all that he is doing.

The satire proceeds from fairly simple and bland forms to the more anguished and disturbing ironic modes. For instance, the list of treatises written by the same author appears at first to be relaxed and amiable buffoonery at the expense of self-satisfied pedants and hack writers, and the age's habit of confusing the large and the trivial:

> A Character of the present Set of *Wits* in this Island.
> A Panegyrical Essay Upon the Number THREE.
> A Dissertation upon the principle Productions of *Grub-street*.
> Lectures upon a Dissection of Human Nature.
> A Panegyrick upon the World.
> An Analytical Discourse upon Zeal, *Histori-theo-physi-logically* considered.
> A general History of *Ears*.

Each mock title touches upon a particular aspect of the triviality of the age: the *soi-disant* wits, the Rosicrucian fad, Grub Street hacks, the fashionable attitudes of the Royal Society and the new science, philosophical optimism, puritanism; but after the comically deflating 'general History of *Ears*' the direction of the satire changes, leading us from the particular to the general, and incidentally anticipating *Gulliver's Travels* in a very pointed way:

> A modest Defence of the Proceedings of the *Rabble* in all ages.
> A Description of the Kingdom of *Absurdities*.
> A Voyage into *England*, by a Person of Quality in *Terra Australis incognita*, translated from the Original.
> A Critical Essay upon the Art of *Canting*, philosophically, physically, and musically considered.

The introduction of the mythical gentleman from the unexplored southern continent (Terra Australis incognita) nudges us into a detached and critical frame of mind, especially when it is so closely linked with the Kingdom of Absurdities – what other kingdom could that be but Swift's

England? The absurd kingdom and its 'Australian' observer are caught between rabble and cant, and follow after triviality, obscurantism and pomposity: we are taught to look with a wondering and sceptical eye upon all that follows.

THE DEDICATIONS

The first dedication, to Lord John Somers, nicely combines the conventionally hyperbolic tribute to a patron (inevitable in an age when the chief benefit of literary industry was some kind of preferment) with general satire on human self-conceit; particularly upon the vanity of false Wits. It's characteristic of Swift that he should combine these two purposes in the form of a lively little fable: his satirical activity invariably involves the setting up of a standard against which the vanity and ephemerality of the world can be measured. The greatest tribute he can make to Somers is to identify him with that necessary standard.

If the first dedication uses a real man to represent an ideal standard, the second dedication playfully personifies an abstract ideal standard: the invention of the infant Prince Posterity, attended by his Governor Time, is a device which invites the reader to stand back from his own time, and see all its feverish activity in a larger context. The *reader* is required to do this, but it's essential to the satiric method that Swift (or his *persona*) should pretend not to be capable of doing so: Swift impersonates the unsuccessful writer, who, failing to satisfy his contemporaries, comforts himself that future readers will be more perceptive. So Swift speaks to us simultaneously with two voices: through the *persona* he mimics the absurdity and inadequacy of a certain sort of representative writer; by means of the concealed ironic voice he makes us step back from the absurdity as if we were able to look back upon it from a hundred years hence.

The most important tool for achieving this double voice is parody: he catches exactly the conventional defensive rhetoric of the inadequate hack. Inevitably the parody is in a rather antique mode: Swift normally avoided elaborate devices of rhetoric and fancy metaphysical metaphor; they were rapidly becoming out of date, anyway; but here he uses the obsolete heroic mannerisms freely to mock his *persona*'s attitude:

> You may be ready to expostulate with Your *Governour* upon the Credit of what I here affirm, and command Him to shew You some of our Productions. To which he will answer, (for I am well informed of his Designs) by asking *Your Highness*, where they are? and what is become of them? and pretend it a Demonstration that there never were any, because they are not then to be found: Not to be found! Who has mislaid them? Are they sunk in the Abyss of Things? 'Tis certain, that in their own Nature they were *light* enough to swim upon the Surface for all Eternity. Therefore the Fault is in Him, who tied Weights so heavy to their Heels, as to depress them to the Center. Is their very Essence destroyed? Who has annihilated them? Were they drowned by *Purges* or martyred by *Pipes*?

Notice how the passage, after approaching a Miltonic eloquence of gesture (though it overplays as Milton never would have done) is deflated by the word-play of *Purges* and *Pipes*. Political purges were then, as they are now, executions of political undesirables; but these papers are to be used for hygienic purposes in privies, and drowned by purges of the bowels. Heroic martyrs have been burned at the stake in their hundreds; these paper martyrs are fated to be spills to light tobacco pipes.

After the sixth paragraph the manner of the satire changes slightly from mock-heroic declaration to injured puzzlement. Notice how the changeableness of the age and the ephemerality of its literature is expressed by an adaptation of Shakespeare; from *Hamlet* and *Antony and Cleopatra*:

> *Hamlet:* Do you see yonder cloud that's almost in shape
> of a camel?
> *Polonius:* By the mass, and 'tis like a camel indeed.
> *Hamlet:* Methinks it is like a weasel.

> *Polonius:* It is backed like a weasel.
> *Hamlet:* Or like a whale?
> *Polonius:* Very like a whale.
>
> (*Hamlet*, Act III, sc. 2)

> Sometimes we see a cloud that's dragonish;
> A vapour sometime like a bear or lion,
> A tower'd citadel, a pendant rock,
> A forked mountain or a blue promontory
> With trees upon't, that nod unto the world
> And mock our eyes with air.
>
> (*Antony and Cleopatra*, Act IV, sc. 14)

The similarities between these passages and Swift is not mere accident, nor is it simply a matter of Swift picking up a handy metaphor:

> So that I can only avow in general to *Your Highness*, that we do abound in Learning and Wit; but to fix upon Particulars, is a Task too slippery for my slender Abilities. If I should venture in a windy Day, to affirm to *Your Highness*, that there is a large Cloud near the *Horizon* in the Form of a *Bear*, another in the *Zenith* with the Head of an *Ass*, a third to the Westward with Claws like a *Dragon*; and *Your Highness* should in a few Minutes think fit to examine the Truth; 'tis certain, they would all be changed in Figure and Position, new ones would arise, and all we could agree upon would be, that Clouds there were, but that I was grosly mistaken in the *Zoography* and *Topography* of them.

Antony and Hamlet are of heroic proportions; in their desperate suffering, their inner world collapsing, they project their own sense of personal unreality on the world around them. Swift's *persona* is anything but heroic, and we have no interest at all in his inward problems: it is *really* the outside world that is collapsing – while Hamlet pretends to be mad Swift's puppet pretends that he is sane and that his world is sane. The reminiscence of Shakespeare is a kind of ironic reversal, but there's another element to the irony, too. The reference to Shakespeare, with his undeniable strength and permanence, provides, in passing, another standard by which the frivolity and impermanence of the present world may be measured.

PREFACE

The *Tale* is addressed 'only to the Men of Wit and Taste', and it already becomes clear that true Wit and Taste must involve a recognition of the failure of contemporary civilization to measure up to certain precious standards of Wit, of Judgement, of stability and permanence. But as part of his strategy, Swift must take advantage of the detached, ironical viewpoint he has cultivated in the reader in order to satirize the pretensions of those who pass as 'Wits' in his own day, while at the same time encouraging true men of Wit to look with a cool ironical eye at all that goes on in their society. The irony opens up the distinction between true and false Wit, encouraging the reader to make clear distinction between the two.

He hits upon the device of pretending to be the great defender of things as they are, the champion of church and state against the rebelliously critical spirit of Wit, employed by government to neutralize Wits by a diversionary tactic. Hence the conceit which gives its name to the book: the tale as a tub thrown out to distract the attention of 'the terrible Wits of our Age' (comically transformed into a whale) away from their proper task of social, religious and political criticism. Of course there is another level to the irony here. The true man of Wit is not distracted from his purpose by such a manoeuvre, though the *soi-disant* 'Wit' might be; further, the irony constantly calls attention to the holes in the side of the ship of state and church, nudging the true man of Wit in us to look and judge. Lastly, Swift constantly reinforces his definition of true Wit and mocks the cheapjack impotence of the false. The comic project for an Academy of Wits, as busy and pretentious as the fashionable Royal Society seemed to be to Swift and some of his friends, is a way of detaching true Wit from the fashionable absurdities which are so often identified with Wit by a superficial social world.

Swift bids us, as 'Men of Wit and Taste', to see things as they really are, not as they appear to be '*today*, or *fasting*, or *in this place*, or *at eight a clock*, or *over a Bottle*, or *spoke by Mr. What d'y' call'm* or *in a Summer's Morning*: Any of which, by the smallest Transposal or Misapplication, is utterly annihilate'. It is the insecurity and vulnerability of the Modern manner which makes it false Wit, in contrast with the stability and poise of the true. 'Thus, *Wit* has its Walks and Purlieus, out of which it may not stray the breadth of an Hair, upon peril of being lost. The *Moderns* have artfully fixed this *Mercury* and reduced it to the Circumstances of Time, Place and Person.'

I. INTRODUCTION

Once again Swift uses an obsolete manner and style as a vehicle for satire: this time the affectations of the mid-seventeenth century pedant. References to Virgil, Aristophanes, Horace, Lucretius, Epicurus and other classical writers tumble over one another; the author affects to find great mysteries and complex significances round every corner, takes every occasion to puff his own forthcoming publications; shows a puppy-like delight in worrying away at his imagination until he has created a scheme, a system, or a discovery; uses always the most pompous words in his effort to impose his own sense of self-importance upon the reader:

> Now this Physico-logical Scheme of Oratorial Receptacles or Machines, contains a great Mystery, being a Type, a Sign, an Emblem, a Shadow, a Symbol, bearing Analogy to the spacious Commonwealth of Writers, and to those Methods by which they must exalt themselves to a certain Eminency above the inferiour World.

This kind of satirical effect is not disturbing because it is pretty obvious; even today we can recognize a certain type of modern scholarship in this, even though the vocabulary and aims of scholarship have changed so much over the years. But there are already aspects of the satirical manner which are less reassuring. As one reads *A Tale of a Tub* new side corridors appear all the time, opening up possible ironies off the main path, blind corridors and cul-de-sacs among the genuine routes. One is never allowed to be quite sure whether this or that ironic suggestion is intended, and this is one of the main sources of Swift's satirical power. He deliberately creates a feeling of insecurity in the reader: if one were to be allowed to feel sure that one had got to the bottom of the satire and understood it completely and in every way, it would not be so effective as it is. One possible reaction to this insecurity is to seize upon some evidence of heresy or moral turpitude in order to have an excuse to dismiss the satire as a whole; even if the pretext is misconceived (perhaps especially if it is misconceived) it will enable you to protect yourself from the effects of the satire with a comforting kind of moral indignation. Swift suffered from this process many times – sometimes, perhaps, justifiably, for one can still not be entirely sure of his meaning sometimes. Passages like the following are in part responsible for his failure to win a bishopric, and his exile to Ireland:

> But if no other Argument could occur . . . it were sufficient that the Admission of them would overthrow a Number which I was resolved to establish, whatever Argument it might cost me; in imitation of that prudent Method observed by many other Philosophers and great Clerks, whose chief Art in Division has been, to grow fond of some proper mystical Number, which their Imaginations have rendred Sacred, to a Degree, that they force common Reason to find room for it in every part of Nature . . . Now among all the rest, the profound Number THREE is that which hath most employ'd my sublimest Speculations, nor ever without wonderful Delight. There is now in the Press, (and will be published next Term) a Panegyrical Essay of mine upon this Number . . .

It's clear to us that in this passage Swift is satirizing the windy and self-important manner of certain clerics and scholars; but this wasn't quite so clear to many of Swift's

contemporaries. To many of Swift's contemporaries it
seemed uncertain whether Swift was tilting at a familiar
kind of cabalistic nonsense or mocking the way in which
Christian dogma and symbolism made such constant use of
the triad: faith, hope and charity, the three wise men, the
three crosses at the Crucifixion and particularly the Trinity
of Father, Son and Holy Ghost. Swift was obliged to explain
himself for this in the Apology which was prefixed to the
fifth edition, shifting the blame to those who had edited the
original version. Nevertheless there is no doubt that he was
playing a most dangerous game. Criticism of any one aspect
of religion as superstitious, ritualistic, pompous or irrelevant
has a way of reflecting on other aspects of religion, especially
in an age in which the drift towards rationalism and scepticism had set strong. Thus, the invention of the three wooden
machines for making one heard above the crowd is primarily
an attack upon Dissenters, who relied far more upon pulpit
oratory than either the Romans or the Anglicans. But,
even though Romans and Anglicans laid greater stress upon
ritual, they used the pulpit as well, and the satirical association of the sermon with the last speeches of murderers and
thieves and the performances of the notoriously loose-living
itinerant players was bound to make many people feel that,
for a Churchman, Swift was dangerously irreverent in his
attitudes.

SECTION II

Swift was by no means irreverent or irreligious, but his
pattern of faith depended very much less upon the comforting
formal structures of dogma and ritual than was common
among the Christians of his age. In the first sentences of the
Tale proper we have Swift's own statement of the foundations
of his belief and motivation, presented with the disarming
simplicity of a fairy-tale:

> Once upon a Time, there was a Man who had Three
> Sons by one Wife, and all at a Birth, neither could the
> Mid-Wife tell certainly which was the Eldest. Their

Father died while they were young, and upon his
Death-Bed, calling the lads to him, spoke thus:

The coats given to the three brothers by the Father – the
Divine Father – are the Christian faith: 'by the Wisdom of
the Divine Founder fitted to all Times, Places and Circumstances', as Swift remarks in his own note. In a word, the
truths of religion are absolute, unchanging, divinely given,
and therefore inaccessible to criticism. It follows that the
only possible aim of satirical criticism is to expose the way in
which individuals, groups and churches pervert the initial
truths through ignorance, folly, vice or ill-will. Swift's
satirical stance here is of a piece with his satirical stance
in other matters: Scholars, Hacks and Wits have all been
pilloried for their pompousness, frivolity and irrelevance,
their neglect of the essential things. Now the whole of the
satire becomes crystallized around the original truths of
Christianity: these are to be the great touchstone, the standard by which all backsliding, absurdity and misdirection
are to be measured. The will of the Father is to stand for the
truths which will last, whether religious, literary, human,
social, stylistic or whatever: and in Swift there is a very
intimate connection between literary, human, social and
stylistic excellence and religious truth.

The fairy-tale simplicity is an important part of the
strategy here. After struggling through the ornate ironic
complexities of the Dedications, the Preface, and particularly
the comic pomposities of the Introduction, we are at last in
clear air. Everything is straightforward, as it is in Aesop,
or in the fairy tales we remember from our childhood. The
naïve epic story of a heroic age is something which always
pleases our imaginations, and it is fitting that the three heroes,
like heroes in any good boy's tale, 'travelled thro' several
Countries, encountred a reasonable Quantity of Gyants, and
slew certain Dragons'. However, the offhand note of 'a
reasonable Quantity of Gyants' clearly signals the fact that
there's an irony at work here which doesn't belong to the
romance story. The great specialists in using the romance
adventure for the purposes of moral parable were the Dissen-

ting Preachers, particularly Bunyan. Swift must have known
Pilgrim's Progress, the great best-seller of his day, and there's
surely a deliberate reference to Bunyan's allegorical method
in the names of the brothers' three mistresses 'The Dutchess
d'Argent, Madame de Grands Titres, and the Countess
d'Orgueil', who represent covetousness, ambition and pride.
Swift pretends briefly that he is going to entertain us with the
kind of strong, simple, powerful moral fable that Bunyan
loved; but this isn't Swift's way; he hurries on as quickly as
he can to sharper, more acid forms of irony. Bunyan's allegory
has a country rhythm about it, slow, strong, clear, assured,
mounting inevitably towards an anticipated climax. Swift is,
like many townsmen, somewhat tricky and evasive at times.
And yet it is precisely the restlessness, the volatility, the lack
of a firm moral sense that he satirizes in the three brothers
and in the society of late seventeenth-century England. Bunyan fights fire with water, Swift fire with fire.

Consider, for instance, the difference between Bunyan's
and Swift's use of the Bible as a source for allegorical images.
In the image of the idol who is worshipped 'especially in the
Grand Monde, and among every Body of good Fashion . . .
who, as their Doctrine delivered did daily create Men, by a
kind of Manufactory Operation' the idol is a tailor, and one
of the means by which Swift pursues his satire against superficiality and love of novelty for its own sake. A considerable
part of the effect (grandly mock-heroic, with all its solemn
reference to *Jupiter Capitolinus* and the *Aegyptian Cercopithecus*)
comes from a concealed reminiscence of the Golden Calf
which the Israelites worshipped in their journey across the
wilderness, turning away from the common search for the
Promised Land until their leader Moses brings them back to
their true purpose. But unlike Bunyan, who converted biblical
images into material for a Christian epic, Swift uses the effect
of grandeur to subvert and mock absurd, evil and insane
attitudes: thus the supposed cult of the tailor is used to
pillory the insane volatility of fashionable society, and the
evil assumption which can lie beneath it that man, and life,
are to be judged only by superficial appearances. Observe
how Swift adopts the conventional manner of a contem-

porary sermon to express this, suggesting the way in which hypocrisy inevitably and unconsciously adopts the language of the pulpit as its natural dialect:

> To conclude from all, what is Man himself but a *Micro-Coat*, or rather a compleat Suit of Cloaths with all its Trimmings? As to his Body, there can be no dispute; but examine even the Acquirements of his Mind, you will find them all contribute in their Order, towards furnishing out an exact Dress: To instance no more; Is not Religion a *Cloak*, Honesty a *Pair of Shoes*, worn out in the Dirt, Self-love a *Surtout*, Vanity a *Shirt*, and Conscience a *Pair of Breeches*, which, tho' a Cover for Lewdness as well as Nastiness, is easily slipt down for the Service of both.

It would be absurd to complain of the unexpected crudeness of the final image: paradoxically it achieves a kind of elegance, rudely deflating all the hypocrisy and cant associated with the manner which is being satirized.

The parody of the manner of the sermon goes further still; Swift concocts his mock theology in terms which are borrowed from certain complex theological disputes which had set seventeenth-century divines at war with each other. The doctrine of traduction is that the soul of a man is transmitted to a man by his parents. Its opponents asserted that each soul is separately created and immortal, and therefore endowed by God at the time of creation, not through the parents at the time of conception. The debate was further stimulated by the recent invention of the microscope, and the discovery, by Antony van Leeuwenhoek, of the spermatozoon, or as he called it, animalcule (1679). Swift pretends to report yet another theory that, whereas the body is inherited from the parents, the soul, far from being immortal, is the most impermanent thing of all, the outward clothing of the body which can be put on and taken off at will:

> That the Soul was the outward, and the Body the inward Cloathing; that the latter was *ex traduce*; but the

> former of daily Creation and Circumfusion. . . . Be-
> sides, said they, separate these two, and you will find
> the Body to be only a sensless unsavory Carcass. By all
> which it is manifest, that the outward Dress must needs
> be the Soul.

The fact that scientific discoveries, and the debates which
followed them, at least partly stimulated the satire here, is
of some significance. Swift continued to find experimental
science a destructive and irrelevant force right until the end
of his career – the most obvious reference is to the Academy
of Lagado in the third book of *Gulliver's Travels* – and this
passage suggests some of the reasons for this hostility.
Leeuwenhoek, with his spermatozoa; Hooke, with his
observations on spores in moulds; Huygens, Malpighi and
other scholars were reducing the mystery of life to a mechanistic explanation: substance, the real and unchanging truth
which underlies all things, was being broken apart into a
complex of accidents, or so it seemed. Science, which to most
of us today seems to offer the most coherent account of
material reality (and one which, for most religious people,
is not inconsistent with their beliefs) seemed to be opening
the way to anarchy. Swift reacted by reasserting the permanence and transcendent importance of the soul and the
insignificance and triviality of outward appearances. It
would be as well for us to bear all this in mind as we approach
the Digression upon Madness, with its images of flaying the
woman and stripping the beau: madness, for Swift, was a
trust in outward appearances rather than the inward
essence, and scientific discovery was but one example of
the growing madness of the age.

III. DIGRESSION CONCERNING CRITICS

This is the first of the digressions, and shares with all the
other digressions the paradox that it is not truly a digression.
Criticism is simply one of the ways in which the essential
principles are now disregarded, and Swift has very little
trouble in summarizing the nature of the abused principles,

when he affects to dismiss the ideas which guided the ancient critics:

> by this Term were understood such Persons as invented or drew up Rules for themselves and the World, by observing which, a careful Reader might be able to pronounce upon the productions of the *Learned*, form his Taste to a true Relish of the *Sublime* and the *Admirable*, and divide every Beauty of Matter or of Style from the Corruption that Apes it.

The modern reader will be cautious, and rightly so, of the implications of this definition; since the late eighteenth century we have become progressively less willing to rely upon formulated rules for the judgement of literature and art, more circumspect about praising 'beauties' of matter and style. The process which has resulted in our caution is one of the things Swift is complaining about.

But we must be careful that we do not reject Swift's attitude because of the conventions of statement he was obliged to use: 'sublime', 'admirable', 'beauty', even 'rule' were words which were part of the neo-classic convention: we must judge the critic, not by the verbal conventions he accepts, but rather by the degree to which he is imprisoned or liberated by them. Essentially, Swift protests against one form of self-imprisonment in criticism; the critic's neglect of his positive functions, his determination to assert his own self-importance by destroying the work of others.

The *Tale* is itself a critical work – though its criticism is not simply of literature, but of religion, society and learning as a whole, and there is no doubt that Swift succeeds in keeping sight of his positive role as a critic throughout the work. He is far finer as a practising critic than as a theorist of criticism; but there is something about his definitions of criticism which indicates some of his own lacks as a writer and as a man. The following passage suggests very well the mixture of prim obsessive self-preservation and fascination with the disgusting which so often prevents Swift from clearing the streets of his own mind:

with the Caution of a Man that walks thro' *Edenborongh* Streets in a Morning, who is indeed as careful as he can, to watch diligently, and spy out the Filth in his Way, not that he is curious to observe the Colour and Complexion of the Ordure, or take its Dimensions, much less to be padling in, or tasting it: but only with a Design to come out as cleanly as he may.

A balancing act like this can only limit the mind and make it shrink away from a full awareness of life, and particularly the life of the body. But in the *Tale* there is another balancing act going on at the same time: one in which Swift sought to use the insanely negative as a way of defining the whole and good. This reminder of the need for critical responsibility comes at precisely the right time, just before the skilful parody of the superstitious excesses, absurdities and abuses which marred the development of the Church and helped to bring about the Reformation.

SECTION IV

Apart from its account of the failings of the Roman Church, the satire in this section has another aspect. It is an account of growing insanity, and a very accurate one too. Peter suffers from what we would today call paranoia. Peter is the Church, but he's also a pattern of the way men become so intoxicated with their own delusions and lies that they quite part company with the world of reality: '*Come Brothers*, said Peter, *fall to, and spare not; here is excellent good Mutton; or hold, now my Hand is in, I'll help you*. At which word, in much Ceremony, with Fork and Knife, he carves out two good Slices of the Loaf.' Of course this is meant to be taken as a satirical account of the Catholic doctrine of transubstantiation, but it is at the same time an account of the insane mind's flight from reality. '*Why, truly*, said the first, *upon more mature Consideration – Ay*, says the other, interrupting him, *now I have thought better on the Thing, your Lordship seems to have a great deal of Reason*' – the responses of Martin and Jack act out the way in which the egotism of the insane affects all around them; how weak mankind is in the face of the energy of madness.

In the context of seventeenth-century religious debate the passage must be seen as arbitrating between Faith and Reason. Swift takes the moderate, Church of England position, neither accepting the wild multiplication of articles of faith which was characteristic of the Roman Church nor the Deistical reduction of all faith by the critical demands of natural reason. But by using a fable like this Swift makes the passage refer not just to the insanity of institutions, but to the behaviour of men when they are cut off, or have cut themselves off, from the original springs of sanity.

V. A DIGRESSION IN THE MODERN KIND

Milton, late Latin Secretary to the Lord Protector Oliver Cromwell, had claimed himself ammanuensis to the heavenly muse. Swift, still affecting to be the great champion of modern literature pretends an even greater self-confidence in a rhetoric so vague and so unctuous that it conveys nothing but the desire to impress: 'This, *O Universe*, is the Adventurous Attempt of me thy Secretary.' The mock-epic inflation satirizes Temple's enemies in the battle of the Ancients and Moderns; so, in a way which is less obvious to the modern reader, does the invocation '*O Universe*' rather than an address to a Christian or a classical deity (like Milton's 'heavenly muse'). Both the Deists and contemporary scientists were rather too fond of this kind of grand abstraction; writers like Glanvill and Wotton were apt to speak of the scientists as 'Nature's secretaries'. Among their list of arguments for the superiority of Moderns over the Ancients were the modern discoveries about the human body: the Ancients knew about bone structure, the positions of the organs and so forth, but the Moderns had begun to understand how the body functions, for instance in the circulation of the blood. It would have been pointless for Swift to deny that there had been progress in this. He doesn't try, but walks round the issue to a more fundamental one. Man was becoming less and less interested in the spiritual nature of man, more and more interested in the material side; the process continues to the point where we hardly understand the division our ancestors made. But Swift finds cause to protest against the tendency to treat man merely as a material mechanism; he points to the anatomy of man's moral and spiritual health as our proper concern:

> To this End, I have some Time since, with a World of Pains and Art, dissected the Carcass of *Humane Nature*, and read many useful Lectures upon the several Parts, both *Containing* and *Contained*; till at last it *smelt* so strong, I could preserve it no longer.

It's quite clear that the experimental method is not a proper method for the investigation of moral or spiritual problems. However, Swift, mimicking the confident, busy manner of the contemporary scientist, makes believe it is, partly in order to define the limitations of experimental science, but partly, also, to shock us with the calculated crudity into considering whether moral stench isn't as disgusting as the putrefaction of the body, before retreating from the unpleasant essentials to the more superficial view of things. Swift is pretending to be a gentleman as well as an experimental scientist, but as satirist (that is, moral anatomist) he can be neither. The gentlemanly assumption of neo-classic criticism was that art should instruct by entertainment or diversion: Swift pretends to have discovered this all by himself, but gives a new slant to the commonplace:

> as Mankind is now disposed, he receives much greater Advantage by being *Diverted* than *Instructed*; His Epidemical Diseases being *Fastidiosity*, *Amorphy* and *Oscitation*; whereas in the present universal Empire of Wit and Learning, there seems but little Matter left for *Instruction*.

Swift manoeuvres us into a position where we seek to disengage ourselves from the pretensions of modern humanity; we hasten to assert that we are much more concerned with a serious inquiry into the truth, the moral and spiritual truth, than with the superficial matters which Swift pretends to be so much more important. The comic pomposity of 'Fastidiosity, Amorphy and Oscitation', which guys the pedantic habit of neutralizing nasty things (squeamishness, shapelessness and yawning boredom) by giving them unfamiliar Latinate names, arrests our attention just long enough for us to grasp what is really wrong in 'the present universal Empire of Wit and Learning'. We are invited to stand outside the superficial and frivolous pre-occupations of contemporary society, and judge it by more permanent standards.

Swift now begins to deal more directly with the controversy between the Ancients and the Moderns; but he does not attempt to do so by answering the arguments of the champions of the Moderns (they were, perhaps, better arguments than those of Swift's patron, Temple). Swift chooses rather to undercut them by associating them with various kinds of pretentious psuedo-scholarly kinds of non-sense: alchemy, Rosicrucianism and mysticism. The odd thing here is that these represent ways of thinking which belonged to the crazier experimental fringes of Renaissance thought; they were the flourishes of the Baroque sensibility, and in full retreat in face of the 'Modern' sensibility. Swift scorns them with all the contempt appropriate to a contemporary of Newton and Boyle, but by a curious trick of association, uses them to condemn the modern way.

Of course there were many ways in which the efforts of scholarship were wasted in triviality and absurdity (there are trivial and absurd scholars in every age, even in our own time) and it is legitimate enough for Swift to measure the lack of dignity and stature of the Bentleys and the Wottons against the genius of Homer. But it's as well for us to understand the ways in which Swift's satire is mischievously inaccurate as well as the ways in which it really does go straight to the point. The contemporary scientist was not infatuated with ways of achieving instant omniscience in the way which Swift implies with his comic recipe; the magical and mystical element in contemporary thought was in full retreat. On the other hand there were ways in which the modern theory of science encouraged the jackdaw mentality, and thus diverted men of science from essential considerations. Thus Swift pretends to have found Homer out in a great deficiency of knowledge: 'I could never yet discover the least Direction about the Structure of that useful Instrument a *Save-all*. For want of which, if the *Moderns* had not lent their Assistance, we might yet have wandred *in the Dark*.' A save-all is a bag or box in which one collects all the bits and pieces one cannot find an immediate use for. The programme of modern science, as laid out by Bacon in the *Novum Organum*, implied the need for years of patient work in collecting information, measuring, comparing and analysing, in order that at some time or other the information collected should provide the material for the processes of inductive reasoning: that fact about the speed of light might lie in the save-all for years before an Einstein uses it to develop the Special Theory of Relativity: in the meanwhile, encouraged by this, common or garden scientists can happily ignore the essential questions by assuming that whatever they do will be useful one day. For Swift, this is the unforgiveable Modern sin; and yet Bacon, too, recognizes the nature of the error, and anticipates the line of criticism which Swift takes: the Aphorism No. XCV of the *Novum Organum* observes:

> Those who have handled sciences have been either men of experiment or men of dogmas. The men of experiment are like the ant; they only collect and use: the reasoners resemble spiders, who make cobwebs out of their own substance. But the bee takes a middle course, it gathers its material from the flowers of the garden and of the field, but transforms and digests it by a power of its own. Not unlike this is the true business of philosophy . . .

Swift is in essential agreement with Bacon about this, except that there are few bees or none at all left in the world's garden for him; we are surrounded by busy ants (like the writer of *A Tale of a Tub*), and spidery theorists like the one in the *Battle of the Books*: all our honey is left to us by the ancient world, unless we can learn once again to comprehend and understand rather than simply collect or invent.

SECTION VI

Swift returns to the tale proper, but this time his subject is not the abuses of the Roman Church, but the extremist zeal for reform of the Dissenters in contrast with the moderation of the Church of England. Swift valued greatly the moderation of the English style both in Church and in temporal government; like many in his age he feared a return to the anarchy of the Civil War and the insecurity of the Commonwealth even more than he feared the arrogant domination of a foreign church. Likewise he saw at least as much danger in the excesses of 'zeal' or 'enthusiasm' as he did in the accumulated corruptions of the Roman dogma and ritual. He therefore matches the madness of Peter with Jack's different kind of madness: the madness of jealousy, spite and hysterical rage. To adapt Bacon's analogy, Peter's is an ant-like madness – the insanity of accumulated habit spilling over into pride and pomp and arrogance. Jack's madness is spun like a spider's web from within himself and spills over into needless rebellion and anarchy. Martin has the busy profitable moderation of the bee.

Swift's language vigorously expresses this insane anarchy by associating Jack with the world of thieves, prostitutes and the criminal poor:

> So that he looked like a drunken *Beau,* half-rifled by Bullies; Or like a fresh Tenant of *Newgate,* when he has refused the Payment of *Garnish*[1]; Or like a discovered *Shoplifter,* left to the Mercy of *Exchange-Women*; Or like a *Bawd* in her old Velvet-Petticoat, resign'd into the secular Hands of the *Mobile*[2].

We are in the world of Hogarth's London here (even though Hogarth was not born until 1697, the year after this was

[1] Garnish: protection money paid by a new prisoner to his fellow prisoners at Newgate.
[2] The mob.

written): Dissent grew out of this disorderly world, and to do it credit, did a great deal to moderate its anarchy; nevertheless there were ways in which it reflected the energy and indecorum of the world it grew from, as against the caution and passion for orderliness of Martin and his Church, and the country squirearchy who were its greatest strength and support.

VII. A DIGRESSION IN PRAISE OF DIGRESSIONS

As we have already remarked, the form of *A Tale of a Tub*, with its medley of digressions running off in all directions, is part of the satire upon the inconsequentiality and indirection of Modern learning. The inconsequentiality is only apparent in *A Tale of a Tub*, but nevertheless Swift enjoys complicating and compounding the shifts and changes in direction: already we have had a digression within a digression, and now, taking the Chinese box principle one stage further, Swift embarks upon a digression in praise of digressions.

Nevertheless Swift is entirely to the point throughout; the opening sentence: 'I have sometimes *heard* of an *Iliad* in a *Nut-Shell*; but it hath been my Fortune to have oftner *seen a Nut-Shell* in an *Iliad*' achieves that neat and telling balance of statement so characteristic of Augustan Wit, an epigrammatic elegance of the kind which Pope was later to seek and find so often in his verse. Some of the images which follow are less like the verse couplet in their balance, but nevertheless attain a compact scornfulness which is a kind of prose equivalent of the couplet's neatness and precision:

> They tell us, that the Fashion of jumbling fifty Things together in a Dish, was at first introduced in Compliance to a depraved and *debauched Appetite*, as well as to a *crazy Constitution*; And to see a Man hunting thro' an Ollio[1], after the *Head* and *Brains* of a *Goose*, a *Wigeon*, or a *Woodcock*, is a Sign, he wants a Stomach

[1] A meat stew, a fashionable culinary import from Italy.

and Digestion for more substantial Victuals. Farther, they affirm, that *Digressions* in a Book, are like *Forein Troops* in a *State*, which argue the Nation to want a *Heart* and *Hands* of its own, and often, either *subdue* the *Natives*, or drive them into the most *unfruitfull Corners*.

Swift excelled at this kind of balanced prose, but it is not the manner he uses for the most intense moments of his satire. By comparison with the Digression upon Madness, or parts of Section VIII, the Digression upon Digressions, neat, pointed and inventive as it is, is comparatively uncreative; his aim is to score points rather than to open minds.

SECTION VIII

So far the tale and the digressions have alternated with each other; in this section the two modes converge. Section VIII is not strictly part of the narrative fable, neither is it in the form of a digression, but it shares some of the characteristics of both kinds. Like the narrative it is a comic parable concerned with religious excess; like the digressions it exploits the manner of self-satisfied and pedantic scholarship as a satiric medium, describing the insane with a wonderful and solemn ignorance of its own madness. The joining of modes is important: for the purposes of the satire Swift has so far pretended to be doing two entirely different things: to be the historian of the three brothers (which is at the same time to be the ironic historian of religion) and to be the scatter-brained pedant who cannot keep his mind on one thing any longer than his audience, which, being full of 'Fastidiosity, Amorphy and Oscitation', cannot bear serious, intelligent and purposeful argument. Now he joins the two pretences in one, making explicit what has been implicit all along, that it is not simply 'the numerous and gross Corruptions in Religion and Learning' which he is concerned with but the prevailing habit of the human mind, in particular the Modern mind, which leads to all corruption and irrelevance: disproportion in values, the lack of a proper sense of priorities, and behind all these a sickness of the gravest kind, a madness which dizzies man's imagination and corrupts him with spiritual vertigo.

The doctrine of the Roman Catholic Church, for all its faults, provided its members with a firm authoritative structure of belief outside themselves to which they could appeal. In rejecting Catholic doctrine, the Dissenters had to find a replacement which had similar authority. The Bible was the ultimate source of truth, but the Bible was a very complex document, and man needed help in interpreting it. The traditions were thrown overboard; the Dissenters sought directly the aid of God: authority was replaced by inspiration as a guide to action and belief.

For the Church of England this was placing too much trust in the oddities and inconsistencies of the human personality; man was too weak to be his own prophet and his own judge. For Swift it was madness: a particular example of the Modern madness of self-will; the madness is satirized in another mock theology – that of Aeolism.

Swift adopts the manner of a windy pedant striving to give dignity to the absurd doctrine by play upon the classical and medieval notions of the four elements and the fifth essence; earth, water, air and fire and the quintessence or principle of life which lies behind the other four. Enjoying himself hugely, he pulls in the Aristotelian doctrine of the soul, with its three aspects, the vegetative, sensitive and intellective, contorts the etymology of all the words for soul to make them mean wind, throws in a fourth kind of wind for good measure, and compounds it all by inventing a fifth, quintessential wind to lie behind the other four. This is parody of an over-exuberant play of mind which was more typical, perhaps, of the sixteenth century and early seventeenth century, but the *parody* is characteristic enough of Swift's time and Swift himself: he laughs at the ornate excesses of this antique kind of imagination, and yet has enough feeling for it to enjoy it and do it well. It serves, as it were, to deflate by over-inflating, but the comically pretentious mystification only partly conceals a very serious point of view. Swift was so very scornful of 'inspiration', perhaps, because it is a branch of, or he would say a perversion of, the imagination, and Swift's attitude to the imagination was profoundly ambivalent. Here we enter into a difficult series of problems of meaning; we have already seen what difficulties the word 'Wit' causes. 'Imagination' was, in Swift's time, a word for something less controllable and sane than Wit, but it had its attractiveness too. One can approach the whole matter from a different angle by thinking about the historical situation of England at the time the *Tale* was written: England still suffered from the shock of the Civil Wars; order and Reason were myths which the age cultivated assiduously as an assurance that the flimsy structures of society would not collapse again, but Reason, like Zeal, led too many to flirt with dangerous ideas which would destroy continuity and tradition and once more lead to anarchy. Wit was a force which could or should make for order, but in its very adventurousness and creativeness it was a danger; these qualities could lead, if unchecked, to the anarchy of Imagination. The Reformation had deprived its dissenting children of a firm structure of belief to restrain Imagination; the English Church tried in its own way to provide the needed checks, but instead of papal authority had to make do with various communal conventions and a spirit of compromise. But there were too many exciting things to tempt the mind out of the secure asylums of faith and civilized behaviour. Wit, like Love, had to be held in by Prudence and cemented by Decency, but Wit, like Love, tended to kick over the traces and go free. Pope followed the pattern of his age by appealing, as judge and disciplinary officer of man's greedy Fancy, to Nature:

> Nature to all Things fix'd the Limits fit,
> And wisely curb'd proud Man's pretending Wit
> (*An Essay on Criticism*, ll. 52–3)

The rewards were great, Swift and Pope agreed; a glorious heady excitement, a creative madness which could by-pass every rule and make something magnificently new:

> Thus *Pegasus*, a nearer way to take,
> May boldly deviate from the common Track.
> Great Wits sometimes may *gloriously offend*
> And *rise* to *Faults* true Criticks *dare not mend*;
> From *vulgar Bounds* with *brave Disorder* part,
> And *snatch* a *Grace* beyond the Reach of Art,
> Which, without passing thro' the *Judgment*, gains
> The Heart, and all its End *at once* attains.
>
> (*An Essay on Criticism*, ll. 150–5)

Swift knew these temptations as well as or better than anyone; his imagination was unusually rich and active, but
then so was his sense of its dangers. The tension thus generated
is the greatest force behind all his work, but particularly
behind the exuberant energy of this celebrated passage:

> And, whereas the mind of Man, when he gives the Spur
> and Bridle to his Thoughts, doth never stop, but
> naturally sallies out into both extreams of High and
> Low, of Good and Evil; His first Flight of Fancy,
> commonly transports Him to Idea's of what is most
> Perfect, finished, and exalted; till having soared out of
> his own Reach and Sight, not well perceiving how near
> the Frontiers of Height and Depth, border upon each
> other; With the same Course and Wing, he falls down
> plum into the lowest Bottom of Things; like one who
> travels the *East* into the *West*; or like a strait Line
> drawn by its own Length into a Circle. Whether a
> tincture of Malice in our Natures, makes us fond of
> furnishing every bright Idea with its Reverse; Or,
> whether Reason reflecting upon the Sum of Things,
> can, like the Sun, serve only to enlighten one half of the
> Globe, leaving the other half, by Necessity, under
> Shade and Darkness: Or, whether Fancy, flying up
> to the imagination of what is Highest and Best, becomes
> over-shot, and spent, and weary, and suddenly falls
> like a dead Bird of Paradise, to the Ground. . . .

Pope is dealing with a more limited subject, and the
Essay on Criticism is one of his less adventurous pieces, so

perhaps any comparison we make between him and Swift on the basis of these passages is partly invalid. (A fairer text for comparison would be the last fifty lines of the *Dunciad*, where Pope imagines the opposite terror to that of over-indulgence of the fancy, that is the extinction of all Art, and Wit and Intelligence, the final triumph of the Goddess Dullness and the coming of her kingdom over the whole world.) However, it is characteristic of Swift that the contemplation of the joys and dangers of the Imagination should raise him to such intensities of energy, while Pope remains comparatively calm about the whole matter, and Dryden, who also saw the problem with great clarity, could encapsulate it, and thus rob it of much of its terror in the celebrated:

> Great wits are sure to madness near allied,
> And thin partitions do their bounds divide
> *(Absalom and Achitophel*, ll. 163–4)

Leavis characterizes the virtues of the Swift passage with the greatest precision; he speaks of 'the spontaneous metaphorical energy of Swift's prose – in the image, action or blow that, leaping out of the prosaic manner, continually surprises and disconcerts the reader', and he goes on to compare its creative force to that of the Metaphysical poets. There is the same exhilaration and boldness of language; a restless energy which fuses together ideas which, were it not for the quickness, the sensitiveness, the agile persuasiveness of the mind which grasps our imaginations so powerfully, we would not think to be related. The resemblance lies partly in the rapid accumulation of images, each contradicting, yet somehow enfolding and continuing the last: the mind is first a rider, his thoughts the mount responsive to spur and bridle. The horse becomes a winged one, but not, like Pegasus, restricted to a material universe – it traverses an abrupt and terrifying moral geography. Then, with one of those strange challenges to logic the metaphysicals delighted in, the rider and his mount soar 'out of his own reach and sight'. The very strange paradox serves to underline the special terrors of the mind-world as opposed to the world of country roads and bridled horses; a world in which one part of the mind may entirely lose contact with the sober controlling judgement-making part, yet still continue to explore, a delighted spirit, despite all misgivings. The paradox leads to another strange ambiguity: 'not well perceiving how near the frontiers of height and depth border on each other' – what height? what depth? and how do they meet in this space-warp? We can supply the pedestrian answer from Dryden: 'Great wits are sure to madness near allied', but Swift's queer science fiction metaphor goes beyond this: if a mind ventures out of its own sight it has no need of a Newtonian universe any more: straight lines curve in the oddest possible anticipation of Einstein (though Swift, clearly, was thinking not of the physical properties of the Universe, and the physical model for his moral paradox was a great-circle line round the terrestrial globe). Swift sails close to Donne's 'south-west discovery' in 'Hymn to God, my God, in my Sickness'; where Donne rejoices in the prospect of traversing the Magellan Straits of death:

> I joy, that in these straits, I see my west;
> For, though their currents yield return to none,
> What shall my west hurt me? As west and east
> In all flat maps (and I am one) are one,
> So death doth touch the resurrection.

But, whereas Donne anticipates a metaphysical rebirth in his physical death, Swift fears the death and madness which will result from the fullest possible exercise of the life of the mind. Losing sight of itself, the horse and rider become a geographer's, then a mathematician's and a metaphysician's line. Then they become the darkness which covers half the earth, and half the mind, the unconscious half best left in darkness, and by a final protean transformation they become a bird of paradise: expelled like Adam and Eve, in the fall which follows the breaking of the great taboos. Like them, the bird, the bird which is, we must remember, the mind expelled from a false paradise of its own, meets death as a consequence of joy and forbidden knowledge. The whole thing, in the change and turn of its flexible rhythms, imitating the flight of a bird, convinces us of the restless, probing, adventurous life of the free mind, and yet its ultimate and inevitable exhaustion and defeat in the halting ebb of 'over-shot, and spent, and weary, and suddenly falls, like a dead Bird of Paradise, to the Ground'.

The passage is a very complex one indeed; a manifestation of one of the most powerful, resilient and irrepressible imaginations ever to express itself in the written word, and yet a passage which, in one sense at least, seems to condemn the Imagination or the Fancy. Again Pope is ready to supply a faintly pedestrian version of the qualifications to this:

> For *Wit* and Judgment often are at strife,
> Tho' meant each other's Aid, like *Man* and *Wife*.
> 'Tis more to *guide* than *spur* the Muse's Steed;
> Restrain his Fury, than provoke his Speed;
> The winged Courser, like a gen'rous Horse,
> Shows most true Mettle when you *check* his Course.
> (*An Essay on Criticism*, ll. 82–7)

It's worth noticing in passing that Pope seems to have written the first version of the *Essay* in 1709, only a few years after Swift published the *Tale*. It's more than likely that there is a connection between the two, but one thing is clear: however heartily Swift would have agreed with the well-turned but frigid sentiments which Pope expresses here, the passionate note of Swift arises from a much more deeply-felt sense of the joys and the dangers of the mind's adventure into forbidden territories of the Imagination. Swift is being negative here only in a superficial sense; he *celebrates* the creative energies of the mind at the same time as bidding us be infinitely more aware of the hazards of being human.

IX. DIGRESSION ON MADNESS

When we believe that an argument is wrong, our first reaction is to look for faults in the basic premises, or errors in the method of reasoning. When, as in a satirical argument such as this, we know that the author is being deliberately wrong, we expect to find the point of the satire in the wrongness of the premises or the wrongness of the methods of reasoning. The author's deliberate errors are in some way a comment on the world of error which surrounds him and surrounds us. Again, we, the readers, find ourselves squinting at reality through the author's distorting glass; we work to correct our vision, reject the bad eye's point of view, and in the process learn to value all the more the angle of vision which we are persuaded is the right one. We tend to believe, when the process is complete, that we have always thought in such a way anyway, but this is sometimes an illusion: by clarifying, sharpening and exaggerating the alternatives the satirist commonly persuades us to shift our angle of vision, even though he may wish us to believe that he is merely confirming our natural good sense.

In 'A Digression Concerning the Original, the Use, and the Improvement of Madness in a Commonwealth', Swift builds on the insecurity he has created in the previous section, our newly acquired or reinforced sense of the hazards of the human imagination, the nearness of the creative intelligence and insanity to each other. He affects the argument that creativeness (or greatness in action, or originality in thought) and insanity are not only near to each other, they are the same, or have a direct causal relationship. They are the wilful and self-centred expression of an individual who neglects the bonds of convention, sentiment and reason which bind him to other men.

But the examples he adduces, with all the solemnity of a white-faced clown, contain the implicit answers to his mock argument. His heroes have certain things in common. For a start they are *not* creative; witness the mighty king 'who, for the space of above Thirty Years, amused himself to take and lose Towns; beat Armies, and be beaten; drive Princes out of their Dominions; fright Children from their Bread and Butter; burn, lay waste, plunder, dragoon, massacre Subject and Stranger, Friend and Foe, Male and Female'. They are *not* great, except in their destructiveness; and they are the slaves of a sickness which, for all the comic pseudo-medical jargon of vapours and tumours which Swift employs to define their ills, is merely the ailment of inflamed self-will, with all its attendant symptoms of arrogance, delusion and arbitrariness. Sanity is not just a matter of self-control, it is a matter of responsibility, and this, ultimately, is what distinguishes true Wit from mere Fancy, or Imagination (we must remember that this word had a less handsome meaning in Swift's day than it does in these post-Romantic times). Man cannot be alone, cannot trust his own fantasies, desires and ambitions, as Dissenting Jack does when he follows the wind of inspiration; to be truly sane is consciously to think and act as part of a human community, living in the present, but honouring the past, and finding one's true individuality in submission to the deeply felt common values of a society rooted in tradition:

Then has this *Madness* been the Parent of all those mighty Revolutions, that have happened in *Empire*, in *Philosophy* and in *Religion*. For, the Brain, in its natural Position and State of Serenity, disposeth its Owner to pass his Life in the common Forms, without any Thought of subduing Multitudes to his own *Power*, his *Reasons* or his *Visions*; and the more he shapes his Understanding by the Pattern of Human Learning, the less he is inclined to form Parties after his particular Notions; because that instructs him in his private Infirmities, as well as in the stubborn Ignorance of the People. But when a Man's Fancy gets *astride* on his Reason, when Imagination is at Cuffs with the Senses and common Understanding, as well as common Sense, is Kickt out of Doors; the first Proselyte he makes, is Himself, and when that is once compass'd, the Difficulty is not so great in bringing over others; A strong Delusion always operating from *without*, as vigorously as from *within*. For, Cant and Vision are to the Ear and Eye, the same that Tickling is to the Touch. Those Entertainments and Pleasures we most value in Life, are such as *Dupe* and play the Wag with the Senses. For if we take an Examination of what is generally understood by *Happiness*, as it has Respect, either to the Understanding or the Senses, we shall find all its Properties and Ad-

juncts will herd under this short Definition: That,
it is a perpetual Possession of being well Deceived.

The passage goes on ironically to praise the capacity for
self-delusion, and more than one reader, like Dr Leavis,
has become less sure about the direction of the irony by
the end of the argument than he was at the beginning: 'It
is as if one found Swift in the place – at the point of view
– where one expected to find his butt.' The nature of the
change of tone, as Leavis agrees, is somewhat difficult to
determine – 'and that is of the essence of the effect'. But
perhaps it is more easy for us, who have become accustomed
to a certain kind of post-Romantic sentiment towards illusion,
to take it seriously than it would have been for one of Swift's
contemporaries. Swift was a master of satirical tones, mar-
vellously apt at counterfeiting emotions which he despised,
but in this case he is not as evasively subtle as he can be in
marking the inadequacy of the sentiment. Swift, in 'A Letter
to a young Gentleman Lately Enter'd into Holy Orders'
advises his novice to follow the example of an acquaintance
who 'made it a Rule in reading, to skip over all Sentences
where he spy'd a Note of Admiration at the End'. And Swift
himself rarely, if ever, uses the exclamation mark or the
emotive rhetorical query for any purpose but to underline
an ironic intention. Swift's stand then, is particularly clear
here:

> How fade and insipid do all Objects accost us that are
> not convey'd in the Vehicle of *Delusion*? How shrunk
> is every Thing, as it appears in the Glass of Nature?
> So, that if it were not for the Assistance of Artificial
> *Mediums*, false Lights, refracted Angles, Varnish and
> Tinsel; there would be a mighty Level in the Felicity
> and Enjoyments of Mortal Men.

The tone of the irony is obvious enough: 'credulity is a
more peaceful possession of the mind than curiosity' begs
questions about peacefulness; perhaps there are more important things than peace; certainly for a satirist of Swift's
stamp, who takes every possible opportunity to disturb

and disillusion us, *that* kind of peacefulness is as undesirable as the happiness which is the '*perpetual Possession of being well Deceived*'. But the more easily-perceived irony can deflect one's attention for a while from a more strenuous and elusive one – the ambiguity which is the essence of the effect and prepares for the hidden ambush. Swift temporarily traps his reader into asserting (unwarily) that curiosity is vastly the better attitude towards all experience; that truth is desirable at all costs; and then he springs his trap, gives the *persona* his ironic ace to play:

> And therefore, in order to save the Charges of all such expensive Anatomy for the Time to come; I do here think fit to inform the Reader, that in such Con- clusions as these, Reason is certainly in the Right; and that in most Corporeal Beings, which have fallen under my Cognizance, the *Outside* hath been in- finitely preferable to the *In*: Whereof I have been farther convinced from some late Experiments. Last Week I saw a Woman *flay'd*, and you will hardly believe, how much it altered her Person for the worse.

The shock of this gross, painful immediate image of horror sets one off balance: one has maintained one's defence against the irony by insisting, against the *persona*'s persuasive rhetoric, that despite all unpleasantness the persistent search for truth should go on. And then one is given a sample of the pain and the horror. The fact that it is strictly irrele- vant to the moral argument doesn't matter for the moment. We have maintained against all opposition our belief that man is a reasonable being; we are confronted with a gross brutality of this kind and made to feel unsure once more: the ground is cut away, we have no firm truth to hold on to.

And yet Swift has salted away many clues to help us recover our moral balance. The play with anatomy, for instance, recalls the Digression in the Modern Kind, where Swift, satirizing the Moderns' proud claim to have super- seded the Ancients in understanding the material structure and functioning of the human animal, hints that we would be better occupied (as the satirist himself is) dissecting 'the Carcass of Human Nature'. 'Yesterday I ordered the Carcass of a *Beau* to be stript in my Presence; when we were all amazed to find so many unsuspected Faults under one Suit of Cloaths': as Swift continues to build on his theme we begin to realize the ways in which we must reject the parallels as illegitimate – shockingly and deliberately so, for to pretend that the disproportion between the superficial and the profound in moral questions is *really* like the difference between clothes and the naked man is to worship that pagan idol, the tailor who presides over Section II of the *Tale*; for 'what is Man himself but a *Micro-Coat* . . . Is not Religion a *Cloak*, Honesty a *Pair of Shoes*?' One is not in the least surprised, really, to find a beau imperfect under his outwardly immaculate appearance; the *persona* is mad to suggest we should be. And we, if we follow him in his cure for the diseases of man, perpetuate the insanity:

> whatever Philosopher or Projector can find out an Art to sodder[1] and patch up the Flaws and Imperfections of Nature, will deserve much better of Mankind, and teach us a more useful Science, than that so much in present Esteem, of widening and exposing them (like him who held *Anatomy* to be the ultimate end of *Physick*). And he, whose Fortunes and Dispositions have placed him in a convenient Station to enjoy the Fruits of this noble Art; He that can with *Epicurus* content his Ideas with the *Films* and *Images* that fly off upon his Senses from the *Superficies* of Things; Such a Man truly wise, creams off Nature, leaving the Sower and the Dregs, for Philosophy and Reason to lap up. This is the sublime and refined Point of Felicity, called, *the Possession of being well-deceived*; The Serene Peaceful State of being a Fool among Knaves.

In the first place, of course, the scornful irony of this is directed against the 'Philosopher or Projector' who so far forgets his duty as to confine himself to the pleasures of the superficial; the action of the satire alerts us to the shape of

[1] Solder.

human infirmities so that we become more and more hesitant about the various devices for concealment which we commonly depend upon. So if the reader demands sanity he is forced to look for something beyond curiosity as well as credulity; something beyond pleasure and pain; beyond 'peacefulness' and 'felicity'; to discover a way of being neither fool nor knave.

Swift writes out of a deep and continuous tradition of morality, and the precept at the heart of his standpoint is one which is shared by both Christian religion and Greek philosophy. According to Plutarch 'Know thyself' was inscribed at the entrance to the Delphic Oracle; the phrase has been attributed to almost every major Greek philosopher, and has been adopted enthusiastically by Christianity and later by the Humanists as a first requisite for true fulness of humanity and understanding. So the epigrammatic concreteness and life, the rich spontaneity of imagery of 'such a Man truly wise, creams off Nature, leaving the Sower and the Dregs, for Philosophy and Reason to lap up' speaks against itself: the irony of wisdom is that whatever sweetness it has proceeds only from a full recognition of the sour, the corrupt, the evil within oneself.

Perhaps the most significant word is 'Nature': another of those words which are keys to a past world of thought and feeling. Nature is not simply the material universe with the products of human artifice subtracted from it; nor is it exactly the wise universal parental spirit beloved of the early English Romantics. It is the sum total of cause and effect, action and response throughout the whole universe; the harmony and unity which lies behind everything, re-conciling ultimately all the disproportions and inconsisten-cies which we, being too close to the object, see in our every day lives. So if to be truly wise is to separate the cream from the buttermilk of Nature it is to flout the whole pattern of creation.

The Digression on Madness works upon confusion and insecurity in the reader; when, at last, London (the centre of the civilized world for an Englishman of Swift's day) becomes a vivid and terrible Bedlam, we are torn between laughter and pity; and both come, ultimately, from a kind of embarrassment. We do not know exactly where *we* stand; we are constantly forced to make more and more effort to retain our self-respect and our balance, and the officious energy of the language, so like Shakespeare's comic prose in its rapidity and headlong balance (like a runner whose centre of gravity is always ahead of his racing feet) refuses to let us disbelieve in the *reality* of the cruel mad parody of ordinary life:

> Behold a Fourth, in much and deep Conversation with himself, biting his Thumbs at proper Junctures; His Countenance chequered with Business and Design; sometimes walking very fast, with his Eyes nailed to a Paper that he holds in his Hands: a great Saver of Time, somewhat thick of Hearing, very short of Sight, but more of Memory. A Man ever in Haste, a great Hatcher and Breeder of Business, and excellent at the Famous Art of *whispering Nothing*. A huge Idolater of Monosyllables and Procrastination; so ready to *Give* his Word to every Body, that he never *keeps* it. One that has forgot the common *Meaning* of Words, but an admirable Retainer of the *Sound*. Extreamly subject to the *Looseness*, for his *Occasions* are perpetually *calling him away*. If you approach his Grate in his familiar Intervals; *Sir*, says he, *Give me a Penny, and I'll sing you a Song; But give me the Penny first*. (Hence comes the common Saying, and commoner Practice of parting with Money for a *Song*.) What a compleat System of *Court-Skill* is here described in every Branch of it, and all utterly lost with wrong Application?

X. A FARTHER DIGRESSION

The Digression on Madness works on our confusion, this, the last Digression, amuses itself at our discomfort. We *have* been provoked to laughter, and so, perhaps, are superficial; we *have* been made to stare, and so perhaps, are ignorant; whether we are truly learned is something which has been profoundly questioned. More than seven Scholars have written more than seven ample Commentaries, and this present one will not be the last piece of 'Scholastick Midwifry' to be practised on a work full of the most fertile possibilities. But characteristically, even the laughter is full of strange echoes and resonances:

> I have a strong Inclination, before I leave the World, to taste a Blessing, which we *mysterious* Writers can seldom reach, till we have got into our Graves. Whether it is, that *Fame* being a Fruit grafted on the Body, can hardly grow, and much less ripen, till the *Stock* is in the Earth: Or, whether she be a Bird of Prey, and is lured among the rest, to pursue after the Scent of a *Carcass*: Or, whether she conceives, her Trumpet sounds best and farthest, when she stands on a *Tomb*, by the Advantage of a rising Ground, and the Echo of a hollow Vault.

It's true that Swift is satirizing, on the one hand the desire for fame, on the other hand the slowness of the world to respond to genius; but it goes beyond this – the copiousness and richness of imagery, which Johnson admired so rightly, produce evocative resonances which go far beyond the surface argument. Here, and elsewhere, Swift contrives to place the satire in the context of truths and values which outlast the writer and the reader, and does it without breaking the continuity of the more immediate satirical argument. He does it in the way that Shakespeare, and Donne, and Marvell had done before him, by making the contrast between the brevity of man's life and the vastness of time, death, eternity, in terms of full, close, immediate and concrete images: the apple-tree graft, the bird of prey, the swell of earth above the grave, the hollow echoing of a trumpet in an enclosed space. If we can hear the echoes, we are more than adequately equipped to deal with the pressures of the vice in which Swift holds us.

SECTION XI AND CONCLUSION

From here onwards the *Tale* is a winding up, the essential part of the satire concluded already. The occasional satire is amusing enough and bites home, even though it would seem to an age like ours (more tolerant of religious beliefs because less deeply interested in religion) that Swift permits himself too cruel a reaction against the Dissenters. It isn't very profound satire, and one of the marks of this is that it depends for its effect upon the reader being in agreement with Swift's point of view. It would never cause a Dissenter to see the error of his ways, to give up the notion of pre-destination or to receive the sacrament with greater cere-mony. The greatness of the *Tale* is in the turbulent experience of the latter part of Section VIII and the whole of Section IX, The Digression on Madness, though all the rest of the book is a necessary framework for this central experience. And, in the Conclusion, Swift has one thing to say about the strange mixture of obscurity and essential clarity, profundity and simplicity which is characteristic of this central part of the satire:

> it is with *Writers*, as with *Wells*; a Person with good Eyes may see to the Bottom of the deepest, provided any *Water* be there; and, that often, when there is nothing in the World at the Bottom, beside *Dryness* and *Dirt*, tho' it be but a Yard and a half under the Ground, it shall pass, however, for wondrous *Deep*, upon no wiser a Reason than because it is wondrous *Dark*.

III

Other Early Satires

The Tale of a Tub is the most complex, sustained, comprehensive, energetic and disturbing prose satire to have been written in English at the time it appeared. It was published together with two other pieces which, though they are overshadowed by the rich profusion of the *Tale*, are remarkable in their own ways. *The Battle of the Books* and *A Discourse Concerning the Mechanical Operation of the Spirit* pursue the same quarry as the *Tale* – 'the numerous and gross Corruptions in Religion and Learning' – and do so with some of the same headlong energy and brilliance. In the *Battle* there is less complexity and variety – the reader is given far more opportunity to preserve his own defences against the restless, probing manoeuvres of the satirical master-strategist – but there are many places where the satire is lively, sharp and memorable. The *Discourse*, on the other hand, is a wonderfully compact masterpiece of the satirist's art.

In *The Battle of the Books*, Swift takes arms in the hotly contested dispute between Temple and Boyle on the one hand and Bentley and Wotton on the other on the contrast between *Ancient and Modern Learning*. Temple had set out to show the superiority of the ancients in prose, instancing Aesop's *Fables* and Phalaris' *Epistles* to support his argument. Wotton had replied with a passionate defence of the modern age as superior to the ancients; Bentley (a distinguished philologist) demonstrated that Aesop and the *Epistles* were not so ancient as Temple had assumed. The quarrel inevitably seems a little pointless to the modern reader. Most of us would now argue that no age has a monopoly of excellence; if the age of Einstein cannot value the age of Aristotle and the age of Newton it is so much the poorer. On the other hand the age of Einstein finds a different value in the age of Newton *because* it is the age of Einstein; because the age of Einstein is built upon the age of Newton, fulfilling some of its potentials, destroying, perhaps, some of its values. Any comparison of the present with the past ought to be a complex affair (more complex still when we realize how much our notion of the past depends on our experience of the present; how much our present experience depends upon the continued presence of the past). So the squabble about the superiority or inferiority of one age's writers to another's looks faintly absurd.

But, as in many other hotly debated arguments, there is an inner contention which is, perhaps, not fully recognized by most of the combatants. In such cases, it is frequently the great artist who is able to pick out and stress the essential problem while the others, engaged in the vehement hand-to-hand fighting, continue helplessly doing as they are forced to do, without ever recognizing the real nature of the dispute. Swift is scornful enough of the actual dispute:

> In this Quarrel, whose Rivulets of *Ink* have been ex-hausted, and the Virulence of both Parties enormously augmented. Now, it must here be understood, that *Ink* is the great missive Weapon, in all Battels of the *Learned*, which, convey'd thro' a sort of Engine, call'd a *Quill*, infinite Numbers of these are darted at the Enemy, by the Valiant on each side, with equal Skill and Violence, as if it were an Engagement of *Porcupines*. This malignant Liquor was compounded by the Engineer, who invented it, of two Ingredients, which are *Gall* and *Copperas*,[1] by its Bitterness and Vemon, to *Suit* in some Degree, as well as to *Foment* the Genius of the Combatants.

One might well ask why Swift himself joins battle if it seems so absurd as this; but by separating himself and the reader

---

[1] The bitter secretions of the gall bladder and copperas (ferrous sulphate), a highly astringent salt, used to be among the main ingredients of ink.

from too close an involvement in the bitter controversy, Swift seeks to concentrate on the broader and deeper problems and ignore the petty details.

Swift hints at the nature of his central concern in the first sentences: war is the child of pride, he says, *that* will readily be granted, but, despite the old aphorism, pride comes from poverty not from wealth. Beneath the surface of the satire, then, with its somewhat repetitive and miscellaneous mock-heroic episodes, there is a drive towards a definition of the genuine richness which is the converse of the pride of poverty: a richness of heart and mind rather than mere prodigality with words and readiness to dispute.

However, Swift's satirical temperament never allows him to argue a positive case in a simply positive way. In the opening remarks of the 'Full and True Account of the Battel fought last Friday, &c' he adopts a tone and a manner which are not precisely his own. A clue to the kind of discourse which he imitates is given in the passing phrase: 'For, to speak in the Phrase of Writers upon the Politicks . . .' The two most distinguished writers on politics of Swift's age were Hobbes and Locke. One of them, Hobbes, was very much concerned with the propensity of human society to conflict, so that in *Leviathan* war tends to be spoken of as the normal state of things, not peace:

> For *war* consisteth not in battle only, or in the act fighting, but in a tract of time wherein the will to contend by battle is sufficiently known. . . . For as the nature of foul weather lieth not in a shower or two of rain, but in an inclination thereto of many days together; so the nature of war consisteth not in actual fighting, but in the known disposition thereto, during all the time there is no assurance to the contrary. All other time is *peace*.
>
> Whatsoever therefore is consequent to a time of war, where every man is enemy to every man; the same is consequent to the time, wherein men live without other security than what their own strength and their own invention shall furnish them withal. In such

> condition there is no place for industry, because the
> fruit thereof is uncertain: and consequently no culture
> of the earth; no navigation, nor use of the commodities
> that may be imported by sea; no commodious building;
> no instruments of moving, and removing, such things as
> require much force; no knowledge of the face of the
> earth; no account of time; no arts; no letters; no
> society; and which is worst of all, continual fear, and
> danger of violent death; and the life of man, solitary,
> poor, nasty, brutish, and short.

Hobbes wrote *Leviathan* in exile, while the English Civil
War was raging. Swift, born seven years after the restoration
of the monarchy, lived in an age in which Hobbes's vision
of the terror of anarchy still seemed all too real. Hobbes
argues, with sceptical bitterness, the paramount need for
authority and control in matters of government. Swift takes
as his starting point the issue which was still among the
greatest of the day, the terrible memory of civil war, the
need for sovereign power to exercise such control as would
protect man against his worst excesses, against his own lust
and avarice and pride, and uses the whole problem as a
metaphor for what seemed to him to be anarchy in the 'Intellectual State, or Commonwealth of Learning'; that is, in
the world of the arts and sciences.

Swift seizes upon the essence of Hobbes's argument and
augments its intensity and bitterness in a way which is
entirely characteristic, anticipating the bitter satiric metaphor of the Yahoos in the fourth book of *Gulliver's Travels*
in a clear enough way:

> The same Reasoning also, holds Place among them, in
> those Dissensions we behold upon a Turgescency in
> any of their Females. For, the Right of Possession
> lying in common (it being impossible to establish a
> Property in so delicate a Case) Jealousies and Suspicions
> do so abound, that the whole Commonwealth of that
> Street, is reduced to a manifest *State* of *War*, of every
> *Citizen* against every *Citizen*; till some One of more
> Courage, Conduct, or Fortune than the rest, seizes and

enjoys the Prize; Upon which, naturally arises Plenty of Heart-burning, and Envy, and Snarling against the *Happy Dog*.

But, whereas Hobbes, even though his view of human integrity is not high (and, in the context of the terrible wars between monarchy and parliament, there was ample reason for doubt about man's capacity for sanity in a state of war), his concern for man's suffering is deep, and expressed with dignity. Swift's satirical voice pushes on far beyond Hobbes towards a savage jeering at man's bestiality; there is no hint of compassion here. The stance is that of a thorough-going cynic (the word is somewhat appropriate, since it is derived from the Greek word for dog-like), and if we were sure that Swift's own view of mankind is being expressed here, in an unqualified way, we could say that Swift debases himself rather than humanity.

But we are not sure of any such thing. The passage acts, as it were, as a satirical probe, exposing a sensitive nerve-ending. We react, as we must, by asserting that human kind is not necessarily, and not always, so poor in spirit as to be afflicted by such mean pride; that man can be generous, open-hearted and creative, that he can achieve poise and richness of spirit. At first the response is defensive; but Swift, in due course, offers us a way of winning greater security. 'SATYR *is a sort of Glass, wherein Beholders do generally discover every body's Face but their Own*' is a shrewd sally, but is, perhaps, too satirical to be strictly true: more often, as in this case, we see a distorted and ugly image, but like our own in too many ways for comfort. The skilful satirist goes on to offer other images, as if in a looking glass, to stimulate our anxiety to understand, not only others, but ourselves.

The mock-epic fable of the battle would have had more interest for a contemporary than it has for us; the episode which continues to engage our attention is the fable of the Spider and the Bee, based appropriately enough on one of the fables of Aesop. Aesop conveys an essential moral economically enough, but Swift (ironically, since he is arguing the greater richness of the ancients, Aesop among them, over the moderns) transforms the fable into something far more subtle and suggestive. Here is an eighteenth century version of Aesop's fable for comparison:

> The Bee and the Spider once entered into a warm debate which was the better artist. The Spider urged her skill in the mathematics; and asserted that no one was half so well acquainted as herself with the construction of lines, angles, squares, and circles: that the web she daily wove was a specimen of art inimitable by any other creature in the universe: and besides, that her works were derived from herself alone, the product of her own bowels; whereas the boasted honey of the bee, was stolen from every herb and flower of the field; nay, that she had obligations even to the meanest weeds. To this the Bee replied, that she was in hopes the art of extracting honey from the meanest weeds, would at least have been allowed her as an excellence; and that as to her stealing sweets from the herbs and flowers of the field, her skill was there so conspicuous, that no flower ever suffered the least diminution of its fragrance from so delicate an operation. Then, as to the Spider's vaunted knowledge in the construction of lines and angles, she believed she might safely rest the merits of her cause, on the regularity alone of her combs; but since she could add to this, the sweetness and excellence of her honey, and the various purposes to which her wax was employed, she had nothing to fear from a comparison of her skill with that of the weaver of a flimsy cobweb; for the *value* of every art, she observed, is chiefly to be estimated by its *use*.

It is a charming enough fable, and one which was in common use: Bacon's Aphorism XCV of the *Novum Organum*, as we have already seen, makes the spider an image of the reasoners 'who make cobwebs out of their own substance', the bee an image of the true philosopher, who transforms what he collects by a creative power of his own. So it is not in the concept of the fable, or in its moral, that the special effectiveness of Swift's episode of Spider and Bee lies:

virtually all his contemporaries would be very familiar with both. The strength of Swift's episode lies in the sharpness of his dramatic talent, and the way he uses it to urge a serious view of right and wrong attitudes towards civilization, tradition and history.

In the first place he uses the calculated disproportion of the mock-epic manner as a kind of measure for the spider, and all the spider represents. The epic was the mode most characteristic of the ancient world, the mode, perhaps, which was most difficult for the modern world (though many of Swift's contemporaries tried it). The traditional epic demands a very deep and intimate identification between the poet and the culture from within which he works. It demands belief, not only in the gods of one's culture, but even more in the men, in the values of a society, its unity and its destiny. In Swift's age this quality of belief had become extraordinarily difficult, though there were two writers, Bunyan and Milton, who caught some of the strength and the dignity, the assuredness and faith of the epic. But Bunyan and Milton, though their lives overlapped Swift's, belonged to a very different world. Swift's habit of irony is a personal quality, but at the same time it is a quality characteristic of the age, a quality demanded by the age, for irony of Swift's kind can only thrive upon insecurity of knowledge and belief, and, for all its stress upon stability and order, Swift's age was a deeply puzzled one. It knew too many ways of looking at the world, and at man; it knew too well that there are more ways than one to cook a carrot; it delighted in the ironies caused by conflicts in understanding between views, each of which have much to recommend them. It learned to look suspiciously at any firm and dogmatic statement of belief, or any work of art which assumed the strength of such belief. And yet it hankered after the strengths of the epic, the stabilities of less thoroughly ironic civilizations.

The description of the Spider's web recalls many of the tricks of epic narrative: 'Thrice he endeavoured to force his passage, and Thrice the Center shook.' It touches, in passing, upon the notion of a return to Chaos, and the sense of the age that Nature, a miraculous balance of harmony and rightness, was always at risk, in danger of collapse under the assault of the forces of Chaos: 'The *Spider* within, feeling the terrible Convulsion, supposed at first, that *Nature* was approaching to her final Dissolution'. It approaches a Miltonic note comparing the Spider's predicament with the war of Heaven and Hell, Beelzebub, the Lord of the Flies, coming to revenge himself upon a Spider-Christ: 'or else, that Beelzebub with all his Legions, was come to revenge the Death of many thousands of his Subjects, whom his Enemy had slain and devoured'.

But, of course, all this bears upon the tiny field of action of a spider's web, at most six inches across. Mock-epic does not mock the epic: on the contrary it depends for its effect upon a continued sense of the dignity of the epic mode, its noble comprehensiveness of vision. It mocks the absurdity and meanness of modern man's pretensions, trapping him in a frame which is too grand for him. Its aim is subversion and its method disproportion.

In passing, Swift satirizes the modern dependence upon artifice. Here the medium of the satire is not precisely mock-epic, but mock romance. The Spider's web as a giant's castle might possibly recall an episode in Spenser or Bunyan: more directly, perhaps, it puts one in mind of a more humble mimic of epic and romance, like the tale of Jack the Giant Killer:

> For, upon the highest Corner of a large Window, there dwelt a certain *Spider*, swollen up to the first Magnitude, by the Destruction of infinite Numbers of *Flies*, whose Spoils lay scattered before the Gates of his Palace, like human Bones before the Cave of some Giant. The Avenues to his Castle were guarded with Turn-pikes, and Palissadoes, all after the *Modern* way of Fortification.

At the time Swift wrote this, and again when it was published, English soldiers were engaged in bloody wars in the Netherlands. They limped home each year after the campaign season, with ghastly mutilations, and told veteran's

tales about marches, counter marches, sieges and forti-
fications; perhaps, like Uncle Toby in *Tristram Shandy*, spent
a life-time re-living a campaign. There were no anti-war
demonstrations, no My Lai trials; just war every year, with
peace a rare and extraordinary interruption of the accustomed pattern.

Of course princes and politicians gained and consolidated
power through war; of course generals made great fortunes
and junior officers lost and made little ones; it was a part of
modern life, a regular habit of mutual destruction which was
the way of things. It must have seemed to a contemporary
that the world of William of Orange and Marlborough was
all 'Turn-pikes and Palissadoes' with no time for honey and
flowers; nothing to set against a world of war but the dream
of a golden age, in which heroes died heroically, and didn't
bring their stumps and blinded eyes home to become beggars
in the market place.

Swift's most powerful weapon is the sudden shift in tone:
the high astounding terms of the mimic epic are followed
suddenly by a vigorous mimicry of vulgar abusive slang:

> At length, casting his Eye upon the *Bee*, and wisely
> gathering Causes from Events, (for they knew each
> other by Sight) *A Plague split you*, said he, *for a giddy
> Son of a Whore; Is it you, with a Vengeance, that have made
> this Litter here? Could you not look before you, and be d – n'd?
> Do you think I have nothing else to do (in the Devil's Name) but
> to Mend and Repair after your Arse?*

The language is deliberately wasteful: out of fifty three
words spoken by the Spider, twenty one are oaths; mono-
tonous and paltry expletives, indicative of a mind's emptiness
more than its anger. The contrast with the mock-dignity
and expansiveness of what has gone before needs no comment.

In the argument which follows, the Spider's claims are all
based upon his superior artifice, upon his independence of
nature: '*This large Castle (to shew my Improvements in the
Mathematicks) is all built with my own Hands, and the Materials
extracted altogether out of my own Person.*' Swift parodies the

modern manner: certainly the age of Newton and Leibniz, Flamsteed and Halley, Galileo, Kepler and Descartes could claim immense superiority in mathematical skills, over any preceding culture. And it was not only in military practice that skills in engineering had opened up a whole new world of possibilities. Primitive steam engines had already begun to be developed; civil engineering had begun to use sophisticated canal systems for drainage and transport; the metallurgical and chemical industries were making great strides; there were dramatic improvements in navigation; the foundations for modern industry and trade were being laid in innumerable ways. No defender of the Ancients could possibly dispute any of this.

What Swift *did* dispute (and what has been disputed by critics of modern society ever since) is whether more intangible qualities have kept pace with technical skills; whether modern man is too absorbed in his own pride, in his own skill, to see where his cleverness should lead; whether, in his absorption with ways of engineering his environment, man is ignoring the larger questions, destroying the balance of Nature, taking too much account of immediate satisfactions and losing the capacity to think in the long-term. The question is still with us:

> *Now, for you and your Skill in Architecture, and other Mathematicks, I have little to say: In that Building of yours, there might, for aught I know, have been Labor and Method enough, but by woful Experience for us both, 'tis too plain, the Materials are nought, and I hope, you will henceforth take Warning, and consider Duration and matter, as well as method and Art. You boast, indeed, of being obliged to no other Creature, but of drawing, and spinning out all from your self; That is to say, if we may judge of the Liquor in the Vessel by what issues out, You possess a good plentiful Store of Dirt and Poison in your Breast; And, tho' I would by no means, lessen or disparage your genuine Stock of either, yet I doubt you are somewhat obliged for an Encrease of both, to a little foreign Assistance. . . . So that in short, the Question comes all to this; Whether is the nobler Being of the two, That which by a lazy Con-*

*templation of four Inches round; by an overweening Pride,
which feeding and engendering on it self, turns all into Excrement and Venom; producing nothing at last, but Fly-bane
and a Cobweb: Or That, which, by an universal Range, with
long Search, much Study, true Judgment, and Distinction of
Things, brings home Honey and Wax.*

Swift returns to the same basic question in *A Discourse
Concerning the Mechanical Operation of the Spirit*; detecting the
same blind satisfaction with artifice, that same inward-
looking pride, which hampers modern arts and sciences in
the most characteristically modern form of religious experience, the Enthusiasm of Dissent.

As a medium for the satire he chooses to use the voice of a
virtuoso; that is, a scholar or savant such as the new scientists
of the Royal Society, eager for knowledge, full of learning,
constantly and busily in communication with other learned
men, whether in his own country or abroad. There are some
obvious ways in which the eye of such a man would be
excellent for observing and exposing the excesses of religious
Enthusiasm; any account of over-emotional or hysterical
behaviour is compromised if the observer's emotions can
be seen to be involved, and the dispassionate, clinical attitude
of the experimental scientist, therefore, suits the occasion
very well. But, as one must expect with Swift's satire, the
irony cuts more than one way. The *virtuoso*'s busy correspondence with fellow intellectuals all over the world has not
done much to cultivate the whole man: in this age of
American colonization the Iroquois would be an instant
image of savage innocence. And the Topinambou, though a
real Brazilian tribe, were best known for having given
their name to the Jerusalem artichoke, so the pretensions of
their *literati* would be somewhat difficult to take seriously.
The perfunctory letter frame serves well enough to convey
the air of busy artless artifice; the concern with ephemeral
fashion, the self-importance and the limitations of vision of
the *virtuoso* who acts as vehicle for the satire; the dispassionate
detachment he claims is already brought into question. When
he reveals his methods of composition (so very like the

methods of certain twentieth-century scholars who never dare show their faces above their card-indexes), he becomes more and more the ass of his *Memorandums*:

> And therefore, whatever in my small Reading, occurs, concerning this our Fellow-Creature, I do never fail to set it down by way of Common-place; and when I have occasion to write upon Human Reason, Politicks, Eloquence, or Knowledge; I lay my *Memorandums* before me, and insert them with a wonderful Facility of Application.

So, we are never allowed to be quite certain of the precise purport of the arguments the *virtuoso* uses: the irony works as often against the pert and busy scepticism of the *persona* as against the Dissenters. Swift provides himself with a system of ironic defences every bit as complex and dangerous for the reader as the Spider's web is for the Bee: and the defences are necessary, for the basic questions at issue are the most solemn of all questions at the root of the contemporary debate about reason and religion.

One of the most relevant discussions of these matters is in *An Essay Concerning Human Understanding*, a work which explores the theoretical and philosophical basis for the kind of scientific activity which we are to imagine the virtuoso is most concerned with. Locke distinguishes between reason and revelation, declaring that revelation must always be tested against reason:

> revelation is natural reason enlarged by a new set of discoveries communicated by God immediately, which reason vouches the truth of, by the testimony and proofs it gives, that they come from God. So that he that takes away reason, to make way for revelation, puts out the light of both, and does much-what the same, as if he would persuade a man to put out his eye, the better to receive the remote light of an invisible star by a telescope.
>
> Immediate revelation being a much easier way for men to establish their opinions, and regulate their

conduct, than the tedious and not always successful labour of strict reasoning, it is no wonder that some have been very apt to pretend to revelation, and to persuade themselves that they are under the peculiar guidance of heaven in their actions and opinions . . . Their minds being thus prepared, whatever groundless opinion comes to settle itself strongly upon their fancies, is an illumination from the spirit of God, and presently of divine authority: and whatsoever odd action they find in themselves a strong inclination to do, that impulse is concluded to be a call or direction from heaven, and must be obeyed . . .

So far, so good, and it must be assumed that Swift shares common cause with Locke, and the *persona* of the *Discourse* would agree with what Locke says, though perhaps the *virtuoso* would be less alive to Locke's ironies (less intricate and subtle than Swift's, but effective none the less). The way Swift develops the argument, making it at once into a farcical exposure of the Enthusiast and a comical parody of the type of reasoning which Locke and his fellow moderns seemed to encourage, is to elaborate with a manic, ant-like intensity, decorating a basically serious argument until the methods, not the purport, of the discourse fall apart in wild confusion.

Locke allows revelation to be an immediate inspiration from God, and so does the *virtuoso*:

> there are three general Ways of ejaculating the Soul, or transporting it beyond the Sphere of Matter. The first, is the immediate Act of God, and is called, *Prophecy* or *Inspiration*.

The academic habit of listing and categorizing, however, pushes our *virtuoso* into instancing the opposite case. Possession by the devil has an equally supernatural cause, but the effect is simply madness. From the supernatural he moves to the next obvious contrast, the natural, and from thence to his real interest, the artificial:

> The second, is the immediate Act of the Devil, and is termed *Possession*. The third, is the Product of natural

Causes, the effect of strong Imagination, Spleen, violent
Anger, Fear, Grief, Pain, and the like. These three
have been abundantly treated on by Authors, and
therefore shall not employ my Enquiry. But, the fourth
Method of *Religious Enthusiasm*, or launching out the
Soul, as it is purely an Effect of Artifice and *Mechanick
Operation*, has been sparingly handled . . .

Divine, diabolic, human, mechanical; the progression marks
out what seemed to Swift and his fellow critics of modern
learning the direction in which all contemporary scholarship
tended: from the most profound to the most trivial; from the
inexplicable mystery of godhead to the obsessive attempt to
explain everything, even religious error or human life, in
terms of the machine. So the *virtuoso*, showing not the slightest
need to inquire after the nature of the soul, or the spiritual
problems of man, contents himself happily with a problem
which is well within his field of understanding, which responds to his accustomed tools of scientific measurement and
scholastic inquiry.

Almost imperceptibly, then, the *Discourse* slides into
speaking of soul or spirit as something which can be physically manipulated, in the same way as the race of Round-
heads, or Puritan extremists, he says 'in its Beginning, was
meerly an Operation of Art, produced by a pair of Cizars,
a Squeeze of the Face, and a black Cap'. At the same time,
though, the spirit remains immaterial – and this paradox
of the physical manipulation of the metaphysical remains
the basis of the humour. Furthermore, the *virtuoso* blandly
assumes that the spirit must be hostile to both sense and
reason. There are many ways in which the scientific *virtuoso*
and the Dissenting Enthusiasts differ; here, at all events,
is something in which they seem to agree (and clearly I am
not speaking of actual people, members of the Royal Society
or the Dissenting congregations, but Swift's satirical versions
of them); that they both behave as if Spirit can only operate
when the senses go astray:

> The Practitioners of this famous Art, proceed in general
> upon the following Fundamental; That, *the Corruption*

of the Senses is the Generation of the Spirit: Because the *Senses* in Men are so many Avenues to the Fort of *Reason*, which in this Operation is wholly block'd up. All Endeavours must be therefore used, either to divert, bind up, stupify, fluster, and amuse the *Senses*, or else to justle them out of their Stations; and while they are either absent, or otherwise employ'd or engaged in a Civil War against each other, the *Spirit* enters and performs its Part.

To Swift, this assumption was disastrously absurd, a distortion of the Natural harmony so dear to the age; and the comparison between man in such a predicament and civil war is significant enough in view of the recent terrible incidents in English history. But it is perhaps equally significant that the complacent discourse of the *virtuoso* recalls very strongly indeed by contrast the discourse of another great expert in matters of the spirit, St Paul, with his insistence:

That there should be no schism in the body; but that the members should have the same care one for another. And whether one member suffer, all the members suffer with it; or one member be honoured, all the members rejoice with it.

The reference to the *Acts of the Apostles* satirically underscores the contrast between the harmony of Spirit and Reason which Swift believes to be characteristic of true Faith, and the inner conflicts which he believes to be characteristic of Enthusiasm:

First, that *the Apostles were gathered together with one accord in one place*; by which is meant, an universal Agreement in Opinion, and Form of Worship; a Harmony (say they) so far from being found between any two Conventicles among Us, that it is vain to expect it between any two Heads in the same.

The *virtuoso*'s gloss is teasingly odd, full of shrewd little hits against the vulgarity and ignorance of Dissenting religion, but it leads towards a vulgarity of the *virtuoso*'s own; one which will easily elude us, because we have come to accept much that Swift would not accept as proper in religious thought. When the *virtuoso* draws a distinction between two possible meanings for the term Spirit, 'a supernatural Assistance, approaching from without' and 'the *Spirit* we treat of here, proceeding entirely from within', we are not meant simply to accept the distinction, and carry on with the argument. The Apostles were visited by the Holy Spirit as a supernatural grace; Swift's eyebrows are raised inquiringly at the idea that something has happened in the intervening centuries to favour us more than the twelve men most intimate with Christ, so that the Spirit need no longer be a supernatural visitation, but can be *entirely* from within. This heresy is, he implies, only too characteristic of the 'modern' manner; a product of self-centredness, pride and triviality rather than divine grace.

Limited though the understanding of the *virtuoso* may be, he is given certain skills of clinically exact description:

> They violently strain their Eye balls inward, half closing the Lids; Then, as they sit, they are in perpetual Motion of *See-saw*, making long Hums at proper Periods, and continuing the Sound at equal Height, chusing their Time in those Intermissions, while the Preacher is at Ebb. . . .

these methods, or methods very like them, are still in use in primitive evangelistic religious practice throughout the world; the rhythms and patterns of mutual hypnosis are caught precisely – too precisely and circumstantially, one would think, for the author never to have experienced something very like ecstatic trance himself (though if he has, he distrusts it profoundly):

> at first, you can see nothing, but after a short pause, a small glimmering Light begins to appear, and dance before you. Then, by frequently moving your Body up and down, you perceive the Vapors to ascend very fast, till you are perfectly dosed and flustred like one who drinks too much in a Morning. Mean while, the

Preacher is also at work; He begins a loud Hum, which
pierces you quite thro'; This is immediately returned by
the Audience, and you find yourself prompted to imitate
them, by a meer spontaneous Impulse, without knowing
what you do.

It is as if Swift himself, out of curiosity, had sampled the
passionate communal experience of the Dissenting conventicle
and drawn back horrified, yet at the same time fascinated
by the pleasures of unreason. As we have seen, Swift had a
markedly ambivalent attitude towards the Imagination,
fearing its excitement as close to madness, but capable of
understanding its intoxicating joys. He is, perhaps, though in
a less obvious way, almost as complex in his feelings about
surrender to the 'meer spontaneous Impulse, without knowing what you do' of mass religious ecstasy. The sharp contempt with which he satirizes the irrelevant ritual and bizarre
stage management of the Dissenting preachers is, possibly,
a measure of its hidden attractions.

In the beginning of Section II he is attacking, rather less
directly, another pattern of religious error. For the Dissenter,
Revelation is a repeated experience; anyone who obeys his
inner light has constant access to divine guidance; Swift
laughs at the Dissenters for becoming intoxicated with
Revelation, and is appalled at the ease and complacency
with which they continually claim it.

The Deists, and proponents of 'Natural' Religion, on the
other hand, attempt to do away with Revelation entirely,
and to substitute Reason for it. There are very few deistical
thinkers who would openly reject Revelation; it was still
shocking, even dangerous, to do so. But they can be recognized by their reservation of the certainties of Revelation
to the very last, their preference for the argument of Reason
taken as far as it will possibly go. And they are distinguished,
too, by their elaborately calm, judicial manner, their careful
tolerance of many points of view. Notice how this bland
scholarly tone is caught in

> You will read it very gravely remarked in the Books
> of those illustrious and right eloquent Pen-men, the

> Modern Travellers; that the fundamental Difference in Point of Religion, between the wild *Indians* and Us, lies in this; that We worship *God*, and they worship the *Devil*. But, there are certain Criticks, who will by no means admit of this Distinction; rather believing, that all Nations whatsoever, adore the *true God*. . . . Others, again, inform us, that . . .

The speaker does not commit himself in the slightest, even when faced with such fundamental questions of faith as these (though one can sense Swift's own ironic presence behind the speaker's voice, guying his academic equanimity by an almost imperceptible excess of moderation). The *persona* approves of a third point of view only because it seems the most 'Universal' (not considering it in terms of truth or falsehood):

> Others, again, inform us, that those Idolaters adore two *Principles*; the *Principle* of *Good*, and That of *Evil*: Which indeed, I am apt to look upon as the most Universal Notion, that Mankind, by the meer Light of Nature, ever entertained of Things Invisible.

But in the early satirical manner of Swift we are never allowed the luxury of consistency; the argument so far has seemed merely to serve a soft and careless fashionable tolerance. The slight tartness of the last few words (the absurd paradox that invisible things can be seen 'by the meer Light of Nature') begins to sour the illusion. Up to now we have been persuaded, or very nearly persuaded – Swift's elusiveness forces us to be wary and keep something in reserve all the time – that the satire only attacks a certain kind of thinker, and not ourselves; we are comfortably seated by the satirist's side, looking at the object satirized. Then suddenly, the satirist deserts us, and goes over to the enemy (or so it seems):

> To me, the difference appears little more than this, That They are put oftener upon their Knees by their *Fears*, and We by our *Desires*; That the former set them a *Praying*, and Us a *Cursing*.

The voice is consistent with the *virtuoso* in its apparent objectivity, but no one is for a moment taken in by the pretence: the epigrammatic balance, the shrewd knock-down wit (vigorously rough in temper, but sharpened by a cultivated economy of statement), pushes through and announces itself as Swift's own. The ironies begin to become quite different in kind now. 'What I applaud them for, is their Discretion, in limiting their Devotions and their Deities to their several Districts, nor ever suffering the Liturgy of the *white* God, to cross or interfere with that of the *Black*' is no longer the voice of the *virtuoso*, even in a remote kind of way: to be sure the real Swift wouldn't applaud a pagan seriously for such delicacy of liturgical protocol; it *is* irony, but irony of the directer, less subtle kind that does not seek the consistency of an imagined *persona*; Swift is angry enough to be carried away from his chosen vehicle and chosen method. And the anger which so engages him is modern Man's pride in his own Reason, and his misuse of Reason to destroy moral sense:

> Not so with Us, who pretending by the Lines and Measures of our Reason, to extend the Dominion of one invisible Power, and contract that of the other, have discovered a gross Ignorance in the Natures of Good and Evil, and most horribly confounded the Frontiers of both. . . . I laugh aloud, to see these Reasoners, at the same time, engaged in wise Dispute, about certain Walks and Purlieus . . . seriously debating, whether such and such Influences come into Mens Minds, from above or below, or whether certain Passions and Affections are guided by the Evil Spirit or the Good.

The tendency of the essential argument by now begins to become quite clear: man is essentially a moral being; he cannot fulfil his moral destiny either by throwing out Reason, as the Enthusiasts do in their conventicles, pretending that Inspiration is enough; but neither can he, like the fashionable Deists, achieve moral rightness and sanity purely through the exercise of Reason. Something else is needed: in the *Tale* it is called the Coat of the Father. Swift was a very orthodox Anglican Christian; at the same time he was a man who, for deep personal reasons, needed something *outside himself* to rely on: not the inner light of the Dissenters, not pure Reason. These were 'Fly-bane and Cobwebs'; 'Honey and Wax' are only brought home by those who recognize their dependence on a vast and marvellous universe outside them; something which they cannot entirely control, but which they can use wisely, if they have humility and wisdom.

'*Pride* is nearly related to Beggary and *Want*' says Swift at the beginning of *The Battle of the Books*; the pride of the Deists in human Reason and the pride of the Dissenters in their inner light of Revelation, is all of a piece:

> However, it is a Sketch of Human Vanity, for every Individual, to imagine the whole Universe is interess'd in his meanest Concern. If he hath got cleanly over a Kennel[1], some Angel, unseen, descended on purpose to help him by the Hand; if he hath knockt his Head against a Post, it was the Devil, for his Sins, let loose from Hell, on purpose to buffet him.

Momentarily, Swift has allowed himself to be carried away. He brings himself back again to the chosen satirical method by means of a hiatus. The side comment is enough to restore the ironic tone: '*Here the whole Scheme of spiritual Mechanism was deduced and explained, with an Appearance of great reading and observation . . .*' Our attention is now turned more towards the folly of the *virtuoso* and his kind. The satisfaction which the *virtuoso* feels in dealing with the *mechanical* operation of the spirit, as I have already suggested, comes from the fact that he is more greatly at ease with mechanics than with things of the spirit. Now Swift allows him to bring forth, with every appearance of complacent satisfaction, a mock-theory of human intelligence which reduces every human activity, every aspect of human excellence, to a sterile soulless mechanism:

> For, it is the Opinion of Choice *Virtuosi*, that the Brain is only a Crowd of little Animals, but with Teeth and

---

[1] A gutter or drain; often in Swift's day a noxious open sewer.

Claws extremely sharp, and therefore, cling together in the Contexture we behold, like the Picture of *Hobbes*'s *Leviathan*, or like Bees in perpendicular swarm upon a Tree, or like a Carrion corrupted into Vermin, still preserving the Shape and Figure of the Mother Animal. That all Invention is formed by the Morsure of two or more of these Animals, upon certain capillary Nerves, which proceed from thence, whereof three Branches spread into the Tongue, and two into the right Hand. They hold also, that these Animals are of a Constitution extremely cold; that their Food is the Air we attract, their Excrement Phlegm; and that what we vulgarly call Rheums, and Colds, and Distillations, is nothing else but an Epidemical Looseness, to which that little Commonwealth is very subject, from the Climate it lyes under. Farther, that nothing less than a violent Heat, can disentangle these Creatures from their hamated Station of Life, or give them Vigor and Humor, to imprint the Marks of their little Teeth. That if the Morsure be Hexagonal, it produces Poetry; the Circular gives Eloquence; If the Bite hath been Conical, the Person, whose Nerve is so affected, shall be disposed to write upon the Politicks; and so of the rest.

There was (as far as I know) no serious theory of intelligence exactly like this, even in the later seventeenth century, which produced some bizarre attempts to explain biological phenomena by means of concepts and methods drawn from physics and mechanics. But these more grotesque physiological theories were by-products of a movement of great importance, which had begun with Galileo, continued through Santorio and Harvey (discoverer of the circulation of the blood), and eventually resulted in a far greater understanding of human and animal physiology and therefore immensely significant advances in medicine.

Among the more fanciful theorists in the movement was the philosopher Descartes, who was one of the first to try to cope with the more disturbing implications of mechanistic approaches to biological organisms. He treated the body as a machine; he illustrated and emphasized the phenomenon of reflex action, in which the body responds to external stimuli without any consciousness being necessarily involved; he believed animals to be entirely governed by such automatic responses; he proposed an elaborate system of co-ordination of bodily activities for these animal automata: the nerves were tubular vessels containing and conveying a 'nervous fluid' which acted upon the muscles to make them contract and extend according to the stimulus applied. But, if animals were machines, there was something unique in man which made him able to initiate action, to put the machinery he shares with other animals to purposes dictated by the will. This raised in a peculiarly acute form the old problem which has confronted almost every philosopher who has ever considered the relationship between mind and body: if the body is a machine which obeys the natural physical laws and no other, what place is there in it for an immaterial, non-physical presence, call it soul, or mind, or spirit, or what you will? And if there is such a presence in the human entity, by what means does it convey its will, or need, or desire, to the machine? Descartes believed that body and soul are related to each other through the pineal gland, but the nature of the connection, and how the pineal gland operates, is, he concedes, a mystery. Descartes' thought led him, in short, to extend the empire of the machine further and further, until it was proper to explain all animal behaviour by mechanical laws, and until almost everything about the human entity could be so explained, but the one thing left unexplained by physical laws could not be explained by any other means either.

Meanwhile Giovanni Borelli was working on his posthumously published classic *On Motion of Animals* (1680), which leaves aside the problem of soul and brings Borelli's knowledge of mathematics and physics to analyse the mechanics of muscular action; other scientists like Sylvius and Stahl were attempting, for the first time, to understand the chemistry of the body, though making no progress at all towards solving the problem of soul. A whole group of workers with the microscope were discovering many things about the structure and behaviour of living beings, and raising the question of the relationship between the material and the spiritual in other ways, for instance, as we have seen, in the problem of the spermatozoon, or animalcule.

Descartes was not the only philosopher to be affected by the movement. Hobbes, for instance, approached much more closely to an uncompromising materialism in his account of human being. For him a man is a collection of material particles in motion, and this is how he speaks of sensation:

> The cause of sense is the external body, or object, which presseth the organ proper to each sense, either immediately, as in the taste and touch; or mediately, as in seeing, hearing, and smelling; which pressure, by the mediation of the nerves, and other strings and membranes of the body, continued inwards to the brain and heart, causeth there a resistance, or counter pressure, or endeavour of the heart to deliver itself, which endeavour, because outward, seemeth to be some matter without.

This leaves a lot of questions unanswered, but clearly Hobbes is not disposed to use the concept of a non-physical, immaterial presence initiating action except as a last resort.

Another influential philosopher whose view of reality was essentially materialistic was Pierre Gassendi, who adapted Epicurus' idea that the universe is composed of innumerable atoms, of various shapes and sizes. Like Descartes, Gassendi thought of animals as entirely material, the animal 'soul' as a material object. And he too conceived of the human soul as something more complex. It is, he believes, composed of two parts, one material, the other immaterial and immortal, derived from God. But, once again, the notion of an immaterial soul is a kind of last resort. Almost everything about human existence, sensation, action and behaviour can be explained by physical processes acting within the brain.

It is speculations of this kind which Swift parodies in the passage last quoted from the *Discourse*. Enthusiasts distort experience by denying reason, Deistical thinkers distort it even more by trusting too much to reason; thinkers of the kind represented by the 'Choice Virtuosi' whose opinions are parodied deny the most essential fact of human existence, or tend to deny it, by eroding the notions of spirit and mind and will, by tending all the time to seek a mechanical explanation of human intellect and feeling.

Notice how Swift's rhetoric persuades the reader into rejection of the materialistic view; we react against the notion that the brain is *only* anything: if we revere life as we should, we think of the human brain as an incredibly complex mystery (imperfect though it is), so fertile of invention and unpredictable in its subtlety and variety that anyone who undertakes to say what it *only* is condemns himself as stupid and inhuman. The 'choiceness' of the *virtuosi* is further made suspect by the rather painful idea that the brain is made up of sharp-toothed animals. No theorist had suggested this, but for the purposes of the satire the notion is close enough, on the one hand, to Gassendi's atoms and on the other to Leeuwenhoek's animalcules to look as if it might well be the next theory to be advanced by the materialists in their campaign to reduce human life to a barren mechanism. By a deft sleight of hand Swift associates this grotesque image with Hobbes's *Leviathan*, as if to suggest that so sceptical a view of human society as Hobbes's must eventually result in some such detestable and intolerable view of human intellect as this one. The images which follow push the image farther and farther into horror, and ourselves into a painful state of horrified amusement. The comparison with swarming bees raises associations of mindless herding, of the loss of individuality to instinct, and also of pain from the bees' stinging; the comparison with vermin on carrion adds associations of corruption, stench and disease. The sequence has led, by an illogical, emotive sequence of metaphor, it is true, but powerfully nevertheless, to the feeling that any such analytical materialism reduces human life to corruption, stench and pain, and nothing else.

Swift proceeds to press the reductive argument still further, using quasi-scientific terms – morsure, capillary, hamated and so on – to give verisimilitude to the parody, and parodying, too, the pert claim to precision of the self-confident virtuoso with details like 'whereof three Branches spread into the Tongue, and two into the right Hand'. So, at last, we are given the final absurdity that all human invention is merely the product of random bites from little sharp-toothed animalcules. The result is laughable (and deplorable) enough, when it is to suggest that poetry is one such automatism. But, characteristically, there is a further level to the irony counter-sunk beneath this, which does not quite reveal itself until the end: 'the Circular gives Eloquence; If the Bite hath been Conical, the Person, whose Nerve is so affected, shall be disposed to write upon the Politicks; and so of the rest'. With this final, sinuous satirical wriggle, Swift contrives to suggest that there are, after all, aspects of human behaviour which might as well be automatism, for all the intelligence one can discover in them.

It is worth our while to stress the scientific and philosophical application of the satire in this way, but we must not lose sight of the fact that it has a very immediate topical interest too; allusion to the incident of Sir Humphrey Edwin, a Dissenter who became Lord Mayor of London, being a good example of the way Swift's satire never strays far away from the experience of living people in a living community. Edwin had gone in his official character to a Presbyterian meeting-house while Lord Mayor, challenging the established religious pattern in a way which many, including Swift, thought grossly improper. Against this official act of approval for 'Canting' Swift employs a highly skilful and purposeful rhetoric to undercut and destroy the rhetoric of unreason. The rhetoric employs, and largely depends upon, the sudden and unexpected juxtaposition of the profound and the absurd, the exalted and the disgusting, forcing us (or at least persuading us with great power, through laughter, uncertainty, disgust and awe at the repeated blasphemy) to reject the mannerisms of Dissent with contempt:

A Master Work-man shall *blow his Nose so powerfully*, as to pierce the Hearts of his People, who are disposed to receive the *Excrements* of his Brain with the same

Reverence, as the *Issue* of it. Hawking, Spitting, and Belching, the defects of other Mens Rhetorick, are the Flowers, and Figures, and Ornaments of his. For, the *Spirit* being the same in all, it is of no Import through what Vehicle it is convey'd.

Swift demonstrates satirically the intimate relationship between flesh and spirit; what is so uncomfortable about his tone is that the irony works consistently towards the degrading of both. In the satirical key he uses here body is simply a collection of functions, excreting, spitting, belching, snuffling, ejaculating. There is nothing disgusting about any of these functions. But when the body of man is described insistently and solely in terms of excretion, and the metaphor of excretion spills over to affect all other bodily actions, particularly sexual activity, then our attitude towards the body is being shoe-horned into a cramped and ill-shaped posture. The rhetoric seeks to persuade us that the spiritual experience of the Dissenters is all of a piece with their physical nature, then, since our attitude to the physical has been so distorted, we find their spiritual behaviour repulsive. If on the contrary we are able to look upon the body as Blake, for instance, looked upon it, then looking at soul and body as parts of each other, all of a piece with each other, will be the opposite of disgusting: it will be joyfully enlightening.

This degrading, devaluating process can be defended as a purposeful and deliberate satirical method. We can say that Swift is speaking through a satirical *persona*, and that neither he nor the reader need necessarily be degraded too by the process. Indeed we could say (and in many senses this would be right) that the experience of degradation forces one to react by asserting a more positive and whole-minded view of man and life. This we can say, but we cannot say precisely how Swift felt. In some sense the satire seems to be defensive – allowing the elaborated expression of inner fears and obsessions and doubts, of pathological states of mind, and yet disclaiming responsibility for them. At the same time part of the object of the satire seems to be his own pathology. In so far as we, the readers, share it with Swift, the satire also pursues a weakness which endangers all of us, distorted as we are by the prudish preoccupations of our culture, by the Platonic dream, by Romantic imaginings, by innumerable factors, but most of all by the problems of living in cities, where, in order to avoid constantly fouling each other's doorsteps, we are forced into more and more sanitary and hygienic ingenuity as time goes on – drains, sewers, septic tanks, water-closets, processing units, clean air acts, river authorities, pollution traps in automobile exhausts. The continual preoccupation with such matters is, in one sense of the word civilization, a mark of the civilized man. And the prime danger of civilization, in *that* sense, is disgust at man. In Swift's day they wore wigs to disguise their filthy hair. In our day we spray deodorants on ourselves to disguise our human odours. Our expressions of disgust are subtler and less recognizable, but for that reason, perhaps, even more dangerous.

But, when we have said all this, the attitude of Swift remains ambivalent. The conclusion that in some way he is forced and crowded into attitudes which are destructive of human values is inescapable; that, aware as he is of the dangers of other attitudes towards the human – that of the Dissenting Saint, the Deist, the Materialist, the Scientific Virtuoso – there is, behind everything, an impulse to avoid humanity altogether, to deny its capacity to fulfil itself, and a deadly reticence about the form which any such fulfilment could take. A passage such as the following, with all its boisterous imagery and satiric reserve, is diagnostic:

> For, some think, that the *Spirit* is apt to feed on the *Flesh*, like hungry Wines on raw Beef. Others rather believe, there is a perpetual Game at *Leap-Frog* between both; and, sometimes, the *Flesh* is uppermost, and sometimes the *Spirit*; adding, that the former, while it is in the State of a *Rider*, wears huge *Rippon* Spurs, and when it comes to the Turn of being *Bearer*, is wonderfully headstrong, and hard-mouth'd.

The assumption of irreconcilable division and conflict between flesh and spirit here is an aspect of the Christian tradition, particularly of the tradition which stems from Pauline Christianity: this is the aspect of Christian orthodoxy which repelled Blake most, and Swift is more deeply affected by it than most orthodox Christians, not because he is more than usually orthodox, but because he was more than usually sick. But notice how vividly the conflict is felt. 'Hungry Wines' were astringently acid wines: the relevant definition of 'hungry' in the *O.E.D.* runs like this:

> Lacking elements which are needful or desirable, and therefore capable of absorbing these to a greater extent; 'more disposed to draw from other substances than to impart to them' (J.); esp. of land etc.: Not rich or fertile, poor; of rivers: not supplying food for fish. Applied formerly also to 'hard' waters and acrid liquids, wines, etc.

An excessively acid wine could 'feed' upon raw meat, reacting chemically with it to destroy some of the meat and sweeten the wine: perhaps such desperate measures were in use by housewives of Swift's time. But to use the image to describe the interaction of soul and body does not flatter the spirit. On one level of the satire this can be explained away; it is the *virtuoso* speaking, and speaking of other peoples' opinions: no-one is committed to support this view of the spirit. But what other views are there? The image changes from acrid wines acting upon raw beef to a game of leap-frog, and from that to the interaction of horse and rider. The question is always one of dominance, control, brutal management of one by the other, assisted by 'huge *Rippon* Spurs'. The relationship described is as aridly wilful as that of Lucky and Pozzo in *Waiting for Godot*, as endless and meaningless as the leap-frogging dialogue of Vladimir and Estragon. But Beckett, avowedly, was writing in the wake of the failure of faith. Swift, avowedly a Christian, seems to assert that balance can only be achieved by a dictatorship of the spirit, not a natural harmony.

Perhaps we have to recall an earlier aspect of the irony here. I have remarked that the *virtuoso* makes a distinction which Swift would not accept, between spirit as 'a supernatural Assistance, approaching from without', and 'the *Spirit* we treat of here, proceeding entirely from within'. It is still the *virtuoso* speaking; the odd and disturbing falsity of the argument, its corrupting infelicities, can only be resolved if we realize that, in *this* account of flesh and spirit, the spirit is not the gift from God, but the spurious illusion of a spirit, a light from within, against which Swift's irony operates all along. What 'some think' and 'others rather believe', which makes flesh and spirit a constant war, acid wine eating into raw beef, is a special kind of pride, and comes from the assumption that we can do without God. We can be sure that Swift would approve of some such orthodox Christian interpretation; it is implicit in his whole argument. But we can also be fairly sure that Swift suffered from that same hostility of flesh and spirit, that same state of pride. The paradox gives the satire its energy.

Thus, for instance, in the episode of the Banbury Saint there is a use of the mock-epic mode every bit as successful as anything in *The Battle of the Books*, its satiric urgency increased a hundredfold by Swift's own acute consciousness of the inner war. He is also conscious, satirically and bitterly conscious, of something which it was at that time only possible to mention, perhaps, in a Rabelaisian or Aristophanic manner, shielded by satiric tensions, but we can today admit without the need for such protection: the closeness of some forms of religious experience to sexual excitement and satisfaction. Sadly, the point of the comparison is to debase the Saints' illusion of ecstasy by tainting it with sexuality, with a 'tentiginous humour' or lecherous disposition which, as the *Discourse* has it, may run into Madness:

> I have been informed by certain Sanguine Brethren of the first Class, that in the Height and *Orgasmus* of their Spiritual exercise it has been frequent with them ****; immediately after which, they found the *Spirit* to relax and flag of a sudden with the Nerves, and they were forced to hasten to a Conclusion.

I say 'sadly' because, of course, there should be no reason why sexual and religious experience should not accompany each other, and be part of each other. But it begins to be clear that the kind of sexual experience he refers to (perhaps the only kind of sexual experience Swift knew) was auto-erotic. The hidden guiding metaphor which gives much of the *Discourse* its absorbed strength and mounting energy begins to be revealed: 'spirit' was a word for semen which was current in the seventeenth century; the criticism of self-centredness and pride which runs through the work has, as its sexual manifestation, the narcissism of the auto-erotic; the images of hawking, spitting, belching, excreting, all tend towards a submerged image of ejaculation of semen. The description of the trance-like experience of the Dissenting Congregation, with its emphasis on rhythmical movement of the body: 'and they move their Bodies up and down, to a Degree, that sometimes their Heads and Points lie parallel to the Horizon' is yet another sample of the tendency of the imagery throughout the *Discourse* to move towards masturbation as an image for the flight from Reason, the surrender of the intellect, absorption with the inner experience. One cannot know how complete Swift's knowledge of his own image-making processes was; one can perceive, however, that an image which is woven into the texture of an argument so closely as this, giving it such intent energy, is of some personal importance to the author. And part of the bitterness and energy of the satire against dissent is, perhaps, transferred from personal guilt and fear by a re-direction of sexual conflict into satire.

IV
The Modes of Satire

Whoever hath an Ambition to be heard in a Crowd,
must press, and squeeze, and thrust, and climb with
indefatigable Pains, till he has exalted himself to a
certain Degree of Altitude above them. Now, in all
Assemblies, tho' you wedge them ever so close, we
may observe this peculiar Property; that, over their
Heads, there is Room enough; but how to reach it, is
the difficult Point; it being as hard to get quit of
Number as of *Hell*;

> ———*Evadere ad auras*
> *Hoc opus, hic labor est.*

> *A Tale of a Tub*, Sect. 1., The Introduction.

My Father had a small Estate in *Nottinghamshire*; I
was the Third of five Sons.

> *Gulliver's Travels*, Part I, Chap. 1.

It is a melancholy Object to those, who walk through
this great Town, or travel in the Country; when they
see the *Streets*, the *Roads*, and *Cabbin-doors* crowded with
Beggars of the Female Sex, followed by three, four, or
six Children, *all in Rags*, and importuning every Passen-
ger for an Alms.

> *A Modest Proposal*

About thirty years passed between the writing of *A Tale of
a Tub* and these two later satires, *Gulliver's Travels* and *A
Modest Proposal*. The change in idiom is remarkable, even
for a writer grown from thirty to sixty, through thirty years
and three reigns in which society had changed in decisive

ways, and the nature of the reading public and the role of the writer had changed decisively too. It seems at first that the change is something to do with the quantum of energy expended; and yet it would be absurd to say that *Gulliver's Travels* or *A Modest Proposal* are lacking in energy: it is not so much the *quanta* of energy which differ as the way in which the essential drive is harnessed.

A Tale of a Tub sets out to satirize 'the numerous and gross Corruptions in Religion and Learning', and does so with remarkable effect; but strong as the motive may be, an even stronger one is in the dominant: a delighted, passionate joy in the qualities and possibilities of the language itself; language as a medium almost in the same way as clay is to the potter a means towards satisfying tactile joy, delight in movement, shaping for its own sake.

'Whoever hath an Ambition to be heard in a Crowd, must . . . [exalt] himself to a certain Degree of Altitude above them.' This in one way would be enough, for the purposes of the discourse; and yet Swift is impelled to dramatize the activity, the tension, the energy of the ambition. This is not simply a matter of an accumulation of verbs. The forceful energies of 'must press, and squeeze, and thrust, and climb' are attached to a ghostly impersonal 'whoever' as subject. If the subject had been Jack, say, who, having 'an Ambition to be heard in a Crowd, must press, and squeeze, and thrust, and climb with indefatigable Pains' to a point of vantage, then we would have learned something about Jack, and the Crowd, and the jostling pressure of human bodies in a mass. But, the subject being 'Whoever hath an Ambition', all the energy, the confusion, the sense of difficulty and single-minded effort bears down upon the ambition to be heard.

Of course Swift is satirizing those who must be heard at all costs; but at the same time his own words thrust and climb from the page, demanding our attention: they are full of 'Ambition to be heard'. Swift treats words as weapons; at least as objects with a weight and presence of their own, like the instruments with which the Flappers demand their masters' attention in Laputa, or the *Things* which Virtuosi (having decided to abolish words altogether) carry around in back-packs in Balnibarbi. Swift says as much (ironically, it is true) in this same Introduction to the *Tale*:

> The deepest Account, and the most fairly digested of any I have yet met with, is this, That Air being a heavy Body, and therefore (according to the System of *Epicurus*) continually descending, must needs be more so, when loaden and press'd down by Words; which are also Bodies of much Weight and Gravity, as it is manifest from those deep *Impressions* they make and leave upon us; and therefore must be delivered from a due Altitude, or else they will neither carry a good Aim, nor fall down with a sufficient Force.

Clearly this satirizes materialism – not only the materialism of Epicurus but also the materialism which threatened the traditional view of things in Swift's own day, particularly the views of Hobbes and Gassendi. Swift exploits the ambiguities of meaning of words like 'Weight', 'Gravity', '*Impressions*' and 'Force', words which, *literally* understood, might be accepted as applying to words by a lunatic extremist of materialism – someone who far outbids Lucretius or Hobbes in this respect – but in a *metaphorical* sense say a good deal about Swift's attitude towards, and practice with, words. It is entirely accurate, for instance, for Leavis to characterize the metaphorical energy of the early Swift as 'the image, action or blow that, leaping out of the prosaic manner, continually surprises and disconcerts the reader'. Thoughts and words are constantly in motion in Swift's early satire; they have dimension, weight and character of their own, while the pressure of the satire, robbing Peter to pay Paul, tends as often as not to strip *people* of their liveliness and give it all to words and ideas, as in the conceit of the theatre:

> For, First; the Pit is sunk below the Stage . . . that whatever *weighty* Matter shall be delivered thence (whether it be *Lead* or *Gold*) may fall plum into the Jaws of certain *Criticks* (as I think they are called) which stand ready open to devour them. Then, the Boxes are

built round, and raised to a Level with the Scene, in
deference to the Ladies, because, That large Portion of
Wit laid out in raising Pruriences and Protuberances,
is observ'd to run much upon a Line, and ever in a
Circle. The whining Passions and little starved Conceits,
are gently wafted up by their own extreme Levity, to
the middle Region, and there fix and are frozen by the
frigid Understandings of the Inhabitants. Bombast and
Buffoonry, by Nature lofty and light, soar highest of all,
and would be lost in the Roof, if the prudent Architect
had not with much Foresight contrived for them a fourth
Place, called the *Twelve-Peny Gallery*, and there planted
a suitable Colony, who greedily intercept them in their
Passage.

Words 'fall plum', 'run much upon a Line, and ever in a
Circle', 'are gently wafted up by their own extreme Levity',
'by Nature lofty and light, soar highest of all'; people, on the
contrary 'stand ready open to devour' (one great unmoving
disembodied mouth), are 'frigid Understandings' which fix
and freeze, or a Colony 'planted' (the word retains associations of vegetable immobility) 'who greedily intercept' the
more volatile words in their passage. This sort of rhetoric
is manifested in its most complex way in the conceit of the
Aeolists: 'At certain Seasons of the Year, you might behold
the Priests amongst them in vast Numbers, with their
Mouths gaping wide against a Storm' and in the whole of *A
Discourse Concerning the Mechanical Operation of the Spirit*, where
the master-conceit is one of the skilful operator putting the
word, or the idea to work upon a passive, torpid, uncritical
human audience:

> A Master Work-man shall *blow his Nose so powerfully*,
> as to pierce the Hearts of his People, who are disposed
> to receive the *Excrements* of his Brain with the same
> Reverence, as the *Issue* of it.

The *Battle*, the Bookseller's Preface warns us, is between
books in the literal sense: 'So, when *Virgil* is mentioned, we
are not to understand the Person of a famous Poet, call'd by

that Name, but only certain Sheets of Paper, bound up in Leather', whereas the three brothers of the *Tale*, though sprightly enough in their behaviour, gain much of their liveliness from the fact that they are ideas personified – ideas which change, develop, conflict, grow grotesque and violent, absurd, diseased and mad, and so have none of the wraith-grey neutrality which personified ideas so often have, for instance, in the Spenserian tradition of verse in the eighteenth century.

The later satires have many of the same objectives as these early ones; Swift still concerns himself very greatly with the dangers which follow when man allows himself to be consumed by an idea so completely that the idea controls man rather than man controlling the idea. But as time goes on, Swift centres his attention more and more upon the man than upon the idea. The episode of the Struldbrugs is characteristic enough of the method of *Gulliver's Travels*: Swift explores the vanity of unrestrained imagination, the superficiality of man, but he does so in an extended fable, in which we are given two simplified points of reference: a Gulliver inflamed by the desire for endless life; and old, toothless, lonely, useless, deformed and desperate men and women who will never find in death an end to their misery. The human (even in a radically distorted or simplified form) is always there: the sentences have definable subjects; human points of reference; so that the ideas, or words, are attached to recognizable emotions.

When the Swift of the *Tale* attacks superficiality he does so at first through a dance of ideas which work towards our confusion, make us into passive subjects for ironic manipulation, focus our attention on the energy and activity of words and ideas rather than upon human feeling. When human feeling is allowed to intrude, it is as often as not for the gross shock effect: 'Last Week I saw a Woman *flay'd*, and you will hardly believe, how much it altered her Person for the worse' – and the purpose of the shock is not to convince us, for instance, of the inhumanity of man to man, the pity and terror of a human being flayed alive by another, but to use that pity and terror for purposes of an argument: in an entirely serious and highly significant debate it is the perfect debating point.

The episode of the Struldbrugs could well be glossed by the two sentences which complete the ironic rhetoric of the flay'd Woman and the stript *Beau*:

> He that can with *Epicurus* content his Ideas with the *Films* and *Images* that fly off upon his Senses from the *Superficies* of Things; Such a Man truly wise, creams off Nature, leaving the Sower and the Dregs, for Philosophy and Reason to lap up. This is the sublime and refined Point of Felicity, called, *the Possession of being well deceived*; The Serene Peaceful State of being a Fool among Knaves.

But the difference in ironic mode between this and the Struldbrug episode is great. Again there is the impersonality of subject: 'He that can . . .', 'Such a Man . . .' which we have seen to be the mark of the early Swiftian manner. The point of reference is the idea rather than the man – in this case a notion which is most fully developed in the fourth book of Lucretius' *De Rerum Natura*. Lucretius, following Epicurus, proposed a theory of vision in which objects constantly slough off a sort of filmy outer skin. This 'image' or 'idol' consists of atoms which are too small to be sensed in themselves, but which get into the eye, jostle the atoms of which the mind consists, and result in vision. It is a serious (though quite unsatisfactory) attempt to explain sight, and by implication the other senses and the activity of mind, by entirely material means. Now, it would be an odd theory of vision which asserted that we see anything *but* the superficies of an opaque object; but Lucretius goes further, suggesting that the imagination consists of amalgamations of these flimsy films or images which lie about in the mind and that all the activities of the mind are functions of material mechanisms, the movement of extremely refined, but still material, soul-atoms responding to the pressures of other incoming atoms.

The principal defender of the Epicurean view of things in the seventeenth century, Pierre Gassendi (who was a prominent Catholic priest) made some attempt to harmonize Epicurean theory with Christian belief. He did not accept wholly the Lucretian theory of vision; but there is enough similarity between it and the more materialistic and free-thinking notions of Swift's day for Swift to use Epicurus as a stick to beat materialism with. His technique is to fasten on to the notion of flimsy films of appearance as characteristic of the whole mode of materialistic thought – making materialism suitable only for the flimsy thinker. Then, by contrast, 'Philosophy and Reason' acquire more body, strength and reality by virtue of the rich, savourful imagery of 'leaving the Sower and the Dregs', and the sensuous sug-gestiveness of 'to lap up'. Thus, in the final epigrammatic turn, the serenity and peacefulness of 'being a Fool among Knaves' associates mechanistic and materialistic views of reality, not just with foolishness, nor just with the peace of complacency, but by a curious sleight of hand, with knavery (this kind of felicity is caused by self-deception, so who is the knave but the fool himself?), and, above all, with unreality. By contrast 'Philosophy and Reason' become very earthy and real indeed.

With Gulliver in Luggnagg it is a different matter: for a start we have accompanied him already through so many adventures that we think of him, with half of our minds, as a real person, as someone 'like us'. He is at all events a good deal more than the impersonal 'He that can . . .' or 'Such a man . . .' of the *Tale*, and the defects exposed in him by his confrontation with the Struldbrugs are not errors in philo-sophical concept, but failures in human wisdom or moral understanding – what we would call philosophical error only in the very loosest sense. In the *Tale* the motive of the satire is, above all, the need for rightness in thinking; here it is more complex. Swift still deplores self-deception, but there is a far deeper, more achieved sense of necessary human in-adequacy and frailty. In the *Tale* or the *Discourse* the mad, the grotesque, the feverish flight from reality, are satirized with an energy, an abandon, and a *self-confidence* which would match any madman's. In the *Travels*, and particularly in Luggnagg, Swift contemplates the decay of human life with a solemnity and a determined fortitude which implies a different idea of wisdom (though one could not in an unqualified way, say it is wise); an idea of wisdom which is deeply involved with his own dreadful consciousness of vulnerability. In some parts of the *Travels* it is vulnerability to insanity or immoderate sensuality, here in Luggnagg to age and decay: 'They were not only opinionative, peevish, covetous, morose, vain, talkative; but incapable of Friendship' – there's a reality about this, as a mirror to Swift's own fears, which nothing in the *Tale* or the *Discourse*, however full of verbal energies or fantastic wit, can begin to equal.

The later satire continually makes wry use of this dark conviction of vulnerability and failing human powers; right thinking becomes more and more of a compromise between pure reason and human weakness, and practical action becomes more and more significant in Swift's system of priorities: his increasing involvement in Irish politics is a measure of this. But his desire to make other people act on their own behalf is qualified ironically by his sense of human weakness. His later ironic *personae* reflect this sense of human fallibility: the *personae* of the *Tale* and the *Discourse*, though Swift doesn't quite hold them to a consistent tone (his own voice keeps on breaking through) are nothing if not facile, pompous and stupid; on the other hand Gulliver is as mixed and variable as any human being – he is facile, pompous and stupid in some situations, wise, humble and tenderly human in others. Gulliver, one might say, is sometimes a brother to the Drapier, at others precious near to the author of *A Modest Proposal*, and even the latter writes out of a desperate though mistaken sense of goodwill: the ironic turn is very light indeed in the following:

> Therefore I repeat, let no Man talk to me of these and the like Expedients; till he hath, at least, a Glimpse of Hope, that there will ever be some hearty and sincere Attempt to put *them in Practice*.
>
> But, as to myself; having been wearied out for many Years with offering vain, idle, visionary Thoughts; and

> at length utterly despairing of Success, I fortunately
> fell upon this Proposal; which, as it is wholly new, so
> it hath something *solid* and *real*, of no Expence, and little
> Trouble, full in our own Power; and whereby we can
> incur no Danger of *disobliging* ENGLAND.

The early satire had been full of irony about those who are
content to follow illusions. Here the bitter irony only partly
masks a deep longing for 'something *solid* and *real* . . . full
in our own Power', a deep sense of frustration that even the
most hopeful and positive attempts to comprehend reality
and to control our own destiny slip away and become 'vain,
idle, visionary'. The longing for 'something *solid* and *real*'
is reflected in the change of idiom which we noticed at the
beginning of this chapter. In the early satire an extraordinary
energy is employed in making the ordinary seem grotesque,
and the fantastic even more insanely unreal. In the later
work even the most bizarre ideas are naturalized to a kind
of reality by the steady, workaday precision of the language:

> The flying or floating Island is exactly circular; its
> Diameter 7837 Yards, or about four Miles and an
> Half, and consequently contains ten Thousand Acres.
> It is three Hundred Yards thick.

> While He and I were thus employed, another Horse
> came up; who applying himself to the first in a very
> formal Manner, they gently struck each others Right
> Hoof before, neighing several times by Turns, and
> varying the Sound, which seemed to be almost articu-
> late.

> Infants Flesh will be in Season throughout the Year;
> but more plentiful in *March*, and a little before and
> after: For we are told by a grave Author, an eminent
> *French* Physician, that *Fish being a prolifick Dyet*, there are
> more Children born in *Roman Catholick Countries* about
> Nine Months after *Lent*, then at any other Season.

By this approach Swift earned a larger audience for himself. In the early satire he wrote of and for wits and scholars,

real or fake; in *Gulliver's Travels* or *A Modest Proposal* he writes for any or every man. One of the most important factors in effecting this change of mode was the experience of writing the group of writings which are called the Irish Tracts, and which will be dealt with in the next chapter.

V

The Irish Tracts

There is no comfort for the any man in the history of
Ireland; 'the Irish Problem' has always been there, not
just for the English, but for the Irish too, ever since the two
nations began to have contacts with each other. Other
nations have been conquered, dispossessed, exploited,
starved, dominated, divided, degraded, pacified and deci-
mated; other nations have been given independence and
yet remain hopelessly dependent economically; other nations
have suffered from recurrent states of declared and un-
declared civil war, and have seen indiscriminate murder
become a way of life; but there is no nation among whom
embittered memories remain so powerful a force, entering
into every aspect of life, impoverishing, distorting and, out
of such contrary passions, breeding both deadly waste and,
from time to time, such extraordinary creative fertility. I, an
Englishman, one of Ireland's hereditary tormentors, can
perhaps resolve to understand my responsibility to my
neighbour nation a little better than my ancestors; I can
even ask as much forgiveness for my country as it deserves,
if it deserves any; I cannot (and this must limit any claims
this chapter may have to deal with its subject fully) feel
the whole force of Ireland's tragic history bearing upon me,
now, as it does, say, upon a resident of the Bogside, or a
prisoner at Long Kesh, or a Belfast shipyard worker, or a
doctor in a Derry hospital emergency ward, or a five-year-
old boy playing war among the ruins.

Swift himself was not, in an unqualified way, an Irishman;
and perhaps because of this, Swift's Irish tracts can be a

better way for an alien to find his way into the terror of
Ireland than his daily newspaper, with its brutalizing, repetitive tale of atrocities and opinionated stubbornness on
every side. Or at least Swift will help us to see some of the
depth of this hell, so that we can no longer dismiss it as a
problem for whichever men have most power now. Sometimes Ireland seems like a cracked record stuck in the one
groove, with the same voices singing the same songs over and
over again, but ever more worn with time; perhaps Swift can
help us in some way to feel how the needle scores and abuses
the desperate, the violent, the unhappy; how deep are the
roots of hatred and despair.

It was in the last quarter of the sixteenth century that
England at last achieved military control over Ireland;
Elizabeth, a great Queen of England in so very many ways,
was a brutal mistress of the Irish; Lord Mountjoy, her general
in Ireland, suppressed the rebellion of Hugh O'Neill, Earl
of Tyrone, and proceeded to confiscate the lands of the
defeated chieftains, dividing them between English ad-
venturers, and thus creating a new Protestant aristocracy.
The early Stuarts continued the process of colonization,
importing large numbers of Scottish presbyterians into Ulster,
dispossessing landlords and persecuting the Catholic priest-
hood. A Catholic rebellion in Ireland in 1641 helped to
precipitate the English Civil Wars, and, as soon as Cromwell
felt sufficiently confident to leave England, in 1649–50, he
devastated Ireland and established a rule of terror. The Act
for the Settlement of Ireland which followed soon after in
1652 dispossessed almost every landowner in Ireland either
wholly or partially; some sixty or seventy per cent of all
the landed property in the island was seized and re-distri-
buted to reward those who had assisted in Ireland's rape.
Dispossessed landlords – whether Catholic or Protestant –
were dumped in the west, and their tenants and labourers
exploited by new and alien masters.

During the next forty years the English government
continued to re-apportion land with regard only to English
political exigencies, never to the needs of unhappy Ireland.
Some land was returned to loyalists at the Restoration,

though most of it remained in the hands of those who had been favoured by Cromwell, and hardly any of it went back to Catholic landlords. James II made his last stand in Ireland after 'the Glorious Revolution' of 1688; his 'patriot parliament' dispossessed some 2,000 supporters of William of Orange; when James was defeated at the Battle of the Boyne (1690) the land changed hands once again, and his supporters lost their lands to the Orangemen, many of whom were neither Irish, English nor Scottish. Even the English protested against this, and once again, in 1700, land was repossessed by the Government and sold to the highest bidder.

The new masters of Ireland found no security in their dominance; they petitioned for union with England in 1707, hoping to gain the benefits, in terms of freedom of trade with England and the colonies and representation in the English parliament, which the Scots had won by their Act of Union in the same year. But Union was not granted. There was, it is true, a separate Irish Parliament. But the Dublin Parliament was subject to a fifteenth-century law which allowed it to pass only those laws which had previously been agreed to by the Privy Council in London. It very rarely submitted itself to the electorate, and therefore was representative of little but itself, and in any case usually only met once every two years to vote supplies.

Nevertheless, with the connivance of the English Government, it managed to pass a series of laws designed to strip Catholics of any vestige of power they still had: Roman Catholics could not vote or stand for Parliament, become lawyers or members of the armed forces; they could not sit on a municipal council. When the owner of one of the few remaining Catholic estates died, the land had to be divided between all the surviving children, and since the families were often large, this meant that Catholic holdings tended to be smaller and smaller, and therefore less viable. If the eldest son turned Protestant, on the other hand, he took all.

But though all this ensured Protestant dominance, it could not ensure prosperity, even for the Protestant landlords. Ireland's economy was in the hands of the English, and the English were determined to avoid any competition they could possibly prevent in industry or trade. The infamous Wool Act of 1699, for instance, prevented Irish exports of wool or cloth to foreign countries or to British Colonies; all woollen products were to be sent to England, where heavy import duties were levied on them. Of course there was a good deal of smuggling from Irish ports to the Continent. But it was a sore blow to the Irish people, both landowner and peasant. The English Parliament took care to consolidate its power to do such things by the Declaratory Act of 1719, which asserted that Ireland 'hath been, is, and of right ought to be, subordinate unto and dependent upon the Imperial Crown of Great Britain, as being inseparably united and annexed thereto; and that the King's Majesty, by and with the advice and consent of the Lords Spiritual and Temporal and the Commons of Great Britain in Parliament assembled, had, hath, and of right ought to have, full power and authority to make laws and statutes of sufficient force and validity to bind the kingdom and people of Ireland'.

These are the bare bones of a terrible story. The detail has to be filled in with the suffering of peasants in loathsome hovels, their handkerchief of land rack-rented from an absentee landlord acting through a voracious agent; a diet of potatoes which would fail in a season of bad weather or blight, causing starvation; lank cattle bled for food; barefoot adults and children; the young men and women emigrating to England or the American Colonies; beggary, theft, murder, prostitution, vicious penal laws, epidemic disease, dirt and cruel bankrupting tax-laws. Ireland was degraded and demoralized; it was also deeply divided, and lacked the kind of dedicated, compassionate and articulate leadership which was necessary if ever Protestant and Catholic, landowner and peasant, Irish and Anglo-Irish, tradesman and farmer were to make common cause about anything; if ever any movement of resistance or protest were to be mounted to ameliorate, in however small a degree, the terrible poverty and the terrible demoralization of the Irish people.

Swift may seem to have been an unlikely candidate for leadership of such a kind. An Anglo-Irishman who would dearly have loved to leave Ireland for good; a minister of the Established Church, hostile both to the Catholics and the Presbyterians; a Tory devoted to tradition and the monarchy he could, perhaps, have devoted his life to port and hunting, mumbling somebody else's sermons every Sunday and intriguing in cloister politics during the week.

Indeed, the first six years of his exile in Ireland passed peacefully enough, to all outward appearance. But his intimacy with Harley and Bolingbroke had given him a taste for action, and he was easily roused to anger by injustice and suffering, though like everyone else he was sometimes blind to some aspects of it. Much of Ireland's suffering could be traced to the Wool Act of 1699 and other related pieces of legislation; Swift recognized this and seized on the fact. However, characteristically he did not attack the Act directly, but proposed a scheme for improving the condition of Ireland without disobeying the law. Even more characteristically, deprived as he was of access to the executive centres of power, he appealed directly to the ultimate source of power, the people. In *A Proposal for the Universal Use of Irish Manufacture* (1720) he argues that, if the manufactures of Ireland may not freely be exported, then the Irish themselves should use them exclusively, and refuse to accept imports of woollen goods from England. One would have thought that, embarrassing as this may have been to the authorities, no one could have considered a proposal for the Irish to wear Irish cloth seditious, treasonable or in any other way actionable at law, but here is Swift's own account of what happened, in a letter to Pope dated a few months after the pamphlet was published:

> This Treatise soon spread very fast, being agreeable to the sentiments of the whole nation, except those gentlemen who had Employments, or were Expectants. Upon which a person in great office here immediately took the alarm; he sent in hast for the Chief Justice, and inform'd him of a seditious, factious, and virulent Pamphlet, lately publish'd with a design of setting the two kingdoms at variance . . . The Printer was seized,

and forced to give great bail: After his tryal, the Jury brought him in Not Guilty, although they had been culled with the utmost industry; The Chief Justice sent them back nine times, and kept them eleven hours, until being perfectly tired out, they were forced to leave the matter to the mercy of the Judge, by what they call a Special Verdict.

As is to be expected, there were accusations of Jacobitism laid against the printer and the author (who was, of course, anonymous) but, after a long and tedious delay, the Lord Lieutenant, the Duke of Grafton, granted a *noli prosequi*, and the case was dropped.

It is possible to read all the most famous of Swift's works, *Gulliver's Travels*, *A Tale of a Tub*, *The Battle of the Books*, *A Discourse Concerning the Mechanical Operation of the Spirit*, even *A Modest Proposal*, as satires of universal application; and this is, indeed, why they are still so famous, and so much read. But each one of these works arises from a particular, local situation, and the concreteness of that situation, the particularity of the problem, gives fulness and energy to the satire: 'the grandeur of generality' in Johnson's phrase, may be what makes art last, but only because it forces itself upon a great variety of readers, living in worlds so different that only the most essential things remain in common between them, as strikingly relevant to their own particular worlds. Universality is not arrived at by a process of reduction, by missing out all the particular detail which gives one age and one culture its unique, unrepeatable colour and flavour, its intricate texture and ambience; it is achieved by re-creating that culture, that time, by fighting the battles which are special to it, but in such a way that everything is related to certain great and abiding issues; so great art has a high degree of convertibility: like good currency, it is backed by ample resources held in the bank of issue.

So, *A Tale of a Tub* is incredibly rich in reference to the London of the last few years of the seventeenth century; its author can be identified as a typical representative of a particular community of a few hundred men and women, living in an acre or two of land in a shabby part of London making money by scribbling for hire. He is a Grub Street hack; but now, when Grub Street no longer exists, we can recognize the character of the hack, with all his habits and pretensions so characteristic of a place and time, as a point of reference for placing similar absurdities in our own, very different time.

Now, if there is one thing obvious about *A Proposal for the Universal Use of Irish Manufacture*, and most of Swift's other Irish Tracts, it is that it is written for a particular purpose at a particular time; it is a very practical document, appealing to the Irish people in the year 1720 to undertake a certain course of action:

> What if we should agree to make *burying in Woollen* a *Fashion*, as our neighbours have made it a *Law*? What if the Ladies should be content with *Irish* Stuffs for the Furniture of their Houses, for Gowns and Petticoats to themselves and their Daughters? Upon the whole, and to crown all the rest, Let a firm Resolution be taken, by *Male* and *Female*, never to appear with one single *Shred* that comes from England; 'and let all the People say, AMEN.'

The tract is as topical as an article in an 'underground' newspaper of today in the United States, Britain or the U.S.S.R. There are, however, several ways in which the pressures of Swift's indignation propels the pamphlet in the direction of a more universal satire; ways, one might say, in which it tends towards the greatest of all English prose satires, *Gulliver's Travels* – particular towards the third book of that masterpiece. The means by which this further reach to the argument is implied is the ironic idiom.

Consider how Swift turns from addressing Parliament to urging, first shopkeepers, then clergy, to do their share; then, with a curious, passing, dismissive irony, deflates all the pomp and circumstance of the army: 'I have not Courage enough to offer one *Syllable* on this subject to *their Honours* of the Army: Neither have I sufficiently considered the great Importance of *Scarlet* and *Gold Lace*.' We are already more than half way towards the tone and manner of Lilliputian satire: 'Whoever performs his Part with most Agility, and holds out the longest in *leaping* and *creeping*, is rewarded with the Blue-coloured Silk . . .', sharing with this later manner the shrewd and light effect of distancing the reader from the subject. The army is made to seem contemptible, in passing, but not in a way that could possibly provoke the army to legal action, or even a brawling duel; so the reader is, partly at least, relieved of his fear of authority and power. Then Swift employs the method of fable for the next stage: notice how he appeals to Ovid, giving a point of reference as remote as may be from the actual sufferings of Ireland, but familiar to most of his readers from their school days. Swift tells the story with simplicity, as if to a schoolboy; he mentions his own reactions to it as a boy, thus suggesting, lightly enough, that no very great experience or wisdom are necessary for judging the case. The fables of Ovid show scant respect for the gods; Olympian power is not necessarily administered with integrity and justice in his tales; in fact the gods generally behave like overgrown babies. The ethos of Ovid is thus entirely suitable to Swift's purpose, which is to adjust the reader's attitude towards power; to re-draw the boundaries of power where that power is administered without respect for justice or morality. Thus, though it would seem to elevate the dignity of England to compare her with Pallas Athene, the goddess of wisdom, in fact the comparison encourages contempt; while the comparison of Ireland with Arachne, the maiden turned into a spider, does not in the least belittle Ireland, but stresses her skill, innocence and injury:

> The Fable, in *Ovid*, of *Arachne* and *Pallas*, is to this Purpose. The Goddess had heard of one *Arachne* a young Virgin, very famous for *Spinning* and *Weaving*: They both met upon a Tryal of Skill; and *Pallas* finding herself almost equalled in her own Art, stung with Rage and Envy, knockt her *Rival* down, turned her into a Spyder, enjoining her to *spin* and *weave* for ever, *out of her own Bowels*, and *in a very narrow Compass*. I confess, that from

a Boy, I always pitied poor *Arachne*, and could never heartily love the Goddess on Account of so *cruel and unjust a Sentence*; which, however is *fully executed* upon *Us* by *England*, with further Additions of *Rigor* and *Severity*. For the greatest Part of *our Bowels and Vitals* is extracted, without allowing us the Liberty of *spinning* and *weaving* them.

What follows is a sinuous little ambiguity which gains a great deal of its inner strength from Swift's obsessive concern with two related ideals, sanity and liberty, and his equally obsessive, indignant fear of their two opposites, madness and oppression or imprisonment (whether the imprisonment be physical or metaphorical). Madness recurs again and again as a leading metaphor in Swift's work, from *A Tale of a Tub* to *The Legion Club*, the horror growing and the laughter acquiring more bitter inflections on each occasion. The hatred of oppression grows greater, and becomes more and more linked with fear of madness, after Swift was obliged to return to Ireland, and after the hated Whigs took power in England. The capture of Gulliver in Lilliput, his impotence and vulnerability in Brobdingnag, the sufferings of Balnibarbi, the desperate uncertainties of Gulliver in Houyhnhnm Land, all these suggest remarkably strong feelings both of protest and fear in the face of power. As these complex feelings are expressed here, they are perhaps too compressed for complete understanding; the words of the Preacher (*Ecclesiastes* 7, 7) are a thought ambiguous, but Swift's development of them chases its own tail in a most disturbing way:

> The Scripture tells us that *Oppression makes a wise Man mad*; therefore, consequently speaking, the Reason why some Men are not *mad*, is because they are not *wise*: However, it were to be wished that *Oppression* would, in Time, teach a little *Wisdom* to *Fools*.

The complexity and disturbing nature of this depends on the ambiguity of the word 'mad'; so much is clear. Mad may mean insane, it may mean very stupid, it may mean terribly angry; and any of these meanings would have been current at Swift's time. But the borderlines between them would have been much hazier for Swift and his audience. A man might have been committed to Bedlam for any of these three reasons: there were none of the fine drawn (though in some ways insensitive) distinctions between levels of intelligence which psychologists and educationalists now employ; no understanding of the physical diseases, like diabetes or epilepsy, which might affect rational behaviour; no distinction between neurotic and psychotic states of mind. 'Mad' was a word of fear: it meant anything which could disturb the proper disposition of things by loosening a man's command over his powers of reason. For a deeply conservative man like Swift it could almost mean not being able to accept life as it is; and yet the life all around him was so clearly not to be accepted that complacency was a more despicable kind of madness. So, oppression of this kind must force upon the sensitive observer, like Swift – himself so much in fear of madness – an odd, almost unbearable distinction: oppression of this degree partitions the kingdom of madness into the madness of the wise and the madness of the foolish, but sanity whole and entire is made impossible.

Some of this ambiguity in attitude towards madness can be recognized in *A Tale of a Tub* already, but there at least there is a Martin who, despite mad Peter's oppression, survives to be sane, and despite mad Jack's frenzy, overcomes his foolishness and preserves his coat entire. But in later life Swift was not so sure of things: *Gulliver's Travels* at several points displays a man sane amidst madness; at several points shows the same man mad amidst sanity. He is sane when, like Gulliver in Lilliput, he does not accept things as they are, and has power to act; sane when, like Gulliver in Laputa, he is an alien and can dissociate himself entirely from things as they are. He is mad, when like Gulliver in Brobdingnag, he is impotent to act, but accepts complacently the world as it is. Again, in Houyhnhnm Land, Gulliver is impotent to act. But on the other hand he is unable to accept the world as it is; man, himself, for what he is. And this terrible combination is something new: impotence without complacency.

Does such a state necessarily lead to madness? If so, Swift implies, wisdom and madness are so close to each other that the first must contain in it a share of the second.

The vigorous sarcasm which follows, of '*how grievously* POOR England *suffers by Impositions from* Ireland', is particularly effective in the way in which it moves from complaints which the English certainly did make – against the smuggling of Irish wool to France, for instance – through ever more unreasonable complaints to the most farcical: '*The Ballad upon* Cotter *is vehemently suspected to be* Irish *Manufacture; and yet is allowed to be sung in our open Streets, under the very* Nose *of the Government*.' By comparison with the *Tale* or the *Discourse* it is crude satire; but it is intensely practical in purpose, designed to accomplish an immediate object by influencing as large a number of people as possible; not only the highly sophisticated reader at whom the earlier satires were aimed, but every shop-keeper, every merchant, anyone with a scruple of patriotic self-interest and a penny piece in his pocket.

For the meanwhile, then, the problem of wisdom and madness is solved by action; and yet Swift has not entirely solved the problem of communication which this kind of action presents. To be sure, his *Proposal* was read widely, most Irishmen agreed with its arguments, and drapers found it harder to shift their English woollens for a while. But Swift writes as if he is not quite sure which audience he is aiming at: at times, as in the reflection upon a text from *Ecclesiastes*, he seems almost to be talking to himself; at times to shop-keepers, at times to landowners; even at times, he returned nostalgically to the old stamping grounds of his early satires, belittling the new English sponsored aristocracy by associating them with Grub Street dullness, and so writing as if he had Pope or Arbuthnot in mind as an audience:

It is not many Years, since I remember a *Person* who, by his Style and Literature seems to have been *Corrector* of a Hedge-Press[1] in some *Blind-Alley* about *Little-*

---

[1] A clandestine printing-house, often engaged in libellous, pornographic or even treasonable work.

Britain, proceed *gradually* to be an *Author*, at least a *Translator* of a lower Rate, although somewhat of a larger Bulk, than any that now *flourishes* in *Grub-street*; and, upon the Strength of this Foundation, come over *here*; *erect* himself up into an *Orator* and *Politician*, and lead a *Kingdom* after him.

But action of the kind that might restore the self-respect of the Irish, and give them a means of living decently, needed more concentration of purpose; an Anglo-Irish *Dunciad* couldn't set matters straight, even if its satiric butts were more substantial than Colonel Bladon, or the 'booby lord', Viscount Grimston. When immediate self-interest, such as the saving of a few pence on an article of clothing or the buying of a smarter hat than one's neighbour's, comes into conflict with a longer-term self-interest, such as helping to restore the economic health of one's nation, then the longer-term consideration usually withdraws from combat early. A very sharp and narrow issue was necessary to focus the attention of the public; it had to be pursued with intense persistence; the manner of persuasion had to be clear enough to convince any man who could read, and many who could not, and above all the recommended course of action had to be one which would not put any man out of pocket or deprive a single pretty woman of a single scrap of lace. It had to be legally defensible as far as was possible in an age which allowed considerable political pressure on courts; it had not to be directly against the king or his principal minister, and yet it had to be an issue sufficiently big to show both England and Ireland the potential strength of the Irish people when they were aroused enough to work together as one.

The perfect issue came along at last; the matter of Wood's halfpence satisfied every one of these requirements. The rights and wrongs of the question hardly matter at all: perhaps Wood's halfpence might have been good honest coin as Sir Isaac Newton and his fellow assayers were prepared to assert after weighing, heating and hammering a random sample and comparing it with other coins of similar value.

That was not important; what was important was that it provided a rallying point for a divided population.

I have remarked on the ways in which *A Proposal for the Universal Use of Irish Manufacture* tends towards the satire of *Gulliver's Travels*, widely different though the tones, methods and purposes of the two works are. The relationship between the *Travels* and *The Drapier's Letters* is even closer: as Harold Williams points out:

> their close relationship is due mainly to the fact that the travels of Gulliver were actually interrupted by the activities of the Drapier in Irish politics. Towards the end of January, 1724, Gulliver was approaching the end of his travels: 'I have left the Country of Horses, and am in the flying Island, where I shall not stay long, and my two last Journyes will be soon over'. But actually two years or more passed before the travels were over, and in that time Gulliver was to learn much from the experience of the Dublin draper, just as the latter was able to profit from the benefits that Gulliver had obtained by reason of his stay among the Brobdingnagians and Houyhnhnms.

However, when we begin to try and define the ways in which Gulliver and 'M.B. Drapier' resemble each other, there begin to be difficulties. They are, both of them, rather ordinary men, practical, patriotic, intelligent; the kind of men most of us would welcome as a neighbour. They are, also, Swiftian *personae*; means by which Swift creates an illusion, persuades us to look at certain events or situations from a special point of view. Swift has used such *personae* before, of course, but never, as in the case of M. B. Drapier, endorsing everything his creation says, using him as a mouthpiece. And, of course, Swift's relationship with Gulliver is far more complex than his relationship with the Drapier. We are made to feel that Gulliver is like us; sometimes we are flattered by the relationship, as when he entertains a nation by letting its army march between his legs: at other times we are humiliated by the similarity, as when the King of Brobdingnag says what odious vermin Gulliver's race must be. *Gulliver's Travels* constantly questions the wisdom of the human animal, and it is Gulliver's job to take us where the questions are. The power of the Drapier, on the other hand, is in our conviction that the ordinary, simple human, the man next door who chats about the weather as he sells a couple of yards of material (all good Irish stuffs and silks, of course) is as good as any man when it comes to political economy. Most men are happy, as they say, to 'listen to common sense', because common sense consists of what one believes is right, or can be persuaded is true, without going too deeply into the matter or seeking expert advice. Sometimes such judgements are right; just as often they are wrong, as anyone who has talked to men in draper's (or tobacconist's, or greengrocer's) shops must know. But, increasingly, such men were becoming the measure of Swift's society, and its core, a fact upon which the extraordinary career of Daniel Defoe was based. The Drapier, perhaps, is even closer to Robinson Crusoe than he is to Gulliver, closer than Gulliver and Crusoe were to each other, despite their common experience of shipwreck. Like Crusoe, he is devised especially to appeal to the man who has won a little comfort and a few possessions by trading in a very competitive world, and is scared of losing it all. Crusoe reassures him that he would make out all right, even if he did lose everything. The Drapier warns him that there is a plot afoot to steal everything he has worked for, and tells him how to fight back:

> What I intend now to say to you, is, next to your Duty to God, and the Care of your Salvation, of the greatest Concern to your selves, and your Children; your *Bread* and *Cloathing*, and every common Necessary of Life entirely depend upon it. Therefore I do most earnestly exhort you as *Men*, as *Christians*, as *Parents*, and as *Lovers of your Country*, to read this Paper with the utmost Attention . . .

Indeed, the soundness of a currency is important. The way in which this soundness used to be guaranteed was by minting coins whose value as metal when melted down was nearly equal to the face value of the coin. Thus, no one would profit by forging in gold or silver of equal quality, and baser alloys could be easily detected by a variety of tests. As the economy began to be based more and more upon trade, more and more coins were needed, and the demand out-stripped the supply of gold and silver. Baser metals began to be used for smaller coins, and gradually it became clear that coins of very little value indeed were greatly useful to the economy as a whole, enabling a finer adjustment of prices, and therefore more competition and more rapid exchange of money and goods. But forgery was made easier, and, perhaps more important than this, it was made easy for governments to increase the money supply at will, and this in its turn could produce inflationary tendencies. Economists still argue about the matter, some stressing the need to stabilize the value of money, others stressing the need to encourage trade and industry by a ready supply of money and credit.

Economists of any school would agree that it was bad practice to license a private individual to issue coin for a whole nation. But there are places where Swift, perhaps, carries his ironies too far, exaggerating the probable effect of the new coinage. The sophisticated would enjoy the joke; the unsophisticated would be scared out of their wits by the prospect of a farmer having to pay his rent with three horse loads of halfpence, a lady having to go out shopping with a carriage full of copper following her, Squire Conally having to pay his rent with two hundred and fifty horse loads, and so on. The mad mathematics assume that there is no other currency, and this is a valid enough distortion for the purposes of satire, but satire depends upon an audience possessed of considerable analytical and critical ability. The *Letter to the Shopkeepers* is, avowedly, addressed to the illiterate as well as the literate, to the simple as well as the sophisticated, and while it does not lie to those who are aware of its satirical aspect, there are ways in which, in addressing its avowed audience, it uses improper methods.

The problem is that Swift is acting more than one role here. He is concerned to give solid, honest advice to the citizens of Ireland. He is concerned to fight irresponsibility and negligence in government. He is concerned to restore self-respect to the Irish nation. But he sees all these concerns in the context of a larger view of the world; in *A Tale of a Tub* he promises *A Description of the Kingdom of Absurdities*; in *Gulliver's Travels* he gives us, not one, but many such absurd kingdoms; but all the time, between writing the *Tale* and the *Travels* and before and after too, he is irresistibly drawn towards the absurd, and to the satirist's habit of giving the naturally absurd a half twist more, until it becomes grotesque caricature. Consider, for instance the progression from Squire Conally, with his two hundred and fifty horse-loads of rent, to this, in the *Letter to Harding*:

> But if I were to buy an hundred Sheep, and the Grazier should bring me one single Weather, fat and well fleeced by way of *Pattern*, and expect the same Price round for the whole hundred, without suffering me to see them before he was paid, or giving me good Security to restore my Money for those that were *Lean*, or *Shorn*, or *Scabby*; I would be none of his Customer. I have heard of a Man who had a Mind to sell his House, and therefore carried a Piece of *Brick* in his Pocket, which he showed as a Pattern to encourage Purchasers: And this is directly the Case in Point with Mr. *Wood*'s *Assay*.

Consider, too, the further progress from this to the various mad projectors of Lagado, particularly those concerned with the 'Scheme for entirely abolishing all Words whatsoever':

> An Expedient was therefore offered, that since Words are only Names for *Things*, it would be more convenient for all Men to carry about them, such *Things* as were necessary to express the particular Business they are to discourse on. . . . many of the most Learned and Wise adhere to the new Scheme of expressing themselves by *Things*; which hath only this Inconvenience attending it; that if a Man's Business be very great, and of various Kinds, he must be obliged in Proportion to

carry a greater Bundle of *Things* upon his Back, unless he can afford one or two strong Servants to attend him.

    All three passages are concerned with the way in which we *represent* things or ideas. Today we are all quite used to the idea that coins and notes are not *in themselves* wealth: they *represent* wealth. If the government which issues a paper currency ceases to guarantee it, it becomes worthless, as did Confederate currency, or Czarist paper money. If the same thing happens to coins which are not made in valuable metals, the only value of the coins, over and above the small value of the metal, is a curiosity value for the collector. Swift's campaign against Wood was based on the idea that this was bad practice; that money should be intrinsically valuable, as the gold sovereign or the old silver dollar are now worth more than face value, even though they are not official coinage any more. So a coin, according to Swift, should be a valuable *thing*; it can be exchanged for other valuable *things*, and its only advantages over other *thing* as a medium for exchange are that it is small, easily carried, and that it is commonly accepted as of a known value, as a measure for the relative value of other *things*. If you take away these two advantages, and have currency consisting of kilos of lead, or gas-filled balloons, or currency of so little intrinsic value in proportion to weight that you have to count it by the horse load; or if a community disagrees about the acceptable value of a coinage, and one man says a six-inch nail is worth a pigeon pie and two cream buns whereas another says it is only worth the iron in a six-inch nail, then the point of coinage is lost.

    In the *Letter to Harding*, Swift explores another angle of this business of representation. We cannot, he says, represent any whole by any one of its parts. Newton's assay only tested a sample of the coins, and therefore need not be reliable as a measure of its worth. Swift emphasizes the point by homely language, easily understandable by either townsman or farmer. What he does not mention here, though he does so elsewhere, is that the assay sample was chosen at random, from several packets of coins, over a period of one year. How else could one test a coinage, if to test it involves destroying it, as Newton's methods did? But ultimately the value of coinage depends upon trust in the authority behind the currency. Swift was attempting to undermine this trust, and was assisted by the ambiguity about who the issuing authority was. Wood guaranteed the money, but was authorized to do so by the English parliament. By distrusting Wood Swift was opening up doubts in the Irish people's minds as to the trustworthiness of the English government, and therefore opening up doubts about its right to authority. In the process some of his arguments may be faulty, even dishonest; but the grand strategy of the process was important enough to justify the aim for Swift, and the grand strategy was this: governments need assent to govern, and assent depends upon trust. If government is bad, trust and assent may be withdrawn. Therefore the process of government is dependent upon winning trust and assent, and this can only be done by a mutual process; by government representing its actions and motives honestly to the people, by the people being allowed to represent its needs and complaints directly to the government. Otherwise a government is a flying island; the governors, wrapped in their own concerns, cannot communicate with their subjects except by force; their subjects are forced to respond in a similar way, and the contract of government is broken, by a failure in communication, by a failure of truth in representation.

The passage from the third book of the *Travels* applies some of these considerations in a different area. One well established theory of language works upon the principle that words *represent* things (or ideas, or actions and so forth). The kind of representative function which words have is not precisely like the function, say, of a paper currency. Currency acts as a standard of value and a medium for exchange, but, according to this ancient theory, each word represents one thing; or, one idea derived from a group of similar things. If this were true, we could, theoretically, do without language altogether; and Swift satirically plays with this idea, unfolding its absurdity: and, of course, one of the ways in which it is absurd is similar to the way in which Wood's halfpence are made to look absurd with the image of Squire Conally carrying his rents on two hundred and fifty pack-horses. Words are even more compact a currency than gold: they occupy no space at all, so it is absurd to imagine doing away with them. Why should Swift go to the trouble of saying this? No contemporary thinker had begun to suggest that one could do away with words: the closest approach was the interest Leibniz showed in a plan to develop a universal language, as logical and rational as mathematics, based upon an ordered analysis of the universe of things. It is most unlikely that Swift had Leibniz in mind; he was thinking of a more widespread tendency in contemporary science: the obsession with the physical aspect of the universe, the growing tendency to disregard the role of the human mind in a moral, intellectual and spiritual universe. The *savants* engaging in conversation with *things* instead of words are not absurd simply because they act in an awkward and unnecessary way; they are absurd because they place crippling limits upon knowledge and communication – precisely the grouse Swift had against contemporary science. This, one aspect of the madness of materialism, is closely linked in Swift's mind to that other aspect, bad government caused by narrow material self-interest, which engages his attention in the *Drapier's Letters*.

Contemporary science and technology, Swift believed, had set out to engineer the universe in such a way as to destroy the accumulated wisdom of man; and one most important aspect of this is language. This same obsession with theory, this disregard of the inherited wealth of knowledge is what leads to the devastation of Balnibarbi: 'The People in the Streets walked fast, looked Wild, their Eyes fixed, and were generally in Rags . . . except in some very few Places, I could not discover one Ear of Corn, or Blade of Grass.' Balnibarbi is a somewhat distant account of Ireland under the domination of an English Parliament in some ways, but in others it is pretty close, allowing for the stretching effect of the satirical rack. The closest match of all is the account of the Lindalinian rebellion:

The People were unanimous, and had laid in Store of Provisions, and a great River runs through the middle of the Town. The King hovered over them several Days to deprive them of the Sun and the Rain . . . not a Person offered to send up a Petition, but instead thereof, very bold Demands . . . This Incident broke entirely the King's Measures and (to dwell no longer on other Circumstances) he was forced to give the Town their own Conditions.

This is not necessarily an account after the event of what happened in the matter of Wood's halfpence: Swift was already 'in the Flying Island' before he began to write as the Drapier. It is, as it were, a model of the kind of action the Irish might take to redress their grievances.

Swift's campaign against Wood's halfpence culminated in the finest of the four letters, *To the whole People of Ireland*, and in this latter he makes clear something which has been implicit in all the other three: that the quarrel about coinage implied an even deeper question – the true relationship between the Crown and the people of Ireland; the status and rights of Ireland as a nation. This was the letter which forced Carteret, the new Lord Lieutenant, to issue a Proclamation, offering three hundred pounds for information about the author, and for publishing which Harding the printer was taken to court.

The reason for this reaction is not difficult to discover: it lies in the assertion that there is 'no Law that makes *Ireland depend* upon *England*; any more than *England* doth upon *Ireland*'. Nor was there any such law; the Declaratory Act of 1719 had only made Ireland 'subordinate unto and dependent upon the Imperial Crown of Great Britain': but everybody knew what that meant. There was no Declaratory Act to say that England or Scotland were 'subordinate unto and dependent upon' the Crown. Instead there were such instruments as the Act of Union with Scotland (1707) which declared that the two kingdoms of England and Scotland shall for ever 'be united into one kingdom by the name of Great Britain'. So the quarrel about Wood's halfpence implies a deep and urgent constitutional question, as well as innumerable social and human problems.

Almost by accident Swift's determined action led to the invention of techniques of civil disobedience (though they were not called that) which have since played an increasing role in the world whenever state and people come into sharp conflict. There are many ways in which the matter of Wood's halfpence prepared the way for the long subsequent history of Irish resistance to English power, and also taught the American colonists a thing or two which they were to remember half a century later. It was a significant incident in the pattern of changing relationship between governor and governed which led eventually, for instance, to the campaign of the Congress movement under Gandhi. But it is only with hindsight that we can see this; radical in effect though Swift's arguments were, they were loyalist, patriotic and conservative in theory: 'next under God, I depend only on the King my Sovereign, and the Laws of my own Country'. The core of his argument, apart from the dispute about the constitutional status of Ireland, was the proper limitations of royal power within the social contract, and this was a matter which had been discussed for some time, by Bacon, Hobbes and Locke, and given constitutional sanction at the accession of William of Orange, in The Bill of Rights (1689) which has the significant sub-title 'An act for declaring the rights and liberties of the subject and settling the succession of the crown'. Swift himself quotes Bacon to support his argument; but notice how the chosen quotation expresses an essentially conservative view of the nature of monarchy; that monarchy is modelled upon divine government:

> as God governs the World by the settled Laws of Nature, which he hath made, and never transcends those Laws, but upon high important Occasions: So among earthly Princes, those are the Wisest and the Best, who govern by the known Laws of the Country, and seldom make Use of their *Prerogative*.

Swift was no democrat; the model of human government which approaches closest to perfection in *Gulliver's Travels* is that of Brobdingnag, where the King is benevolent, intelligent and governs by consent, but where the King *is* a king. A Houyhnhnm democracy, based upon the total integrity, intelligence and freedom from malice of each member of society, is not put forward as a serious model for mankind, and yet neither is Lilliputian society, where the governors in whom the king trusts are distinguished by their malice, envy and narrowness of vision. This is the kind of perspective in which the *Drapier's Letters* are written; the boycott of Wood's halfpence was not a bid for popular power, the first stage in a rebellion—Swift would have been terribly shocked if it had turned out that way. It was an attempt to restore a proper relationship between monarch and subject, the kind of desperate act which should be as rare as the monarch's use of his prerogative, but was just as necessary to the health of the state. And its intended social effects were not what we should think of as social justice or civil rights: equality of opportunity, freedom of religion, or anything of the sort. Swift would want the Protestant squirearchy in control of the land again, and the Protestant tradesman prosperous in the towns. The following shows clearly enough for whom he spoke:

> One great Merit I am sure we have, which those of *English* Birth can have no Pretence to; that our Ancestors reduced this Kingdom to the Obedience of ENGLAND; for which we have been rewarded with a worse Climate, the Privilege of being governed by Laws to which we do not consent; a ruined Trade, a House of *Peers* without *Jurisdiction*; almost an incapacity for all Employments, and the Dread of *Wood's* Half-pence.

VI
Gulliver's Travels

In the list of forthcoming publications at the beginning of
A Tale of a Tub Swift (or his shadowy *persona*) promises 'A
Voyage into *England*, by a Person of Quality in *Terra Australis incognita*, translated from the Original'. This is a formula
for satirical observation which has always been attractive,
and still is. Fifty years ago Swift's 'Australian' would have
been a little green man from Mars, nowadays he would be an
alien humanoid from Rigel V, but in principle he would still
be precisely the same kind of vehicle for satire. He offers very
considerable possibilities: he can be endowed with exactly
the right blend of innocence and wisdom, great powers of
perception and analysis, but at the same time a profound
ignorance of human emotions and manners. We can excuse
a marked absence of compassion or understanding in such an
observer; the author can, if he wishes, shelter behind these
privileges – indeed, this may be why he chooses this kind of
vehicle in the first place. The 'Australian' would seem to be
totally detached, uninvolved, and therefore unprejudiced.
But the trick only works because of his simplicity: we know
nothing, or next to nothing, about *his* society, *his* work, *his*
hopes, *his* fears, *his* ambitions, *his* family life, *his* education;
only what the author is prepared to let us know as a foil
to his satirical account of terrestrial mismanagement. The
advantages of Swift's 'Australian', had he elected to use him,
would have arisen from the fact that he was *unreal*.

In the event, Swift chose to use a totally different framework. Instead of an unreal alien he takes as his vehicle
Gulliver, an Englishman who is neither rich nor very poor;

neither a fool nor a genius; resourceful, energetic and brave, though not on the grand heroic scale; possessed of many of the strengths and virtues the average Englishman would pride himself on, but also a ready prey at times to self-deception and the comforting half-truth. In short, Swift chooses a man whom all his audience would know, or think they knew.

Swift makes Gulliver begin by giving us a brief auto-biographical sketch. It is *very* brief – five hundred words or so for the thirty nine years from Gulliver's birth to the sailing of the *Antelope* from Bristol in May 1699. But the facts are made to seem so clear, the places so familiar even to a twentieth century English reader that we can fill in innumerable details and give body to the sketch. Swift resembles Defoe in his trick of the unremarkable detail reported with faithful accuracy. The commonplace name with parish-register details of relationship, occupation, address: '*Mary Burton*, second Daughter to Mr. *Edmond Burton*, Hosier, in *Newgate-Street*'; '*Mr. James Bates*, an eminent Surgeon in London'; the exact accounting of money given, borrowed, lent and earned: 'where, by the Assistance of him and my Uncle *John*, and some other Relations, I got Forty Pounds, and a Promise of Thirty Pounds a Year to maintain me at Leyden'; the detailed record of house removals and business ventures: 'I took Part of a small House in the *Old Jury* . . . from the *Old Jury* to *Fetter-Lane*, and from thence to *Wapping*, hoping to get Business among the Sailors; but it would not turn to account' – all these concrete details, little hard facts pressed into a mosaic which convinces us (or nearly convinces us) of the reality of the narrative, could well have come from Defoe. *Robinson Crusoe* had been selling like hot cakes for two years when Swift began the *Travels*, and *Captain Singleton*, *A Journal of the Plague Year*, *Moll Flanders* and the others made their several impacts on the reading public in quick succession as Swift continued to write. Swift has left us only one parenthetic reference to Defoe: 'one of those authors (the fellow that was pilloried I have forgot his name) . . .' but we need not be deceived by the offhandedness of this. Swift may perhaps not have possessed Defoe's novels, may have not read them through, but he remembered Defoe's name all right, and it is very difficult to believe that he did not have a good idea of what went on in his novels.

All this detail convinces us of the substantiality of Gulliver; he does not exist in a vacuum (as does our alien humanoid from *Terra incognita*); on the contrary he is given an exact place in a social structure which we can understand. He is given understandable problems and relationships; despite his real talents he has professional difficulties; despite his difficulties he is able to rely on good friends and a loyal wife. It is, then, a very ordinary middle-aged man of what we would now call the middle class; somebody with whom we can identify or at least sympathize, who is made to look in turn through the several carefully prepared distorting glasses of the four books at human, European, English, particularly eighteenth century English, society – at the society of which he, Gulliver, is so much a part. This is the first given condition of the satirical structure of *Gulliver's Travels*, and this first condition defines the range and methods of the satire as very different indeed from any possible satire which employs the unreal alien gentleman from *Terra Australis incognita*.

Gulliver is not the simple, ideal, detached, alien, outward observer; but then neither is he the complex, real, involved, inward actor. His 'reality' is largely a matter of being 'typical', and being surrounded by a large number of believable details. Very little indeed is given of Gulliver's inward life, except when Swift finds it necessary to evoke certain characteristic human emotions from the reader; common self-deceptions, illusions, emotions which evade reality, or horror and disgust at physical humanity; in each case it is not Gulliver Swift is interested in so much as the reader, who is to be made to recognize the ways in which Gulliver's inner life resembles his own. Gulliver swells with patriotic pride before the Brobdingnagian king; he dreams of immortality when told about the Struldbrugs. The reader recognizes Gulliver's emotions as a generalized pattern of his own, but there is never a case in which Gulliver's reactions set him apart from other men, make him into an individual in his own right. The only thing which is unusual about him is the things which happen *to* him; he's a way of putting a common factor of humanity, the 'ordinary man' within the reader, into odd situations. At the same time he is a way of testing the behaviour of the average human animal (and the reader can think of himself as at least partly the average) under extreme conditions of stress and fatigue.

But 'typical' and 'ordinary' are very slippery concepts when we speak of humanity. If you undertake experiments on, say, an alloy of manganese and aluminium with small measured quantities of molybdenum and tungsten under carefully defined conditions of stress, you are able to guarantee a certain consistency in molecular structure, tensile strength and so forth in your metal. You are testing something which you can measure and weigh; if the experiment is properly conducted it can be repeated and within certain narrow limits the result will be exactly the same. With the human metal the task is more difficult: the reader contributes to the experiment by co-operating or by resisting; emotional structures and moral strengths are what is at issue, and these will be altered in the reader as you test them (and as he tests them, for the reader is experimenter as well as experimented upon): indeed it is the avowed purpose of the satirist to change as well as to test his material. In one sense Gulliver must remain the same person throughout because the reader must continue to accept Gulliver as his representative within the action, or at least the representative of the common man within him. In another way, though, Gulliver must change repeatedly in order to expose new areas of that common humanity to the continuing satirical experiment.

The paradox leads to certain inconsistencies. The most obvious one is this: the book is supposed to have been written by Gulliver after his travels are over; after his travels are over he is so totally disenchanted by humanity that he can scarcely bear to sit down to dinner with his wife at the other end of a long table, and even then must stop his nose with powerful aromatics; and yet in the first three books of the *Travels* Gulliver writes of other men with affection and respect. The first three books, and even the first half of the fourth book, are clearly not written by the sour hermetic misanthrope of the conclusion to the fourth book.

One accepts the paradox without much trouble because, though Gulliver is real enough for us to identify with him *partially*, we are always conscious that it is only part of ourselves that we can identify with him. The satire repeatedly stimulates us to detach ourselves from him and his reactions to the world which he observes; we recognize that those reactions could possibly be our own, and therefore, as we detach ourselves from Gulliver we become detached, too, from those parts of ourselves in which we most resemble Gulliver. To be critical of Gulliver is (if the satire works properly on us) to become critical of ourselves. Thus, though Gulliver is made to be 'real' in a certain way and to a certain degree, we never look upon him as complete. At a given time we see him as representing some *aspect* of humanity, or of ourselves, never the whole. When these aspects contradict each other we don't set about looking for ways in which the contradictions can be reconciled by a deeper and fuller understanding of the complexities of the human personality as we do in real life situations, or in novels or plays which seek to reflect the complex situations of real life. We accept Gulliver as what he really is: a tool which the author uses to warp our vision of ourselves and reality; a means by which we can be brought to look at things through several distorting mediums in a carefully prepared series of experiments. To put it in another, completely different, metaphor; Gulliver is a mount, who carries us to several different bizarre vantage points from which we can re-examine various aspects of our consciousness and experience.

Each of these chosen vantage points involves a deliberate and consistent exaggeration. In Lilliput we are asked to put ourselves in the position of a benevolent giant looking at a society very much like our own, or an unusually clear-sighted man of normal size inspecting his own society, through the wrong end of a telescope. The eighteenth century term for a magnifying or diminishing lens, 'perspective glass', is a useful way of suggesting the nature of the conceit: we are looking at our society in an altered perspective. Our identification with Gulliver is one of detachment; we persuade ourselves that we are bigger, not so much physically as morally and spiritually, than the world as it is observed in Lilliput – and that is, we recognize, in some sense *our* world.

In Brobdingnag the position is reversed: it is we who are small. Instead of being the observer, we are the observed. In Lilliput the satire has been primarily external, that is, a criticism of absurdities and evils which we think of as outside ourselves. In Brobdingnag the satire turns inwards for its primary targets; our own failings are probed and exposed by the mercilessly detached gigantic presences around us. Gulliver is constantly on show in both Lilliput and Brobdingnag, but whereas in Lilliput he is a marvel of strength and dignity, in Brobdingnag his pretensions to dignity and strength are mocked by his littleness: by implication it is our own puny vanity and helplessness that we are required to observe.

In Laputa and Balnibarbi Gulliver is once more observer rather than observed, and so are we. It is society at large, the world outside us, that is being pilloried, and since the satire is mainly external, our self-respect is allowed to refresh itself for a while. However, the latter part of the third book somewhat unexpectedly alters the vantage point. In Glubbdubdrib, and even more remarkably in Luggnagg, the satire points inward again. Gulliver is once more the object of the satire, the observed rather than the observer; his vanity and impotence are exposed, and we are ambushed into an unwelcome (though perhaps incomplete) identification with his human silliness.

So far the point of view has alternated between observer and observed, external and internal, superior and inferior. Each of these warps in vision has in one way or another been an example of the 'polarization' effect we discussed in our first chapter. In Lilliput human vice and folly are streamed off and concentrated in a little people; we can examine and criticize this little people with amused detachment. It is our own absurdity and malice we see reflected in the little people, but our own failings made diagrammatically simple and placed at a safe distance.

In Brobdingnag most of the vice and folly tend to concentrate in Gulliver as the plenipotentiary representative of our own race. We are challenged to scramble up and see ourselves through a giant's eye while at the same time seeing the coarse horror of the giants' bodies through little Gulliver's squeamish sensibilities. We could develop this, I suppose, by treating the physical horror as an image of the moral horror; the wens and the lice representing the moral corruption of man, but that would, I think, be making Swift too tidy an author. The physical disgust and the moral indignation are, as always in Swift, closely connected with each other, but the physical disgust has a life of its own, too; and we can never be certain how conscious Swift was of the illogic of his revulsion, the degree to which it trespassed upon and clouded his moral feelings. The uncertainty assists the satire; it confuses us, and makes us more vulnerable to ambush; at the same time it makes us more anxious to find a secure point of moral vantage.

So there is very little comfort for us little-worlders in Brobdingnag; nevertheless it does allow us the consolation that *something* in human form – giants, or ourselves so enlarged in moral experience as to be able to perceive with giants' eyes, may see the full depravity of the human race, and yet be tolerantly affectionate towards its members. The king is fond of Gulliver; and love, of an innocent and engaging kind, is possible between Glumdalclitch and her little charge. But even here there is a snare which is difficult to negotiate safely: Swift seems to suggest that a childish affection of this kind, innocent of any awareness of human depravity or adult sexuality, is the only possible basis for human love. Swift himself was odd enough to believe this, and his own hesitant amorous history might very well suggest that a fearful and childish scepticism of this kind hedged in his emotional life. We are reluctant (and rightly so) to grasp at this slender kind of love as a counterbalance to all the fear and doubt and humiliation we suffer through Gulliver; but small as it is, the comfort is there.

The fourth book doesn't offer even this comfort. It is the most extreme experiment in polarization which Swift ever attempted, and the sharpness and brutality of the diffraction excludes a great part of human experience. Man *seems* to be split into two, and the two halves propelled to their extremes, rational intellect and passionate beast, each half with no admixture of the other, and therefore neither of them really man. Gulliver, still our representative, though we have been given reasons to distrust his reliability in that role on many occasions, is dropped into a situation which *appears* to be offered as a radical analysis of the whole nature of man. Man has always claimed to be *animal rationale*, the rational animal, but as a deliberate affront to this proud boast, reason is given the shape of a horse while brutish passion is still recognizable as man. Gulliver is faced with a choice of identification: he chooses reason and is rejected by it, rejects brutishness and yet is accepted by it. The irony was particularly cruel for a eighteenth century reader; but not because the philosophy of Locke, or the experiments of the Royal Society, or the rationalizing theologies of the Deists had convinced the average contemporary of his perfection, the victory of sweet reason over the sinfulness of the body. Quite the reverse; the new developments in philosophy and science had given men a novel system of ideals, and so had made the more perceptive uncomfortably aware of their failure to match their own ideal concept of themselves.

Thirty or forty years ago very few readers of Swift had any doubt at all that Swift was entirely behind Gulliver in his love affair with Reason. It was, perhaps, Dr Leavis's fine essay, 'The Irony of Swift' which began to make readers of Swift uncertain about Swift's attitude to Reason, and his attitude to Gulliver's idealism. Leavis argues that:

> The Houyhnhnms, of course, stand for Reason, Truth and Nature, the Augustan positives, and it was in deadly earnest that Swift appealed to these; but how little at best they were anything solidly realized comparison with Pope brings out. Swift did his best for the Houyhnhnms, and they have all the reason, but the Yahoos have all the life. Gulliver's master 'thought Nature and Reason were sufficient guides for a reasonable animal,' but nature and reason as Gulliver exhibits them are curiously negative, and the reasonable animals appear to have nothing in them to guide.

It would have been difficult for the defender of Swift to

counter-attack by arguing that the ideals represented by the Houyhnhmns are sufficient in themselves, or that the kind of society Swift makes them create is an acceptable model for the way humans should organize their affairs. It would have been difficult, too, for the defender of Swift to argue that Swift wasn't 'in deadly earnest' about Reason, Truth and Nature. Gradually a more complex defence of Swift evolved: Kathleen Williams is representative of this view. Miss Williams does not argue that the Houyhnhnms are models for human behaviour: 'The Houyhnhnms do not strike the reader as altogether admirable beings; indeed they are sometimes absurd, and even repellent, and we are disgusted by Gulliver's exaggerated devotion to them.' She agrees that the Houyhnhnms are negative, and that Swift's method, too is fundamentally negative:

> The characteristic of Swift's satire is precisely his inability, or his refusal, to present us straightforwardly with a positive to aim at. It may be, at bottom, a psychological or a spiritual weakness; he turns it to satiric strength . . .

And yet, it seems, the 'psychological or spiritual weakness' which Miss Williams discovers is not in any way a lack of sureness about what the positives should be; the Houyhnhnms, she says, 'far from being a model of perfection, are intended to show the inadequacy of the life of reason'. When Gulliver returns to Rotherhithe after his last voyage, according to this view, he is a living indictment of the view that man can live by reason alone. He has been maddened by insane pride in his reason; 'He has become inhuman, losing the specifically human virtues in his attempt to achieve something for which humanity is not fitted.' Swift himself is sometimes quoted to support this interpretation of his moral viewpoint; in a letter to Pope he writes: 'I tell you, after all, that I do not hate mankind: it is "vous autres" who hate them, because you would have them reasonable animals, and are angry for being disappointed.' Writers are never entirely reliable when writing about their own intentions and attitudes, and Swift, the satirist, clearly cannot resist the temptation of an ironic inflection in this, a letter to another master of irony. Taken out of context (as it usually is) this passage would surely do something more than exonerate Swift from the crime of hatred of humanity; it would substitute contempt for hatred as the ruling passion in his attitude to men. And perhaps, after all, this is not far off the mark – contempt is an emotion which comes very easily to Swift – as I have remarked, there are places, as in 'A Beautiful Young Nymph Going to Bed' where Swift becomes entirely despicable, where his satire becomes ungenerous, carping, dirty and low. And there is no escaping the fact that this motive is present in the fourth book of *Gulliver's Travels*: rage at the body, obsessive fear of filth, unlovely distress with the idea of human sexuality. The version of Swift which Miss Williams urges is far too tidy; it places Swift too far above the satire, puts him far too securely in control of his own emotions and credits him with a much more modern attitude to Reason than he could possibly have had.

I believe that if we are to understand the fourth book of the *Travels*, indeed if we are to understand any of Swift, we must recognize that there are severe and unresolved moral conflicts at issue throughout the whole book, and also we must recognize the degree to which satirical discourse may be, for the writer himself, a way of exploring such conflicts. Swift, like Dr Sloper in James's *Washington Square*, was possessed by the idea of the beauty of Reason; unlike Dr Sloper he was not coldly capable of attempting to force such an idea upon real humans; on the contrary he despaired of humanity ever achieving such an aim. He took pleasure, as any of us might in daydreams, in constructing a model for human society, supposing human beings might be persuaded to behave as he would like them to do; and yet he was not able for long to indulge the daydream without allowing his consciousness of human failure, his fearful and sombre sense of his own inadequacies, and those of other men, to intrude upon the dream, betraying its absurdity.

The daydream is of a democracy, but a peculiar one, a democracy with no individuals, so that each Houyhnhnm is subject to a control far stricter and more thoroughgoing than any totalitarian autocracy could achieve. It is a perfect democracy, and in its perfection it swings full circle, becoming in a way the opposite of what most of us would think a democracy must be – it becomes a dictatorship of the intellect. In part Swift's imagination is taken up by the dream – he indulges himself in it; but right from the beginning the Yahoos are there to challenge the ordered simplicity and peace of the phantasy. In part Swift's imagination is taken up by the furious negative passions which the Yahoo myth embodies. The Yahoos are as much a dream as the Houyhnhnms, and, taken by itself, each dream is as discreditable to Swift's imagination as the other. But when the two dreams are put together, and Gulliver is dropped in the middle of them to blunder his way through to some conclusion, something happens to modify the power of each dream. The question whether this really is the choice before man – whether we have to decide between brutish passion and dispassionate reason, with no third way – begins to clamour for the reader's attention, as it visibly clamours for Swift's attention as he writes.

It is made abundantly clear what makes the Houyhnhnms and the Yahoos differ from each other: if the difference doesn't point the way to the real question, then it seems clear that the satire directs us to the things that the two races have in common. The unimpassioned intellect and the vile body each by itself lacks love. The lack implies another lack: neither race has any capacity for moral choice, neither can conceive of either good or evil. It is only Gulliver who can construe the problem of Houyhnhnm Land morally: just as the Houyhnhnm language lacks a word for evil, one would imagine any possible Yahoo language would lack a word for good. Thus neither Yahoo nor Houyhnhnm has any use for religion; neither faith nor doubt have any part to play in that imagined moral universe.

Swift's final experiment, then, is to conduct us, with Gulliver, into an anti-paradise; to confuse us by peopling it with two races which appear to be moral antitheses, but in reality are not: reason, however noble and clear and precise; the body, however ugly or foul-smelling, have no moral significance at all. It is only Gulliver who is potentially a moral agent, and it is he who fails disastrously, while in the Land of the Houyhnhnms, to realize that the choice does not really lie in the terms offered by the two island races. His real choice begins when he returns to a human world, and his failure there, too, is an angry and intense image of humanity's failure to live at peace with itself, in tolerance, generosity and understanding. Whether we can treat this as a perfect cadence or a triumphant, positive, moral statement, is another matter. The rage of disappointment, the lack of faith in human capacity for truth and self-understanding, remain the dominant emotions; however he struggles, Swift remains caught in a trap of his own devising.

A VOYAGE TO LILLIPUT

Each of the four voyages employs a fantasy or dream situation as a framework for the satirical distortion of reality. In latitude and longitude Lilliput is right in *Terra Australis incognita* (somewhere in the vicinity of the Woomera rocket range); in terms of moral and political geography it is a very elaborate metaphor of eighteenth century London, but only one in a thousand of those who read of Gulliver's adventures in Lilliput is interested in either the physical or political geography of it. It's by far the most clearly topical of the four books, and yet paradoxically it is the one which has always reached the largest audiences among people of every age, every cultural and social background, and most of its readers know nothing and care nothing about Bolingbroke, Walpole, Oxford, Marlborough, the War of the Spanish Succession, the Peace of Utrecht, Tories, Whigs, Hanoverians, Jacobites, all the issues, incidents and personalities which engaged Swift's passionate interest as he wrote the book. In particular it has been read and enjoyed (often in abridged and bowdlerized versions) by children, and has thus acquired the character of a folk-myth, at least as deeply part of our every day mythology as the tales of Hans Andersen and the brothers Grimm.

It is a very striking fact that this lasting mythical power does not depend upon a specific story-plot, as do the tales of Aladdin, Cinderella or the Little Mermaid. It does not depend upon a romantic idea, like Atlantis, Utopia or the American West. It does not depend upon a striking, uniquely individual character, like Cyrano de Bergerac, Falstaff or Baron von Munchausen. It depends upon something very much more basic than any of these – upon a simple and primitive dream situation which every reader recognizes immediately as part of his own fantasy world. It is somewhat curious that Swift's age – an age which seems to us to have been so deeply committed to the idea of reason, and which so assiduously cultivated the powers of the conscious mind, should have produced at least two lasting myths of this kind; *Robinson Crusoe* is the other. Neither Gulliver nor Crusoe are very special or unusual people; we could change the sequence of their adventures, even change the incidents themselves, without harming the power of either tale much. What matters in each case is the situation: we are asked to enter a dream; we are a shipwrecked sailor on a desert island, fighting to survive; we are surrounded by a world of little people, a world of animated dolls. However materialistic and practical the ethic of *Robinson Crusoe* is, it catches its small-shopkeeper, do-it-yourself reader in a moment when he is neither selling anything nor making anything, but when he allows himself time out for day-dreams. However strongly Swift may wish to wean his reader from illusion and self-deception and bring him to recognize reality, he takes advantage of the reader's weakness. He decoys the reader by allowing him the pleasure of escaping for a while from the present reality.

Every child loves to hear tales of little people living in a scale-model world. Coping with the problems of growing up, adjusting to grown-ups and imitating their ways is a continuing strain, and play with dolls and toy soldiers, or imaginative fantasies about fairies and the like provide outlets for all kinds of emotions which are kindled or balked by the process of growing up. Very complex things happen in child's play: the small girl is satisfying her protective instinct by bathing, feeding and dressing a doll; at the same time she is preparing for her role as a mother. The boy with toy soldiers is working out aggressive instincts; at the same time he is learning how to make plans, strategies for action, preparing himself for his adult work-life. Other children (or perhaps the same) might swing from affection to aggression in a moment unpredictably, and display their own unhappiness and insecurity by nursing a doll one moment and breaking it the next.

Whatever the detail of the game, the child is reacting to the real world at one remove, putting himself into a fantasy situation where he has the power to produce whatever result he desires. More often than not the result will be mixed; the child will be preparing to deal with reality in a constructive way at the same time as getting his own back on the real world by destroying something in a fantasy world.

The adult never quite overcomes this kind of play. It can result in serious illness; it can also be transformed into serious art which, far from being a retreat from the problems of reality may be a way of enriching life, bringing the reader to see the realities of his own world more clearly and steadily than before.

The average child, when reading 'A Voyage to Lilliput' will not respond to it as art, but simply as fantasy; the tale gives him a means of entering into the world of play. The adult will never be immune to this kind of fascination; Swift certainly was not. But Swift and the adult reader can relate the play or fantasy to the reality in an infinitely more conscious and critical way than the child. The emotions the child feels – amusement, wonder, protective affection, imagined power, the constructive and the destructive motives of play – all these remain, but change in their relationship with each other. The boundary lines between constructiveness and destructiveness become far more subtle.

For instance, there is the matter of the Tramecksan and Slamecksan, or High-Heel party and Low-Heel party. This is a fantasy or play account of a real situation which was of the greatest importance of Swift and all his English contemporaries. The High-Heels represent the Tory Party, which had been out of office for twelve years when the *Travels* were first published, but which Swift continued obstinately to support. On the level of political allegory 'A Voyage to Lilliput' is intended as a defence of Tory principles and an attack on Walpole (Flimnap) and the Whigs (Slamecksan). Parts of the satire are quite straightforward in their mockery of the petty irrelevances, the ceremonial absurdities which cloud the real issues and responsibilities of government – for instance there is the account of the rope-jumping competitions at which Flimnap/Walpole is so skilful. But the account of the Tramecksan/Slamecksan dispute goes much further, belittling not only the personalities and the rituals of politics, but the issues too.

It must be said that these were profoundly important. The Whigs had committed England to a series of expensive and bloody trade wars; the Tories in their brief period of office had secured a peace settlement which changed the map of Europe and gave Britain the chance to win real stability and prosperity. The Tories, however, drew most of their support from the landed gentry, the traditionalists in religion, agriculture, economics and values. The Whigs advanced the cause of those groups upon whom the future prosperity of English society depended: bourgeois tradesmen, often dissenters in religion, progressive in their ideas about economics, agriculture and trade, and with changing ideas about morality and values. The Whigs were identified with the Hanoverian monarchy; the Tories were suspected, often rightly, of hankering after the Jacobite cause, and therefore supporting those forces which threatened to divide the country in civil war once again. The issues were profoundly important, but by miniaturizing them Swift makes them, for the moment, appear absurd and insignificant: 'his Majesty's Imperial Heels are lower by at least a *Drurr* than any of his Court. . . . We apprehend his Imperial Highness, the Heir to the Crown, to have some Tendency towards the High-Heels; at least we can plainly discover one of his Heels higher than the other; which gives him a Hobble in his Gait.' The issues raised by the schism in Christianity at the Reformation were even more important still for Swift and his contemporaries; but when Swift translates the enmity between Catholic and Protestant into a Lilliputian dispute about whether one should break one's egg at the big or the little end, the whole terrible problem, which had been made the cause for persecution, rebellion and war for centuries, seems to be dismissed with contempt. Even the sufferings of religious martyrs and the tyranny of their persecutors is belittled: 'It is computed, that eleven Thousand Persons have, at several Times, suffered Death, rather than submit to break their Eggs at the smaller End.'

But the final effect is not to persuade us that these problems are insignificant. The diminishing perspective glass of fantasy shows us a world which is *not* exactly the same as eighteenth-century England; a conscious and deliberate distortion, though the parallels are witty and ingenious. The reader is conscious all the time of the ways in which the real world and the Lilliputian microcosm match; at the same time he realizes the ways in which they do *not* match. They match in absurdity, pomposity and lack of self understanding, but they do not match in that happenings in the real world are sometimes of the most profound importance; in Lilliput they must always be absurd, even if they are malicious, vicious and mad. So the reader is forced, implicitly, to seek out the ways in which humanity is constantly betraying itself into ridiculous disproportion; to try once again, with a fresh mind, to seek out what the real problems are, and imagine what courses of action beings of dignity, moderation and intelligence would take to solve them. It gives us a standard from which to judge real human actions: is this a Lilliputian act, or has it the dignity, the generosity and the moderation characteristic of Gulliver? The question is a flattering one, for Gulliver is the ordinary man, and the satire assumes that the ordinary man is capable (in some situations) of a great deal of wisdom and moderation.

There are points, however, at which Swift's satirical method alters; where he pockets the diminishing glass, as it were, and indulges in a different kind of fantasy. The sixth chapter begins in a rather miscellaneous way, which is all to the good because it gives the opportunity for some delightfully irrelevant strokes of humour.

their Manner of Writing is very peculiar; being neither from the Left to the Right, like the *Europeans*; nor from the Right to the Left, like the *Arabians*; nor from up to down, like the *Chinese*, nor from down to up, like the *Cascagians*; but aslant from one Corner of the Paper to the other like Ladies in *England*.

But this is all merely preliminary to more serious business; most of the rest of the chapter holds up certain Lilliputian customs as superior to English practice. Some of Swift's reforms, particularly the intolerance of barring unbelievers from public office, will seem unenlightened to the modern reader; the repeated recourse to the death penalty will sicken most of us; but in the context of his time most of the legal reforms he suggests are brave challenges to the accepted structure of moral values and unusually shrewd criticisms of the basis of common law. Swift has allowed Gulliver to shift his vantage point; he is no longer simply the practical man, observing, recording and acting. He has become an Utopian radical, a Hythlodaeus returning from Utopia with news of how much better they do things over there. It is in this mood that he reports on Lilliputian traditions of education and the rearing of children.

This is not the mad ravings of a Gulliver retired to Rotherhithe and living in a horse box. Swift is not ironically describing a rational arrangement which it would be absurd for an irrational animal like man to attempt; Lilliputians are humans, irrational and absurd ones at that, and there they are, practising this draconian educational system with every sign of Gulliver's (and Swift's) approval. These are part of 'the original Institutions, and not the most scandalous Corruptions into which these People are fallen by the degenerate Nature of Man'. And so we are asked to accept that it would be best to separate children from their parents at a very early age, deprive them of love and affection, allow them no time for play, rigidly separate the sexes, restrict education solely to instruction suitable for the child's 'station in life', regiment and restrict the child in an impersonal institutional life. These, we are asked to believe, are the only ways of instilling those 'Principles of Honour, Justice, Courage, Modesty, Clemency, Religion, and Love of their Country' for which family love is to be sacrificed.

Not even the most rigidly disciplinarian defender of the British public school system would accept such a stern programme; at least they play games, even at Eton. Can we, against all the evidence, contend that Swift ironically directs the reader to seek out the one thing lacking, to respond to the clinical savageries of Lilliputian education by protesting that love, after all, is the one essential thing in a child's upbringing? I do not believe that we can. It is, I think, rather feeble to argue that Swift is merely taking advantage of satirical licence to overstate his case. For the moment Swift no longer controls the fantasy, but is controlled by it. The calmness of the passage is deceptive; there is a deep and bitter fury against the normal patterns of family life here. Swift becomes in some ways like the child who rebels in his fantasy life against the incomprehension and aloofness of his parents by breaking his toys.

It is, I believe, important that we should make up our minds what our attitudes to this passage are, because our decision upon this passage will have a bearing on what we decide about Swift's attitude towards the Houyhnhnms in Book IV. The Lilliputian programme of education is Houyhnhnm-like in its calculating inhumanity, and yet, if I am right, Swift is capable of being attracted, one might even say infatuated, by its grey and loveless discipline. Even so, this does not mean that Swift was incapable of rising above the infatuation. There is clearly a continuing tension in his work. On the one hand there is his prudish infatuation with discipline, decency and cleanliness, to the point that he is at times prepared to sacrifice humour, faith, compassion and love to these antiseptic idols. But there are, too, moments in which the satirical crucible reaches white heat, when everything is melted down into the essential emotions, and the antiseptic idols themselves are melted down. The sixth chapter of 'A Voyage to Lilliput' does not reach this point of intensity. The fourth book does.

The satire of the first book of the *Travels*, then, engages our attention at a profound level of fantasy, but there are ways in which Swift puts himself at risk in the fantasy. That it works, triumphantly, as fantasy, has been proved by more readers, young and old, than one could possibly calculate; that it works as political satire is only slightly less sure, but very much less important. As a work of art, however, judged by the very *highest* standards, it is not completely successful. Questions crowd in, impatient for an answer, once one begins to doubt whether Swift possesses, in this book, that extremely high degree of control over his material and of self-understanding which he himself would demand as the necessary standard for a satirist. But, for the most part, Swift succeeds triumphantly.

For instance, one of the most pointed and poignant effects of the satire is the way in which the little people, absurd, delightful and doll-like in their diminutiveness, are yet vicious, corrupt, malicious and deceitful on a fully human scale – the perspective glass makes us larger morally, as well as physically, but cannot diminish the evil of the little people. As the book progresses the human evil becomes more and more distinct; our eyes are focused on this as we accustom ourselves to the novelty of the Lilliputians' size. Their viciousness, which has seemed little more than absurd and laughable when they practise it on each other, becomes more serious when it begins to be directed against Gulliver – the 'ordinary' man, through whose eyes we see.

On the level of political metaphor the articles of impeachment against Gulliver represent the way in which Bolingbroke was treated by the Whig administration after his escape to the continent. But the feelings of pity and horror evoked by the fate proposed for Gulliver suggest something more than this; there is a strong element of tragic fantasy; blindness like Samson's; starvation on a heroic scale, more concretely imagined than that of Tantalus; the division and dispersal of the body like that of Osiris; the bleak white monstrous skeleton remaining behind like a statue brooding over the capital city for ever:

But his Imperial Majesty, fully determined against

capital Punishment, was graciously pleased to say, that
since the Council thought the Loss of your Eyes too
easy a Censure, some other may be inflicted hereafter.
And your Friend the Secretary humbly desiring to be
heard again, in Answer to what the Treasurer had
objected concerning the great Charge his Majesty was
at in maintaining you; said, that his Excellency . . .
might easily provide against this Evil, by gradually
lessening your Establishment; by which, for want of
sufficient Food, you would grow weak and faint, and
lose your Appetite, and consequently decay and con-
sume in a few Months; neither would the Stench of
your Carcass be then so dangerous, when it should
become more than half diminished; and immediately
upon your Death, five or six Thousand of his Majesty's
Subjects might, in two or three Days, cut your Flesh
from your Bones, take it away by Cart-loads, and bury
it in distant Parts to prevent Infection; leaving the
Skeleton as a Monument of Admiration to Posterity.

One may speculate on the question how much of this
intensity of horror (stressed rather than diminished by the
matter-of-fact manner of Gulliver's informant) is, as it were,
transferred from Swift's own feelings of isolation, neglect,
impotence and deprivation at being exiled to the Deanery of
St Patrick's after having known the excitement of being a
friend of the greatest men in the land. Indeed, it is very
probable that some of the energy of imagination comes from
self-pity: probable, but not particularly important. Both the
historical metaphor and the possible biographical factor
recede in importance before the thing which gives the satire
its permanent moral relevance. Society always has been, and
remains to this day, incredibly wasteful of its human resources, destroying its best and most far-sighted servants;
blinding them as the Philistines blinded Samson, exiling
them as Virgil and Dante and Swift were exiled, imprisoning,
maiming or murdering them from envy, malice or greed.
The mean and puny Lilliputians rejecting the kindly giant
is a better metaphor for the murder of Martin Luther King

or Gandhi, the long imprisonment of Luthuli, Nelson Mandela or Helen Joseph, the sufferings of Solzhenitsyn or Pasternak, the death of the Kennedy brothers, the suicide of Masaryk, the humiliation of Dubcek, than it is for Bolingbroke or Swift himself. The immediate occasion for the satire recedes quickly, but if it possesses the right kind of intensity of concern and compassion it remains applicable to innumerable occasions in any age.

A VOYAGE TO BROBDINGNAG

The second voyage keeps the scale differential exactly the same; it is the point of view which is changed. In Lilliput Gulliver's vantage point is so lofty that he can see the whole nation at a glance; the emperor's army can march between his legs; he can pull an enemy's fleet across a narrow sea; even his urine can save a royal palace from burning. Through Gulliver we are enabled to experience, vicariously, a power which is almost, but not quite, unlimited. The only limitation to his power is the pettiness of the material tools available to him, but even more than this the pettiness of his human surroundings. He has to use all his resourcefulness to overcome the fragility of the available tools – cables as slender as packthread, the stoutest trees as thin as canes, the only available shield against arrows and shot a pair of spectacles. But in the end it is the fragility of his human surroundings that defeats his good will. Overcoming the material problems is, quite literally, play: whether it is a matter of participating in the pomp and ceremony of court ritual (and finding a way of getting unexpected results with his pocket-handkerchief) or capturing fifty men-of-war single-handed. Overcoming the human problems is far more formidable a difficulty, for though Gulliver has the physical advantage by a factor of one thousand seven hundred and twenty eight, each little Lilliputian possesses his full adult human measure of malice, hypocrisy, envy, pride, treachery, blood-lust, greed and ingratitude. What began as play for the reader as well as Gulliver, becomes deadly serious, and we come to realize that the little people are not simply toys;

they are, like any man, capable of a deadly destructiveness.

In Brobdingnag, everything is reversed with deliberate care. Gulliver is so tiny that a stile is as impassable an obstacle as a sea-cliff; far from being able to straddle across an army he confesses he cannot calculate the size of one, they occupy so vast an area; his naval skills are restricted to navigating a toy boat in a tub. Not that his resourcefulness and courage are any the less than in Lilliput: few men could survive an attack by two rats each as big as mastiffs, or defend themselves so stoutly against monstrous wasps; few could be so skilful and agile as to entertain a court by such athletic displays as Gulliver with his sword-play, spinet-playing, sailing and the like. Even fewer could remain so cheerful and so self-reliant despite constant humiliation, mockery and terrible danger. In Brobdingnag Gulliver is a representative of the average man, but very much better than average in very many ways: he has the skills and abilities we give ourselves in day-dreams. The only aspect in which he remains merely the average is in his complacent acceptance of the values of his own society. Gulliver, the courageous little toy-man is in many ways admirable personally, but as our ambassador and representative he takes pride in a society in which malice, hypocrisy, envy, pride, treachery, blood-lust, greed and ingratitude are the norm. What begins as play for the king and court becomes somewhat sour as Gulliver reveals that his own race of people are not simply amiable toys; they are wilfully and criminally destructive when they mass together in a society.

Because Gulliver is in a different position, the reader is placed in a different position too. But at the beginning of the book Swift prepares his ground by persuading us once again that Gulliver's adventures are in continuity with the unremarkable real world; this time by an absorbed and determined use of nautical language (how exact I do not know, but most of us are landlubbers enough to be convinced):

Finding it was likely to overblow, we took in our Sprit-sail, and stood by to hand the Fore-sail; but making foul Weather, we looked the Guns were all fast, and handed the Missen. The Ship lay very broad off, so we thought it better spooning before the Sea, than trying or hulling. . . .

The reader is more wary this time, but the sheer opacity of the technical jargon goes a great way to persuading us once more that Gulliver is an ordinary shipman, involved in the techniques and trials of his trade; someone capable of sober judgement and precise, even unimaginative reporting on his experiences. The description of the Brobdingnagian country-side which follows confirms this, and its busy accuracy of detail almost conceals for us the way in which our perspective is being altered. Now, instead of being the gigantic power who must tread carefully in order not to destroy whole villages, Gulliver is vulnerable, impotent, absurd and insignificant. Whereas in Lilliput we have accepted a welcome, engaging kind of fantasy – the dream situation in which the hero has the power to bend everything to his will – in Brobdingnag the fantasy situation is one of sheer terror. This is the dream situation in which our wills are useless, in which we are totally dependent upon the benevolence of others and a good share of luck for our continued existence. Someone with less courage and more imagination than Gulliver would have been driven mad by fear and horror. But Gulliver, practical and unemotional as he is, is perfect for reporting the close and vivid specific detail which gives the fantasy its solidity and fullness:

> . . . the Stalks of the Corn were sometimes not above a Foot distant, so that I could hardly squeeze my Body betwixt them. However, I made a shift to go forward till I came to a part of the Field where the Corn had been laid by the Rain and the Wind: Here it was impossible for me to advance a step; for the Stalks were so interwoven that I could not creep through, and the Beards of the fallen Ears so strong and pointed, that they pierced through my Cloaths into my Flesh.

This, or the description of the labourer picking Gulliver

off the ground, demand a peculiar detail and fidelity of imagination, eidetic in hallucinatory exactness, as does the description of the farmer examining Gulliver's gold:

> I pulled off my Hat, and made a low Bow towards the Farmer: I fell on my Knees, and lifted up my Hands and Eyes, and spoke several Words as loud as I could: I took a Purse of Gold out of my Pocket, and humbly presented it to him. He received it on the Palm of his Hand, then applied it close to his Eye, to see what it was, and afterwards turned it several times with the Point of a Pin, (which he took out of his Sleeve,) but could make nothing of it. . . . I saw him wet the Tip of his little Finger upon his Tongue, and take up one of my largest Pieces, and then another; but he seemed to be wholly ignorant what they were.

It's interesting to compare the kind of description with that of the first book: there, perforce, description frequently tends to be generalized, since even the largest Lilliputian action or feature is so tiny, and Gulliver reports his observations rather like a genial but short-sighted man who has mislaid his spectacles: 'He acted every part of an Orator; and I could observe many Periods of Threatnings, and others of Promises, Pity, and Kindness', whereas here in Brobdingnag even the tiniest detail of movement becomes significant, like the wetting of the farmer's finger (one can see the monstrous curling of the great pink tongue), or the picking of the pin from the sleeve. The tiny Lilliputian orator is depersonalized by his littleness; we are aware only of the conventions within which he acts; he represents the way in which orators behave. Everything the Brobdingnagian farmer does, however insignificant, is the action of an individual to be reckoned with by himself. The Lilliputian orator is on his guard; the formal mannerisms are a defence, an attempt at self-enlargement in front of the giant Gulliver; the Brobdingnagian farmer has no need to protect himself in this way, formalities are absent, he is at ease all the time and his smallest action is necessarily immense in its ominousness. In Lilliput it was Gulliver who possessed this ease; now it is he who has to try

to overcome the insignificance of his person by the extrava-
gance of his gestures, as when he recovers from stumbling
over a crust and 'got up immediately, and observing the good
People to be in much Concern, I took my Hat (which I held
under my Arm out of good Manners) and waving it over
my Head, made three Huzza's, to shew that I had got no
Mischief by the Fall'. The giants, on the other hand, behave
in the most natural and unguarded way possible.

But, to the eye of Gulliver, the most simple and natural
things become distorted; Swift uses Gulliver's naïvely im-
pressionable and distinctly prudish view of things to carry
on his war against the flesh; and it must be admitted that
this leads Swift into some unnecessarily morbid postures.
The same obsessive, hallucinatory concern with detail which
gives such an air of reality to Gulliver's account of the farmer
is used to make the nurse's breast gross and disgusting when
she gives suck:

> I must confess no Object ever disgusted me so much as
> the Sight of her monstrous Breast, which I cannot tell
> what to compare with, so as to give the curious Reader
> an Idea of its Bulk, Shape and Colour. It stood pro-
> minent six Foot, and could not be less than sixteen in
> Circumference. The Nipple was about half the Bigness
> of my Head, and the Hue both of that and the Dug so
> varified with Spots, Pimples and Freckles, that nothing
> could appear more nauseous: For I had a near Sight
> of her, she sitting down the more conveniently to give
> Suck, and I standing on the Table. This made me reflect
> upon the fair skins of our *English* Ladies . . .

Like so much of Swift's satire, the effect of this is deeply
ambiguous. It conveys disgust at the human body. At the
same time it conveys a sense of the absurdity of the disgust.
We see through the eyes of Gulliver. At the same time we
stand aside from Gulliver and see the priggishness of the
voyeur disillusioned; Gulliver as the prim little peeping Tom
seeing things for the first time as they really are. As they
really are? The question, inevitable as it is, prompts an

immediate response; we do not live that way unless we are mad: seeing, especially the haunted, obsessive fixation with the detail of seeing which Gulliver displays here, plays only a part in our total consciousness of others. Seeing is absorbed into a whole complex of sensations, not just hearing, feeling, smelling, but sensations from memory, emotions triggered by touch or sight, the rich and complex traffic of the mind and heart. The problem of this passage is very similar to the problems posed by poems like 'The Lady's Dressing Room', 'Strephon and Chloe', 'Cassinus and Peter'; like these poems, this passage sets out to criticize an amorous obsession with external and superficial beauty by shock, by setting the amorous sentiment against the animal facts. Like those poems, it may betray a gross failure in Swift himself to overcome the problems he sets himself because it merely replaces one obsession – a romantic obsession with beauty – by another obsession. And yet Swift, though possibly he shares Gulliver's absurd failure, sees it as a failure; a ridiculous meanness of apprehension, a ridiculous bondage to the body despite a longing for the kind of decency and beauty which can be imagined only; despite fragile cerebral ideals which cannot survive exposure to reality.

Perhaps the clearest signal of Gulliver's absurd failure and Swift's awareness of it is in the incident which follows the battle with the rats. Observe the evasive primness of the euphemisms, and the even more elaborate excuses with which Gulliver seeks to justify dwelling upon the matter:

> I was pressed to do more than one Thing, which another could not do for me; and therefore endeavoured to make my Mistress understand that I desired to be set down on the Floor; which after she had done, my Bashfulness would not suffer me to express myself farther than by pointing to the Door, and bowing several Times. The good Woman with much Difficulty at last perceived what I would be at; and taking me up again in her Hand, walked into the Garden where she set me down. I went on one Side about two Hundred Yards; and beckoning to her not to look or to follow me, I hid my

self between two Leaves of Sorrel, and there discharged
the Necessities of Nature.

I hope, the gentle Reader will excuse me for dwelling
on these and the like Particulars; which however
insignificant they may appear to grovelling vulgar
Minds, yet will certainly help a Philosopher to enlarge
his Thoughts and Imagination; and apply them to the
Benefit of publick as well as private Life. . . .

The irony here, of course, is that it is little Gulliver who
is entirely unphilosophical and more than a little vulgar in
his conventional modesty and in his pompous manner. His
elaborate euphemisms and fussy prudish precautions are a
mirror of the behaviour society demands of us, and its stern
suppression of obvious and necessary realities. Gulliver's
obsession with the grossness of the giants' flesh, their stench
and the coarseness of their complexions, reflects more upon
Gulliver than it does upon the giants. The 'pleasant frolic-
some Girl of sixteen', the Maid of Honour who affronts
Gulliver's dignity by setting him astride one of her nipples
comes out of the episode far better than he does. She is
somewhat lacking in sensitivity to the feelings of others, but
she is without doubt a warm and spirited lass, and Gulliver
is, once again, comically, morbidly obsessed with flesh and
imprisoned by pride. The special sting the satire has here,
is that we are forced to recognize that, in however small a
degree, we share Gulliver's absurdity. We share in the conspiracies of convention every time we employ a euphemism,
every time we behave in the oblique ways which are the
equivalents of euphemism in action, and however necessary
we feel such delicate evasions are, they all involve some kind
of lie.

Swift is far from presenting the Brobdingnagians as morally
perfect creatures to counterbalance their physical imper-
fections. In Lilliput the 'considerable person at Court' who
warns Gulliver of his impeachment and the honest Reldresal
are leaven, as it were, to the wickedness of Lilliput; they put
the malice of Flimnap and Skyresh Bolgolam into the context of a potential goodness. In the same way in Brobdingnag

there is a mixture of vice and virtue, thoughtlessness and consideration, folly and wisdom. The farmer nearly works Gulliver to death, a foolish mother gives him as a plaything to her baby, a schoolboy nearly knocks out his brains with a hazel-nut, the King's dwarf endangers his life twice out of malice and envy. Male and female beggars are obliged to live in the most appalling conditions of dirt and disease, public executions are treated as a public entertainment: in innumerable ways personal and public morality is as unenlightened as it was in eighteenth-century England. Swift is neither criticizing Brobdingnagian society by importing an observer of superior virtue and understanding, nor satirizing European society by inventing a perfectly organized society peopled with god-like paragons. Brobdingnagians are very ordinary people made into giants, but with about the same range of natural vices and virtues as Gulliver-sized men, that is, ourselves. The comparative smallness of Gulliver helps to exaggerate some of the vices, such as the farmer's thoughtless cruelty. On the other hand the giant's society is less sophisticated in organized vice; in war, intrigue, corruption and politics, than either Europe or Lilliput. Whereas Lilliput is a diminished parody of London under the Whigs and Hanoverians, Brobdingnagian society (even the Brobdingnagian court) is much more the world of Tory squires and country gentlemen as Swift, the Tory, saw them. They are a little rough and ready, modest in pretensions, easy-going and genial in manner. They are honest enough in general, though fallible; they prefer the comforts of peace to the glories of war; they make up for their lack of refinement by plain good sense. But they are not above the human average in their cleanliness, intelligence, or sensitivity towards the feelings of others.

The King, who is, as Gulliver remarks 'a Prince of excellent Understanding' is a fitting monarch for such a people. He is distinguished by sanity rather than genius, worthiness rather than saintliness, shrewdness and good sense rather than any prophetic gift of far-sightedness. This is the judge before whom Swift makes Gulliver plead the cause of Europe; a judge whose authority, wisdom and experience are great, but not out of our range completely: we can hope to be able to emulate him (as we cannot hope to imitate the Houyhnhnms). And so, when the King invites Gulliver to give a full account of the government and customs of his beloved England, it is possible for us to be divided in our loyalties.

We understand, and may very well share, the anxiety of Gulliver to do justice to his native land. But, as we follow the bare outline which Gulliver gives of his oratory, we gradually become as acutely aware of the silent judge as we are of the eloquent advocate. It is this splitting of our attention that is the basis of the irony, the cause of the satirical squint. We begin, rather warily, with at least some part of Gulliver's patriotic pride, but this gives way more and more to intelligent doubt; we begin to formulate the kind of question that a sceptical alien might ask – and we realize increasingly how difficult such questions would be to answer.

The ironic pressure builds up further when the King begins to formulate his questions. We have anticipated many of them, but the King pursues them with a relentless persistence which sharpens our doubts. It is now the advocate's turn to be silent, but, as before we were constantly conscious of the silent King and imagining his responses, so we are now equally conscious of the silent Gulliver, who has become defendant now rather than advocate, and his lack of any reasonable grounds for defence.

It does not matter very much that the particular institutions which are brought under scrutiny are of another age and another world: if Swift's satire were merely directed against an England governed by hereditary peers, bishops appointed by political patronage and representatives of rotten boroughs, then the satire would be historically interesting and little more than that. The essence of the satirical effect is that Swift leaves the reader to supply the details of Gulliver's defence, and so we can adapt the broad outlines of his argument to a variety of situations. 'He asked, what Methods were used to cultivate the Minds and Bodies of our young Nobility; and in what kind of Business they commonly spent the first and teachable Part of their Lives.'

Surely this is far more pointed as a means of satirizing educational methods – not only the education of the eighteenth-century aristocrat, but the educational arrangements of any society – than the elaborate educational scheme described in the sixth chapter of the Voyage to Lilliput? It challenges us to test our own educational experience against the very highest standards; to test whether our educational institutions really do make for the enrichment of our society, or contribute to its greater awareness and creativity. The challenges continue: 'Whether Advocates and Orators had Liberty to plead in Causes manifestly known to be unjust, vexatious or oppressive. Whether Party in Religion or Politicks were observed to be of any Weight in the Scale of Justice. Whether those pleading Orators were Persons educated in the general Knowledge of Equity; or only in provincial, national, and other local Customs.' Here the questions raised are rather more complex in their effect, and would seem to a modern reader to work in opposite directions at the same time. For instance 'manifestly known to be unjust' seems to beg the question; courts are there to decide what is and what is not just, and what is 'manifestly known' can often turn out to be merely prejudice or mis-understanding. However, the questions remain relevant. If any man can assemble his memories of court judgements which he has read or heard about and say that none of them has served injustice or oppression; that none of them has been influenced by prejudice or hatred, then either his memory is very selective or his sense of justice very limited.

We in the twentieth century have little defence against the King of Brobdingnag; our century too is 'a Heap of Conspiracies, Rebellions, Murders, Massacres, Revolutions, Banishments; the very worst Effects that Avarice, Faction, Hypocrisy, Perfidiousness, Cruelty, Rage, Madness, Hatred, Envy, Lust, Malice, and Ambition could produce'. The only advance, perhaps, is that more of us know it and are un-happy because of it. We simply cannot withstand the King's summing up to Gulliver.

As for yourself . . . who have spent the greatest Part of

your Life in travelling; I am well disposed to hope you
may hitherto have escaped many Vices of your Country.
But, by what I have gathered from your own Relation,
and the Answers I have with much Pains wringed and
extorted from you; I cannot but conclude the Bulk of
your Natives, to be the most pernicious Race of little
odious Vermin that Nature ever suffered to crawl upon
the Surface of the Earth.

It would be incorrect to say that this is an ambush of the
kind which Swift so often prepares. We have prepared ourselves at length for this judgement by involving ourselves in
the satirical situation, imagining Gulliver's panegyric and
the King's reactions, applying the King's questions to our
own world with increasing awareness of the inadequacies of
mankind. However, it should not escape our attention that
Gulliver's role has been changing as his audiences with the
King proceed.

Gulliver begins the interviews a simple-minded patriot,
but not vicious or corrupt in his love of his country. By the
seventh chapter the ironic process has pushed him into quite
a different position. He is no longer the naïve patriot, but the
vicious and evil representative of a vicious and corrupt
humanity. The coarsening of the irony forces the reader
into a different position too; we are prised away from
Gulliver; as he praises himself for hiding some of the truth
and condemns the King for his narrowness of thinking, we
hasten to dissociate ourselves from him. His offer to reveal
the secret of gunpowder to the King completes the process;
I suppose that in this more sophisticated age we silently
replace gunpowder by other, more technically elegant means
of destruction; either way we come to reject Gulliver for his
brutality. And this is strange, for most of us accept, in the
name of security, defence, deterrent power, negotiation from
strength or some such euphemism, both Gulliver's arguments
and weapons more terrible than his.

It would seem, almost, that in dissociating ourselves from
Gulliver we are dissociating ourselves from the human race;
but this is not really what happens. As I have argued, the

King is a being whose intelligence, sanity and moral worthiness are by no means superhuman; he is well within the range of humanity, and there is relatively little difficulty for us in transferring our point of view to his, seeing through the giant's eye rather than the puny mannikin's. Swift has accomplished a radical change in the reader's attitude, one in which we are forced to separate the mean and vicious conforming animal in us from the wise and responsible critic and judge.

The process is one special version of the polarization effect which we have observed so many times. We are encouraged to distinguish and separate two aspects of humanity, to condemn one and accept or identify with the other. The process inevitably involves a certain amount of forcing; Swift wrenches the truth because man is simultaneously wise and stupid, both sane and mad, and the two aspects of man are more closely and subtly inter-related than the satirical diagram can possibly allow. Satire of this kind necessarily involves a certain distortion because its aim, ultimately, is to challenge the reader into a moral re-evaluation of his own; the satirist's strategy is to analyse the problem in extreme, even intolerable terms and to leave the reader to cope with the distress this causes by making his own synthesis as best he can.

The King is the embodiment of good sense; with all their limitations and inadequacies his people are a sensible, moderate, intelligent folk. It is worth while to see the way Swift defines their good sense. The Gulliver of Brobdingnag – so different from the very pragmatic Gulliver of Laputa and Balnibarbi – criticizes the giants for their lack of abstract and theoretical scholarship.

> The Learning of this People is very defective; consisting only in Morality, History, Poetry and Mathematicks; wherein they must be allowed to excel. But the last of these is wholly applied to what may be useful in Life; to the Improvement of Agriculture and all mechanical Arts; so that among us it would be little esteemed. And as to Ideas, Entities, Abstractions and Transcendentals,

I could never drive the least Conception into their Heads.

The reader by this time recognizes that his loyalties lie with the giants rather than Gulliver, and so understands that Swift has no time for theory; this in an age which began the great concerted effort to understand and develop the theoretical basis of our physical world upon which all our present practice depends. We are bound to admit that Swift was appallingly ignorant and stubborn in his attitude to such changes; the greatest practical advantages commonly follow apparently recondite theoretical discoveries. Nevertheless, the King's summary of the aim of science and technology; his notion of good sense and the proper priorities, is a sound enough one, even to this day (we allow Swift the satirist's licence to flay the poor politician, who is useful sometimes):

> And, he gave it for his Opinion; that whoever could make two Ears of Corn, or two Blades of Grass to grow upon a Spot of Ground where only one grew before; would deserve better of Mankind, and do more essential Service to his Country, than the whole Race of Politicians put together.

A VOYAGE TO LAPUTA ETC.

The third volume of the *Travels* advances this practical ethic further. It is a curious book. Each of the other three could stand on its own (though each of them would lose a great deal by being detached from the others). The third book has no such independence; by itself it would seem miscellaneous and episodic. We can understand a great deal more about its structure and purpose when we realize that it was the last book of the four to be written. The third book provides a kind of bridge between the satirical methods of the first two books and that of Book IV.

If the *Voyage to the Houyhnhnms* had followed directly after Gulliver's return from Brobdingnag the effect upon the reader would have been so abrupt and distressing that it would have interfered with the satirical processes. The absurd pride and meanness of Man's spirit – not individual *men*, but *Man*, in the mass – is attacked in both the Voyages, to Lilliput and Brobdingnag. But both of the first two voyages offer the reader a fairly safe avenue of retreat so that he can detach himself from the satirical criticism, at least partially. In Lilliput we can congratulate ourselves that we are like Gulliver, benign, tolerant, far-sighted; in Brobdingnag the giants are human too; we can comfort ourselves by being giants for the while. But in the land of the Houyhnhnms we dare not and cannot identify ourselves with the horses and refuse to identify ourselves with the Yahoos; Gulliver is himself so completely confused, bewildered and denatured by the experience that we can't use him as a lifeline any more. So the fourth book offers no relief for our self-respect, unless we can do what Swift deliberately makes difficult for us, unless we can go right outside the terms of analysis which are offered in Book IV, and assert our humanity in terms which that book (for the purposes of satirical strategy) does not allow.

The third book, then, effects a difficult change of key. It begins with satire which is amusing but somewhat superficial, and wholly external in that Gulliver remains the outsider in a crazy fantasy society, possessed of all his senses, and able to see clearly and judge well. The reader's self-respect is left untouched. But after Gulliver leaves Balnibarbi and as he travels through Glubbdubdrib and Luggnagg, the satire strikes deeper, becomes more inward in its effect, involving both Gulliver and ourselves in an embarrassing admission that we, too, share an unreal fantasy world, that we, too, deceive ourselves daily with illusions which rob us of some part of our sanity. In Luggnagg, particularly, we are brought to a point where we are no longer willing to trust ourselves, where we are vulnerable to the satiric method of Book IV, but at the same time we are made more than ever aware of the need to know some firm and steady vantage point, a rock on which we can build our faith and our hope in ourselves and in our fellow men.

Just as Swift employs a common fantasy or dream situation in the Voyages to Lilliput and Brobdingnag, so, in the Voyage to Laputa, he uses the universal dreams of unlimited power and the flying machine. The invention of the aeroplane didn't really change the power of the dream; the little boy who runs about the school playground with his arms outstretched making noises like a jet fighter is not entirely unlike the older dreamers who invented magic carpets, flying horses, gods with winged heels or djinns with unlimited magical powers; Icarus dreamed the same dream, and so did Leonardo. And when the little boy gets tired of aeroplanes and becomes Superman he reverts entirely to the original pattern of the myth.

What Swift does in inventing the flying island of Laputa is to create the image of a whole society possessed by a fantastic dream. In Lilliput we have been invited to join in the fantasy, and given as a lollipop bribe the pleasant imaginary prospect of great power without real responsibility. In Brobdingnag we join in the fantasy again, but it's not so pleasant a dream this time and we struggle to climb out of it to escape the humiliation and anguish of poor Gulliver. Here in Laputa both Gulliver and the reader stay outside the fantasy situation altogether. However high the island flies Gulliver's feet stay on the ground, and we, too, are allowed to feel that we remain down to earth, untouched by illusion and self-deception.

The satire in the Laputan and Balnibarbian episodes is, as it were, fraternal; if all the rest of the world is mad, at least we can stay sane, and join forces against a common, absurd enemy who has both unlimited power and unlimited foolishness. As in the Voyage to Lilliput the immediate object of the satirical discourse is contemporary attitudes and institutions. But the parallels between historical reality and the satirical myth are not always so clear and straightforward as they are in Lilliput. In Lilliput the satire goes straight for its mark, like a rifle; in Laputa and Balnibarbi Swift lets off a shot gun, peppering the Hanoverian Court, the Walpole administration, theoretical scientists, agricultural improvers, projectors of any and every kind almost indiscriminately. He seems concerned, not so much to satirize particular people or policies, as the general anarchy of values, the feverish hunt for novelty, the lack of realism and common sense which lie behind all the more particular symptoms of the disease.

There's another marked difference in method between the Laputan episode and the Voyage to Lilliput. In Lilliput Gulliver has a part to play in the action; he represents a particular historical and political point of view. He acts and he suffers as Oxford and Bolingbroke, their ministry and their party, acted and suffered during and after their few short years of power. In Laputa and Balnibarbi Gulliver has no such active role to play; he is entirely the outsider, the bewildered and sceptical alien observing the oddness of his surroundings as a visitor to Bedlam in Swift's day would watch the ravings of the madman with mixed amusement and fear; amusement which arises out of the fear. The Bedlamite metaphor is a familiar one in Swift: he uses it right at the beginning of his career in the Digression on Madness in *A Tale of a Tub*; he is still using it at the very end of his career in that remarkable poem 'The Legion Club' (1736). And of course it is implicit in the account of Laputa, explicit in the account of the great Academy of Lagado.

There are remarkable parallels between all three of these works; the basic situation is one which haunted Swift; fear, sorrow, madness and laughter fused into one acutely disturbing experience; the visitor from the outside world looking down upon the insane, guffawing at their oddities, yet realizing all the time how close he and they are in the essence of their humanity; how little divides the whole mind from the broken. So, in *A Tale of a Tub* he pretends to suggest that we should not waste the talents of the Bedlamites, who are clearly so well suited to be courtiers, lawyers, scientists and the like. And here the flying island is a sad, abstract, unworldly Bedlam which not only rules the solid earth, but becomes the lodestar which attracts the imaginations and the intellects of those beneath, turning Balnibarbi itself into a madhouse of crazy speculative activity. Whereas in Lilliput Gulliver had done what he could to cure the madness, here in Laputa and Balnibarbi he can do nothing but stand by and watch.

Gulliver is entirely passive, merely the observer. His friendship with the Lord Munodi stresses the point. Munodi is the idealized Tory landowner, traditional and conservative in his ideas about agriculture, economics and morality, but unlike the King of Brobdingnag he is not secure and certain, supported by the whole of his civilization. In a crazy world sanity becomes madness; Munodi is the social outcast, a passive resister, a maverick waiting for the madness of the world to pass, doing his best within a limited sphere of action and not attempting to influence others.

The reader's attitude is affected by all this. In Lilliput, we react, perhaps, by saying 'We can do better than this; we can change the world around us.' In Brobdingnag our reaction might be 'We could hardly do worse; but perhaps by changing ourselves we can do something to change the world.' In Balnibarbi the reaction which Swift encourages in us is 'In such a world we can do nothing at all but cultivate our gardens.' Candide's 'il faut cultiver notre jardin' is metaphorical; this is more literal. The proper use of the land was one of the most important themes of the Tory and traditionalist. It is an important theme again in our own day, though the similarity is disguised a good deal by terms like 'the environment', 'conservation' and 'ecology'. 'Conservationist' isn't a party label; it is probable that most people who are the most concerned about the matter think of themselves as radicals in politics. But they are, in fact, like Swift, literally to be described as reactionaries, and the things they are in reaction against are the same things that Swift reacted against. The modern conservationist though, reacts with hindsight, and Swift, writing in an age when man had only begun to ruin his environment, is oddly prophetic: 'I never knew a Soil so unhappily cultivated, Houses so ill contrived and so ruinous, or a People whose Countenances and Habit expressed so much Misery and Want.'

This being said, we must draw back a bit and take a rather more careful look at Swift's Tory traditionalism and our own reactionary conservationism. Swift expresses a deeply-felt sentiment, not only about the use of the land, but about the relationship of people to each other in society. As in other writers in the same vein (Ben Jonson in 'Penshurst', Andrew Marvell in 'The Garden' and 'Upon Nun Appleton House', Pope in the fourth Moral Essay addressed to Burlington) conservation of the land is bound up closely with conservation of the Landlord. The movements which Swift satirized have since done precisely what the Brobdingnagian King said man should do: make two blades of grass, two ears of corn grow where only one grew before. Some of the experiments of Jethro Tull, 'Turnip' Townshend, Coke of Norfolk and others like them were unrealistic, but the use of the seed-drill and the horse-hoe, better use of manuring, stocking of winter feed, the selective breeding of cattle and sheep, all these began a process which we could not reverse even if we wanted to. Better and more plentiful food led to a more even distribution of wealth, a more even distribution of wealth led to a collapse of the old social hierarchies, the collapse of the hierarchy led to the end of the old system of landlord and squire. Swift fought a desperate rear-guard action; his prophecies had no future to recommend but a stale copy of the past.

In the same way there was necessarily a great deal of incomprehension, even fear, at the strange activities of the Royal Society. The same Tory squires who exercised their tongues about the new methods of Tull over a bottle of port would doubtless be sardonic about cats in air pumps too. Nowadays we tend only to remember the activities of geniuses like Newton and Boyle, and the way in which they set the patterns of thought of modern science which were to dominate the intellectual life of the world for centuries. But members of the Royal Society sometimes did silly things, too, sometimes chased wild whims and delusions in the fashionable name of experimental science. Swift, like other reactionaries (I use the term neutrally, not as an adverse judgement) picked on the excesses and the absurdities, but perhaps the real problem for him lay deeper. The new science seemed to be tainted with irreverence for the old truths, and even with irreligion. The members of the Royal Society excluded Thomas Hobbes from membership because he was an atheist; they cultivated clerics like poor Thomas Sprat, their historian; they indulged in bizarre attempts to prove experimentally the reality of the spirit and of ghosts, but try as they might the suspicion always remained that their experimental, analytical and inductive methods either challenged revealed religion or were going to do so before long. In fact, like Newton, most of the members of the Royal Society were deeply religious, but the conservative and traditionalist half-glimpsed the fact that they were going to change irrevocably the whole fabric of society. The truths of religion depend so intimately upon the believer's daily experience that any such radical change as the scientist prepared for was bound to seem counter to religion.

In a word the impulse behind the satire in the Laputan and Balnibarbian episodes is fear of change, and this is the motive which binds together the diverse elements of the satire. Characteristically, Swift builds his satirical parable out of elements provided by his enemies. Both the Hanoverian court and the Whig administration were very favourably inclined towards science and scientists; one of their great interests, like that of the Laputans, was astronomy. Charles II had set up the Greenwich Observatory for John Flamsteed to map the stars: Flamsteed and Halley, who succeeded him, did so with such success that British ships had for many, many years a tremendous superiority over ships of other nations in navigating the high seas. Indirectly their labour stimulated the development of the first accurate chronometers; the government and the crown directly stimulated this work by offering prizes. The tiny basis of fact for the elaborate joke of the magnetic flying island was provided by the work of another, earlier British scientist, William Gilbert, who first demonstrated the magnetic properties of the earth; a discovery which led to results of the greatest practical significance in marine navigation. All this was hardly impractical; it did much to lay the foundations of Britain's mercantile power. But it did involve fundamental investigations into the physical nature of the universe which were bound to disturb the old ways of life, the old certainties and truths.

For all the reactionary stubbornness of Swift's attitude in all this, there are ways in which the satire remains relevant. The Lord Munodi sees his own estate as a whole; he refuses to alter the balance of things for the satisfaction of a whim. To him, everything is inter-related, and to change one thing without due thought and care is, frequently, to change everything in unpredictable and sometimes disastrous ways. The message anticipates that of the modern conservationist; but *he* uses all the tools and methods, all the patient collecting of data, all the paraphernalia of theory and analysis which was pioneered by the Royal Society. Otherwise he would merely be expressing personal opinion and sentiment, merely reacting against the inevitable rather than planning to make the inevitable more acceptable.

Gulliver's short visit to Glubdubbdrib pivots a change in the satirical method of the book. Again, as in Laputa, the satire takes as its starting point a dream of extraordinary power; in this case the power of sorcery. But, whereas in Laputa Gulliver has been the entirely passive observer of power used unwisely, here in Glubdubbdrib he is allowed to indulge in the dream himself, briefly, and call up ghosts from the past, see for himself what the past really was like. Obviously one of the things behind this particular satirical use of the fantasy is the battle between the Ancients and Moderns, Temple and Boyle against Bentley and Wotton, in which Swift engaged so spiritedly in *The Battle of the Books* and *A Tale of a Tub*. Swift makes the fact fit with his prejudice; Gulliver learns that history was as Swift always had argued it was. The Roman senate is set against the modern parliament: 'The first seemed to be an Assembly of Heroes and Demy-Gods; the other a Knot of Pedlars, Pick-pockets, Highwaymen and Bullies.' And yet the Ancients don't always turn out as well as one might expect them to; Swift takes the opportunity to tease the nostalgic veneration for antiquity which he largely shared himself. Alexander the Great, who conquered a greater Empire than had ever been known 'assured me upon his

Honour that he was not poisoned, but dyed of a Fever by excessive Drinking'. Hannibal, who nearly defeated the Romans by his heroic march across the Alps, is worried because there isn't a drop of vinegar in the camp. Swift hovers and hesitates between saying that history is bunk and that the past is so glorious that we cannot begin to compete with our ancestors.

The one Modern he does allow to compete on equal terms with the Ancients is Sir Thomas More, the only modern member of the great Sextumvirate of Philosophers and Men of Honour who are together with each other for all eternity:

> I was struck with a profound Veneration at the Sight of *Brutus*; and could easily discover the most con-summate Virtue, the greatest Intrepidity, and Firmness of Mind, the truest Love of his Country, and general Benevolence for Mankind in every Lineament of his Countenance. I observed with much Pleasure, that these two Persons were in good Intelligence with each other; and *Caesar* freely confessed to me, that the greatest Actions of his own Life were not equal by many Degrees to the Glory of taking it away. I had the Honour to have much Conversation with *Brutus*; and was told that his Ancestor *Junius*, *Socrates*, *Epaminondas*, *Cato* the Younger, Sir *Thomas More* and himself, were perpetually together: A *Sextumvirate* to which all the Ages of the World cannot add a Seventh.

The Six were all men who are reputed to have held honour and truth above other, lesser kinds of duty, and suffered for their pains; in this way the passage is a blow against compromise and servility in the service of the state. But it helps to define certain virtues as having priority over others; they are the Roman virtues of Courage, Fortitude and Honour rather than the prime Christian virtues of Faith, Hope and Charity. The two notions of virtue can be recon-ciled; but in this context, and for the time being, it is the Roman virtues which Swift chooses to stress: the Greeks Epaminondas and Socrates and the only Christian Sir Thomas More are, as it were, assimilated to the virtuous

Romans, Junius, Cato the Younger, and 'the noblest Roman of them all', Brutus. The sentiment of the passage echoes that which runs through the Lilliputian Voyage: Gulliver, like More, Socrates and the rest, suffered grievously for his greater integrity and greater far-sightedness, and in the Tory interpretation of things, so did Bolingbroke, the historical figure who most closely parallels Gulliver's career.

The curious thing is the way in which Swift allows his nostalgic conservative idealism to go to such extremes that he disparages and condemns the whole history of the Christian era, which becomes a record of disastrous and progressive moral and spiritual decline relieved only by the one bright exception of More. And it is not for his humanism or his Christian principles that More is honoured so much as his willingness to oppose tyrannical power to the point of martyrdom.

Chapter VIII continues the tale of decline. It's understandable that Homer should be preferred to his commentators, Aristotle to Scotus and Ramus, though these two later philosophers have more to offer than Swift would suggest. It is to be expected, given Swift's reactionary sentiments, that he should use old Aristotle as a stick to beat modern philosophers like Descartes and Gassendi, and that he should carry on his private war against the Royal Society by making Aristotle predict (with unhappy inaccuracy) that Newton's theory of gravitation (or 'Attraction') would prove to be as wrong as Descartes' notion of vortices. What is so very interesting are the heroes who are missing: Sir Thomas More imitated Socrates in dying for the truth; Brutus and Cato the Younger took their own lives for the sake of honour; where are those who imitated Christ and died for love? Aristotle lasted as the standard of excellence in intellect for two thousand years; his analytic methods were copied, adapted and naturalized to the Christian and Muslim faiths; but if all those who copied and adapted them were coarse dolts, the Christian faith is simply a corrupted Aristotelianism. Once again, I believe, this is a place where Swift puts himself at risk in the fantasy, and allows it to run away with him: the digression reveals with unusual clarity some of the problems which injured his moral understanding at times, though at other times he was able to rise above them. Swift spent his life as a servant of the Christian church, but seems, at moments like these, not to understand what Christianity required of him. The point will become of the greatest significance when we begin our discussion of the fourth book of the *Travels*.

Another fantasy situation lies at the root of the satirical method in the visit to Luggnagg; but there's no question of Swift himself becoming involved too deeply in it; neither are the inhabitants of the island deluded by the dream. It is Gulliver only who suffers from the delusion that immortality will bring unlimited power, unlimited happiness, unlimited wisdom; Gulliver alone if we do not count the sympathetic string in our own emotional make-up which responds to Gulliver's enthusiasm. The mode of the satire takes a decisive turn. It is no longer in any way satire upon society, upon the follies of conventional behaviour and human relationships, government, politics, war, education, law, the court; all these targets disappear after the brief black humour of the Royal audience, and we are left with secret follies and delusions which we all know because in some degree we share them.

So far, in Book III Gulliver has escaped serious criticism; in fact he has almost entirely escaped definition, being merely a neutral vehicle enabling the reader to observe. As a result we are less wary than perhaps we should be when Gulliver begins to be enthusiastic about the magnificent opportunities offered to the immortal Struldbrugs. The fantasy of personal immortality is too strong in most of us to resist the temptation; very few of us can reconcile ourselves to the idea of our own deaths, and in the secret places of our dream worlds – perhaps you may recall it, can you? – most of us are convinced that we will live for ever.

> I freely own myself to have been struck with inexpressible Delight upon hearing this Account: And the Person who gave it me happening to understand the *Balni-barbian* Language, which I spoke very well, I could not

forbear breaking into Expressions perhaps a little too
extravagant. I cryed out as in a Rapture; Happy
Nation, where every Child hath at least a Chance for
being immortal! Happy People who enjoy so many
living Examples of antient Virtue, and have Masters
ready to instruct them in the Wisdom of all former
Ages! But, happiest beyond all Comparison are those
excellent *Struldbruggs*, who being born exempt from that
universal Calamity of human Nature, have their Minds
free and disingaged, without the Weight and Depression
of Spirits caused by the continual Apprehension of
Death.

Gulliver's extravagant rhetoric; the free use of the exclamation mark, the rhetorical inversions and syntactical
parallelisms – 'Happy Nation . . . Happy People . . . But,
happiest beyond all . . .' should be enough to warn us to
withdraw from Gulliver a little; indeed Gulliver himself tells
us that he was overdoing it: 'breaking into Expressions
perhaps a little too extravagant'. The satirical caution which
Swift delivers in this way and in his account of the reactions
of the Luggnaggians pushes us into a defensively critical
position: 'The Gentleman . . . said to me with a Sort of a
Smile which usually ariseth from Pity to the Ignorant . . .',
and so when Gulliver is invited to lavish his eloquence on
the theme of endless life, we have already become suspicious
of our own desires, in so far as we share them with the good
Lemuel.

So we are manoeuvred into a position where we accept
Swift's own satirical position, taking the pathos and the
horror of the Immortals as the final, terrible blow to concealed and only half-admitted inner fantasies. Nevertheless,
for all its power and poignancy, there are ways in which the
episode does more, and at the same time less, than it offers
to do; ways in which one could almost say it cheats. The
desire for continued life, the fear of death, is a harmless
biological necessity; it can only make us cautious of danger
and avid for life. Swift counters the fear of death with something quite different; the fear of impotent, painful and weari-

some old age. He dismisses the idea that extreme old age may be happy and wise, and paradoxically tends to confirm the illusion it sets out to destroy. Fear of age as terrible as this would keep us all Peter Pans clinging desperately to the memory of youth; it would make age even more distressing and difficult.

The last curiosity about the episode (and it is among the most powerful and memorable things that Swift ever did; entirely characteristic of his great genius as well as his curious shortcomings) is this: Swift seeks to reconcile us to mortality, but does so by terrorizing us and shows his own terror in doing so:

> When they come to Fourscore Years . . . they had not only all the Follies and Infirmities of other old Men, but many more which arose from the dreadful Prospect of never dying. They were not only opinionative, peevish, covetous, morose, vain, talkative; but uncapable of Friendship, and dead to all natural Affection, which never descended below their Grand-children. Envy and impotent Desires, are their prevailing Passions. But those Objects against which their Envy seems principally directed, are the Vices of the younger Sort, and the Deaths of the old. By reflecting on the former, they find themselves cut off from all Possibility of Pleasure; and whenever they see a Funeral, they lament and repine that others are gone to an Harbour of Rest, to which they themselves can never hope to arrive.

It is one of the constant themes both of religion and philosophy that man must reconcile himself to his own death; but within the moral tradition inherited by Swift, the moral tradition which springs equally from Plato and the New Testament, there is consolation for physical death in an immortal life. At this point Swift seems to proceed in the opposite direction. In a way like the Buddhists, he offers death as a release from the horror and corruption of life. Once again he seems to be adopting a profoundly un-Christian viewpoint; in Glubbdubdrib discovering justice, temperance and fortitude as the cardinal virtues, in Luggnagg death as a negative release rather than, as the traditional Christian would have it, the assumption of eternal life.

Swift wrote the third book of the *Travels* after the fourth: in some way these last episodes must be seen as preparing us for the satire of the Voyage to Houyhnhnmland. Certainly the movement of the satire from the external to the internal prepares us; certainly Gulliver's transposition from the sane observer to the absurd dreamer prepares us. I would argue that the system of values and emotional and moral priorities which we have been discussing prepares us too. Notice that in the last passage I have quoted the terror of age is not only presented in terms of the loss of the senses, the loss of the intellect, the persistence of sensual desire; one of the most terrible fates the Struldbrugs suffer is the loss of Friendship and natural Affection. The Struldbrugs, as their bodies and their minds decay, become *isolated* from their fellow men, and this is the last and most terrible injury that age can offer. We must remember this as we read Gulliver's account of his increasing isolation from humanity – from his own humanity – in Book Four.

A VOYAGE TO THE COUNTRY OF THE HOUYHNHNMS

The last voyage begins in a way which is slightly different from the beginnings of the other voyages. Gulliver has always been presented as a somewhat restless and impulsive man, apt to leave wife, family and home at the shortest of notice whenever a new chance to travel comes up. In the fourth book, however, for the first time he shows some remorse for his restlessness, some sense of conflict in his responsibilities: 'I continued at home with my Wife and and Children about five Months in a very happy Condition, if I could have learned the Lesson of knowing when I was well. I left my poor Wife big with Child, and accepted an advantageous Offer . . .'

This hint at the dangers of wilfulness is strengthened when Gulliver mentions the good Captain Pocock: 'He was an honest Man, and a good Sailor, but a little too positive in his own Opinions, which was the Cause of his Destruction, as it hath been of several others.' The irony is muted so far: 'several others' might include Gulliver, and then again it might not; but the irony of the following sentence is inescapable, in the light of Gulliver's final fate: 'For if he had followed my Advice, he might at this Time have been safe at home with his Family as well as my self.' Safe at home, that is, in the stable, talking to horses, unable to endure physical contact with either wife or children.

Immediately after this there is another significant little hint which it is very easy to miss: 'I had several Men died in my Ship of Calentures . . .' The 'calenture' is a tropical fever accompanied by a strange hallucinatory delirium: Dryden wrote of sailors imagining the ocean to be a lush green pasture and throwing themselves into it in suicidal ecstasy. Swift uses it as a significant metaphor for other kinds of deception and illusion in his Ballad 'Upon the South-Sea Project', written in 1720, a few years before the *Travels*:

> Thus, the deluded Bankrupt raves;
> Puts all upon a desp'rate Bet
> Then plunges in the *Southern* Waves,
> Dipt over Head and Ears – in Debt.

> So, by a Calenture misled,
> The Mariner with Rapture sees,
> On the smooth Ocean's azure Bed
> Enamel'd Fields, and verdant Trees.

> With eager Haste he longs to rove
> In that fantastick Scene, and thinks
> It must be some enchanted Grove;
> And *in* he leaps, and *down* he sinks.

These stanzas might stand as a summary of Gulliver's progress through the fourth book; wilful, opinionated, restless, still incapable of learning all the lessons he has been taught, this son of Adam plunges into a false paradise, and drowns in it; not physically as the fevered sailors do, but spiritually and morally.

Once again the basic satirical structure exploits a common dream or fantasy; or in this case two. There are innumerable folk tales and children's stories about talking and reasoning animals. And only slightly less common in fantasy is the idea of the wild, half-animal man.

Characteristically, however, Swift makes some adjustments to the fantasy situation to suit his own purposes. In the folk tale or children's story the talking animal flatters humanity in one way or another. In some cases the talking horse or cat or dog is the hero's servant in a magical adventure: the most familiar example is Dick Whittington's cat. In others, for instance Aesop's fables or the Brer Rabbit stories, talking animals are ways of moralizing about human behaviour. Puss in Boots is a clever little man dressed as a cat, not a cat who has found out how to reason – such an animal would be far stranger, far more surprising and perhaps far more frightening than the pantomime cat. Chauntecleer isn't a real farmyard cock; he's a foolish little man made even more foolish by his bright tail and strutting walk.

The Houyhnhnms are neither pantomime horses nor real horses who can think: they haven't an ounce of horse in them. They are, even, far removed from the traditional stereotype idea of a horse, which man has always sentimentally thought of as pure passion, easy flowing movement unthinking strength and nobility, never, like a fox or monkey as mimic of man's capacity to reason. Except in their outward form, they are not a bit like horses, but they *are* admirable, morally; they *are* in their own way a perfect adaptation to the natural world; they *are* careful, calm, deliberate and intelligent in the way in which they organize their lives. In short they are an expression of something which we would all, in some moods and moments, wish to be; an expression of a human ideal, an ideal which was very much prized in Swift's day. There is no doubt that Swift shares the ideal they represent in some degree; but though they represent a human ideal they do *not* represent a human fact, an aspect of the human in reality. Far from flattering humanity they are a calculated affront to man's proud image of himself.

Tales of wild men commonly flatter our humanity, too. Caliban helps us believe in the fullness of our humanity by offering a contrast to Prospero and Ferdinand and Miranda – Ariel too – they are all possibilities within the human. We react to the tale of the wild man, the Yeti, the Missing Link, the Orang Utan (or wild man of the woods) with congratulations to ourselves upon our humanity.

Nowadays there is a fashionable attitude, both in scholarship and sensational journalism, which is every bit as conservative in its outlook as Swift: it is argued that we can understand human behaviour by comparison with animal behaviour in such matters as territorial rights, systems of precedence and power and the like. The approach is dramatic and seems largely valid: for instance a University Faculty meeting or a Student's Union debate can be analysed in terms of the structural parallels between it and the social life, say, of a troop of baboons, with remarkably revealing results. I don't intend to discuss the value, for instance, of Robert Ardrey's books *African Genesis*, *The Territorial Imperative*, and *The Social Contract*, but any criticism of him would inevitably depend upon two things. First, whether he is working with a sufficiently large body of sound experimental data; secondly whether his own attitudes towards society are sufficiently objective, or whether they colour his analysis, suppressing certain facts, stressing others too greatly, or making relationships between facts in an illegitimate way.

We can't criticize Swift in this way. The evidences he works with *are* his own impressions, his own attitude to man's social arrangements and his moral experience. Swift uses the idea of the savage, as Rousseau does, to persuade us to look at our present human condition in a certain way, though Rousseau and Swift are clean counter to each other in the attitudes they wish to convey. The contrast between Rousseau's 'noble savage' and Swift's Yahoo neatly underlines not only the contrast between the two attitudes the two men represent, but also a curious ultimate similarity between the ways in which they think. Rousseau, the arch-Romantic, creates the noble savage as a criticism of modern man corrupted by his own complex civilization, with its tight structures based upon power, greed, suspicion and hatred. Swift's Yahoo is a criticism of modern man as a degenerate, who has been backsliding for generations from his original nobility and strength. Both Rousseau and Swift are alike in that they set the real man and his society against an ideal man of their imaginations: they are, as it were, Platonists in their convictions of Man's present inadequacies. They differ most markedly in the fact that Rousseau believes it possible to construct a society in which man can approach his original innocent nobility once more, whereas Swift appears to see the downward slide of Man and his societies into the abyss of corruption, nastiness and death as irreversible, and the only alleviation of this process in the individual achieving a tenuous, fragile, vulnerable poise and sanity in the midst of all the hell and horror around him. Oddly, it is Rousseau the Romantic who believes in Reason and in the saving power of Civilization, Swift the Classicist who despairs of collective human Reason and of Civilization and puts his only faith in the individual.

Swift, then, invents two races, which indicate diagrammatically a scale on which it is possible to judge the human animal. The scale operates in three ways; aesthetic, moral and intellectual or rational. The Yahoos are aesthetically revolting – they are ugly, they smell, they are noisy, incontinent and dirty. They excrete and copulate copiously, which, in the context of the peculiarly intense physical revulsion which is characteristic of the book, makes them very nasty indeed. The Houyhnhnms are handsome, graceful, clean smelling, quiet, and if they do copulate or excrete we are allowed to know nothing about it.

The Yahoos are morally foul – covetous, angry, envious, proud, lazy, greedy and lustful; the Houyhnhnms have not one of the Seven Deadly Sins.

The Yahoos are intellectually null and totally irrational; The Houyhnhnms are entirely rational and intelligent in all their behaviour, their beliefs and their emotions.

There are two curious things about this simplified scheme of antitheses. One is that the aesthetic and moral contrasts

are presented as following from the differences in the ration-
ality of the two races. The Houyhnhnms are good and
beautiful because it is rational to be so. The Yahoos are bad
and ugly because they totally lack reason. It follows that, in
the scale of values which is created, nothing which is
irrational, like special personal affection (as opposed to love
for the race as a whole), or fear of death, or enthusiasm, or
fancy, can be aesthetically pleasing or morally good. The
other curious thing is that, whereas the Yahoos possess all
the Seven Deadly Sins of the Christian faith, and the
Houyhnhnms possess the four Cardinal Virtues of the
Ancients, Prudence, Justice, Temperance and Fortitude,
there is no place in the moral scheme provided for the three
great Christian virtues – at least in the way that they are felt
and seen and experienced by the Christian – Faith, Hope and
Love.

Of course not; Christianity is an irrational system of
beliefs, so the Houyhnhnms have no need for it: they are
'endowed by Nature with a general Disposition to all
Virtues, and have no Conceptions or Ideas of what is evil in
a rational Creature; so their grand Maxim is, to cultivate
Reason, and to be wholly governed by it'. The idea of Reason
as a basis for ethics, as opposed to revealed truth, or faith,
was one which was much discussed during the later part of
the seventeenth century and the first half of the eighteenth.
Locke, for instance, in the second of the *Two Treatises of
Government*, conceives of an ideal 'State of Nature', in which
the restrictions of government and the ethical guidance of
the church are alike absent: 'The State of Nature hath a
Law of Nature to govern it, which obliges everyone; and
Reason, which is that Law, teaches all Mankind who will
but consult it, that, being all equal and independent, no one
ought to harm another in his Life, Health, Liberty or
Possessions.' Locke used the idea of the State of Nature and
the Laws of Nature to help set off and define the idea of the
civil state in which civil laws were necessary to restrain man;
man enters into a social contract in which he surrenders
some of his right to behave freely in return for protection by
government and the law.

Elsewhere Locke is severely scornful of the irrational element in belief. Swift would have smiled with the keenest ironic pleasure when Locke, in *An Essay Concerning Human Understanding*, writes:

> Religion, which should most distinguish us from Beasts, and ought most peculiarly to elevate us as rational Creatures above Brutes, is that wherein Men often appear most irrational, and more senseless than Beasts themselves. *Credo quia impossibile est*: 'I believe because it is impossible,' might, in a good Man, pass for a Sally of Zeal, but would prove a very ill Rule for Men to chose their Opinions or Religion by.

In the fourth book of *Gulliver's Travels*, then, Swift creates a 'State of Nature' and populates it with two possible sets of inhabitants. The Houyhnhnms take reason as far as it will go, but it does not lead them to a God or to Love, merely to Reason (or, Nature) and to Benevolence. Yahoo, the parody Man, on the other hand, takes unreason as far as it will go, and it leads him to squalour, anarchy, filth and greed.

From the moment when Gulliver lands on Houyhnhnm Land there are hints that what is being described is Locke's 'State of Nature'. This is neither the absurd waste land of the Balnibarbian projector, nor is it the neat, ordered, rich, cultivated agricultural land of the Lord Munodi:

> The Land was divided by long Rows of Trees, not regularly planted, but naturally growing; there was great Plenty of Grass, and several Fields of Oats.

The Houyhnhnm houses, too, suggest the kind of life which was popularly associated with the 'State of Nature' in Swift's day. Locke, Rousseau and many others, turned to the American Indian as an example of the Natural Society (arguing, it must be said, with more enthusiasm than knowledge) and it is quite significant that Gulliver, too, should think of the 'Savage *Indians* of *America*' as he pulls out baubles for peace-offerings when he sees the first Houyhnhnm house:

Having travelled about three Miles, we came to a long Kind of Building, made of Timber, stuck in the Ground, and wattled a-cross; the Roof was low, and covered with Straw. I now began to be a little comforted; and took out some Toys, which Travellers usually carry for Presents to the Savage *Indians* of *America* and other Parts, in hopes the People of the House would be thereby encouraged to receive me kindly.

It is a small step from Locke's 'State of Nature' to a State of Innocence; the Houyhnhnms are only capable of knowing evil in the person of the Yahoos. Their language contains no word for evil (except Yahoo); they are forced to use elaborate circumlocutions to express the concept of falsehood. The closest approximation to their state of being in human history or myth is the state of Adam and Eve in Paradise; their goodness is not a result of moral decision, but of moral innocence, or ignorance:

> My Master heard me with great Appearances of Un-easiness in his Countenance; because *Doubting* or *not believing*, are so little known in this Country, that the Inhabitants cannot tell how to behave themselves under such Circumstances. And I remember in frequent Discourses with my Master concerning the Nature of Manhood, in other Parts of the World; having Occasion to talk of *Lying*, and *false Representation*, it was with much Difficulty that he comprehended what I meant; although he had otherwise a most acute Judgment. For he argued thus; That the Use of Speech was to make us understand one another, and to receive Information of Facts; now if any one *said the Thing which was not*, these Ends were defeated; because I cannot properly be said to understand him.

Houyhnhnms and Yahoos, therefore, share one further characteristic; they lack the capacity for moral choice. Yahoos cannot choose but be foul, and evil and irrational. Houyhnhnms cannot choose but be graceful, good and entirely rational in all their actions. Only one creature on the island can make any significant moral choice at all, and that is Gulliver.

We have reached a point where we must inevitably touch upon some of the most profound of all problems of Christian theology and ethics. Gulliver, the son of Adam as I have called him, is posed with a problem, and by the same token poses a problem for the reader, which *can* be stated in the traditional language of theology. Whether we use the language of theology or not, the problem remains the same: Gulliver gives another hint to it in the passage just quoted, when he speaks of the 'frequent Discourses with my Master concerning the Nature of Manhood'. The special faculty which distinguishes man from other animals, according to Locke and almost every thinker of the time, is Reason: *that* is the key factor in 'the Nature of Manhood'. But we can hardly argue that to a Houyhnhnm. Confronted with the similarities between the real world as we know it and the microcosmic society of the Yahoos, we might come to the conclusion that the key to 'the Nature of Manhood' is man's helpless tendency to foulness and evil – and this is the conclusion both Gulliver and the Houyhnhnms come to. Man, after all, is the most destructive animal which has ever populated the earth; the havoc he wreaks upon the land, the seas, the rivers, the air, the plants, the other animals; the way he fouls and destroys his surroundings with methodical efficiency, exceeds anything that, say, the rat can do. We surely cannot resist this conclusion any more than we could resist the King of Brobdingnag's summary description of the little-worlders as odious vermin.

But most of us – I hope all of us – would hold back and say, with a very deep sense of conviction, that this is not by any means all the truth. Swift expects us to; wants us to. We are forced back again to consider what it is that distinguishes Gulliver from the Yahoos. At first Gulliver manages to practise a mild deception on his master by wearing his clothes at all times; but this will not answer as a way of asserting his difference from the Yahoos. This recalls the satire upon superficiality in *A Tale of a Tub*, with the religion of Clothes and the image of the Tailor worshipped

as a deity. Gulliver is nervously anxious to stress the point
that he is neither so dirty nor so malformed as the Yahoos.
His master is ready to agree:

> He said, I differed indeed from other *Yahoos*, being
> much more cleanly, and not altogether so deformed;
> but in point of real Advantage, he thought I differed
> for the worse. That my Nails were of no Use either to
> my fore or hinder Feet: As to my fore Feet . . . they
> were too soft to bear the Ground. . . . That I could not
> walk with any Security; for if either of my hinder
> Feet slipped, I must inevitably fall. He then began to
> find fault with other Parts of my Body . . .

Clothes don't make a man, neither does cleanliness or beauty;
we cannot take any special pride in that admittedly in-
efficient machine, our body. We are pushed back still further,
and rise the third time from drowning with one straw clutched
in our hand: the only distinguishing thing that Gulliver can
lay claim to is a knowledge both of good and evil, and the
capacity to choose between them.

The special faculty of Man is not Reason, but the capacity
for moral choice; and in so far as the way of Reason coin-
cides with the way of goodness, this means the capacity to
choose to be reasonable. From this follows Swift's carefully
phrased distinction of terms in the letter to Pope I have
quoted elsewhere: 'I have got materials towards a treatise,
proving the falsity of that definition *animal rationale*, and to
show it would be only *rationis capax*.' Not a rational animal,
but an animal capable of choosing Reason.

Once again, Gulliver is in some sense or other our representative, since he is the only human on the island. If we
believe the essential human faculty is the faculty of choice,
then the choices Gulliver makes are important to us, as some
kind of comment upon the way humans make use of their
freedom. And perhaps the most important thing about
moral choice, the thing which precedes all else, is to be able
to discern where and when there is a choice to be made.

Yahoo and Houyhnhnm represent aspects of humanity;
aspects which are deliberately exaggerated until they no

longer fall within the range of the human. They seem to be offered as a radical analysis of man into his essential elements. We can recognize, in some way or other, that the 'Yahoo' refers to us: it sounds like a scornful, drawnout, whinnied 'You'. 'Houyhnhnm' too, in some way refers to some part of us: it is a neighing, twisted parody of 'human'. If the two races do, between them, share out all that there is to humanity, it would seem that we have to make a choice between them. Certainly Gulliver tries to do so.

He sees the contrast between the two races simultaneously in aesthetic, in moral and in intellectual terms. As we read we follow him, inevitably, at least part of the way in the way he interprets what he sees. The good, the beautiful and the reasonable are one and the same; they have four legs, eat oats and neigh. The bad, the ugly and the irrational are one and the same; they have two legs, eat meat and copulate. However much I wriggle from the fact, I am an animal with two legs, who eats meat, and I copulate. Am I therefore bad, and ugly, and irrational? Gulliver doesn't decide the answer for himself; it seems to him that it is decided for him:

> Being one Day abroad with my Protector the Sorrel Nag, and the Weather exceeding hot, I entreated him to let me bathe in a River that was near. He consented, and I immediately stripped myself stark naked, and went down softly into the Stream. It happened that a young Female *Yahoo* standing behind a Bank, saw the whole Proceeding; and inflamed by Desire, as the Nag and I conjectured, came running with all Speed, and leaped into the Water within five Yards of the Place where I bathed. I was never in my Life so terribly frighted . . . She embraced me after a most fulsome Manner; I roared as loud as I could, and the Nag came galloping towards me, whereupon she quitted her Grasp. . . . This was a Matter of Diversion to my Master and his Family, as well as Mortification to my self. For now I could no longer deny, that I was a real *Yahoo*, in every Limb and Feature, since the Females

had a natural Propensity to me as one of their own
Species: Neither was the Hair of this Brute of a Red
Colour, (which might have been some Excuse for an
Appetite a little irregular) but black as a Sloe, and her
Countenance did not make an Appearance altogether
so hideous as the rest of the Kind; for, I think, she could
not be above Eleven Years old.

Gulliver feels that he is forced to accept identification with
the Yahoos because he has two legs and is desirable to a
Yahoo girl. To make it even more conclusive he tries to
make allowances for her: there is a special poignancy in
'her Countenance did not make an Appearance altogether
so hideous as the rest of the Kind', Gulliver learning to
recognize degrees of attractiveness, or if you will, repellent-
ness, among Yahookind. There is a curious doubleness of
effect in 'for, I think, she could not be above Eleven Years
old', hinting, on the one hand, at the kind of preference for
the childish relationship which we saw in Gulliver's love
for Glumdalclitch, on the other hand at the horror of infant
sexuality – a horror which many people still feel even in our
more tolerant post-Freudian age. But the whole effect is
one of high comedy: the absurd Gulliver affronted at being
forced to recognize that he possesses the body he possesses.

On the other hand he continues to attempt to identify
himself with the Houyhnhnms; a choice, as it seems to
Gulliver a moral choice, which he persists in despite all the
obstacles. Let us take another look at the direction in
which the Houyhnhnm logic takes the mind. The
Houyhnhnms are ignorant of evil; their constant aim is to
follow the dictates of Reason; and this results in an un-
exceptionable rightness of behaviour and certainty of belief:

> Neither is *Reason* among them a Point problematical
> as with us, where Men can argue with Plausibility on
> both Sides of a Question; but strikes you with im-
> mediate Conviction; as it must needs do where it is
> not mingled, obscured, or discoloured by Passion and
> Interest. I remember it was with extreme Difficulty
> that I could bring my Master to understand the Meaning

of the word *Opinion* . . . In the like Manner when I
used to explain to him our several Systems of *Natural
Philosophy*, he would laugh that a Creature pretending to
Reason, should value itself upon the Knowledge of other
Peoples Conjectures, and in Things, where that Know-
ledge, if it were certain, could be of no Use. Wherein
he agreed entirely with the Sentiments of *Socrates*, as
Plato delivers them; which I mention as the highest
Honour I can do that Prince of Philosophers. I have
often since reflected what Destruction such a Doctrine
would make in the Libraries of *Europe*; and how many
Paths to Fame would be then shut up in the Learned
World.

At first sight this seems to be just another shrewd blow
against the pretentiousness and pomposity of disputant
scholars. But as we have seen, it is often unwise to allow first
impressions to stay unaltered when we are reading Swift.
Let us take the passage a little more slowly and carefully,
weighing its consequences and implications. The 'Libraries
of Europe' would give up a great deal more than Bentley
and Wotton; Plato himself would be of uncertain status;
the Fathers and Doctors of the Church would be difficult
to justify.

The argument against 'opinion' would work equally
against Faith, where that Faith is justified by other means
than Reason. Swift, as part of his professional duties, made
a statement of belief at regular intervals throughout his
adult life. One wonders how a Houyhnhnm would assay its
claim to Reason; or whether he would judge, even if it
were certain, that the Knowledge it pretends to convey
could be of any possible 'Use'?

I believe in God the Father Almighty, Maker of heaven
and earth:
And in Jesus Christ his only Son our Lord, Who was
conceived by the Holy Ghost, Born of the Virgin
Mary, Suffered under Pontius Pilate, Was crucified,
dead, and buried: He descended into hell; The third
day he rose again from the dead; He ascended into

heaven, And sitteth on the right hand of God the Father Almighty; from thence he shall come to judge the quick and the dead.

I believe in the Holy Ghost; the holy Catholick Church; the Communion of Saints; The Forgiveness of sins; The Resurrection of the body, And the life everlasting. Amen.

Locke, as we have seen, remarked that religion 'is that wherein Men often appear most irrational'. In so far as the Houyhnhnms have a religion it is a rational one; carefully constructed to meet the demands of Reason, and nothing else: implicitly this careful, brittle and cold structure is set against the strictly irrational religious structures constructed, not merely to satisfy Reason, but to satisfy Man. 'Friendship and *Benevolence* are the two principle Virtues among the Houyhnhnms; and these not confined to particular Objects, but universal to the whole Race.' Let us say, for argument's sake, that Gulliver is correct in implying that Reason dictates these two virtues as pre-eminent over others, over Faith, Hope and Love, for instance. If these are Gulliver's ideals, then perhaps he should be judged by them. Gulliver returns to Rotherhithe:

As soon as I entered the House, my Wife took me in her Arms, and kissed me; at which, having not been used to the Touch of that odious Animal for so many Years, I fell in a Swoon for almost an Hour. At the Time I am writing, it is five Years since my last Return to *England*: During the first Year I could not endure my Wife or Children in my Presence, the very Smell of them was intolerable; much less could I suffer them to eat in the same Room. To this Hour they dare not presume to touch my Bread, or drink out of the same Cup; neither was I ever able to let one of them take me by the Hand. The first Money I laid out was to buy two young Stone-Horses, which I keep in a good Stable . . . they live in great Amity with me, and Friendship to each other.

Friendship and Benevolence remain the principal virtues; but only towards horses: even the religion of Reason becomes irrational in Gulliver, the son of Adam. Gulliver has suffered from his calenture; plunged into a sea of rational idealism, and is incapable of bringing back anything from the experience but friendship and benevolence for horses, and a heightened sense of disgust for the physical and moral properties of his own kind. He has sacrificed his freedom, his humanity even, to a mad delusion.

Through Gulliver, Swift offers to contradict certain fundamental axioms, not only of Christianity, but of Greek thought. The Houyhnhnm Master finds sympathy only with Socrates, as he is reported by Plato; but Socrates and Plato agree in treating 'man as the measure of all things', as the *Theaetetus* has it; the familiar Hebraic precept is: 'So God created Man in his own image.' The effect of the Voyage to the Houyhnhnms is to displace, or appear to displace man for a while from this, his central role. Instead of Plato's Man-centred universe and instead of the God-centred universe of the Hebrews, in which man is given a privileged role as mirror of the divine, we are offered a modern barbarism: a Reason-centred universe. Swift tests the notion against Gulliver, and shows it destroying his sanity.

This, perhaps, is the moment to look back upon the various incidents in which Swift has, as I have expressed it, put himself at risk in the fantasy: those terrible Spartan schools of Lilliput; the contemptuous dismissal of the whole moral and intellectual history of mankind since antiquity (with the single exception of Sir Thomas More) in Glubbdubdrib; the fear of death attacked by the fear of age, decrepitude and decay in Luggnagg. In all these incidents the Houyhnhnm virtues have been in control of things; Swift has shown how very strong their hold is over his imagination. They form a third element in a triumvirate of influences over Swift— as indeed over the mind of any European; to the Athenian spirit and the Hebrew spirit we have to add the powerful disciplinary influence of the Roman mind. 'Friendship and Benevolence', the whole range of Houyhnhnm virtues, arise from the *control* of the natural affections through the exercise of Prudence, Justice, Temperance and Fortitude; and there is no doubt at all that Swift – for complex reasons of his own which we have not the right or the knowledge to discuss – felt the need for himself, and for man as a whole, to subject the natural affections to as iron a control as was humanly possible. *Humanly* possible – and this is the key to the whole question of Book IV. Swift allows free rein to a fantasy of Reason. But the fantasy which attracts Swift is not simply of Reason; Reason becomes identified with an absence of all powerful emotion, all the disturbing energies of natural affection. He allows the reader (and, perhaps, allows himself) to dream of the simplicity, and elegance, and tranquillity, of such a paradise, but then at last admits its failure in face of certain other essential human needs. I have remarked elsewhere that satire is fundamentally dishonest unless the satirist directs his artillery as much against himself as against the reader, or the world which surrounds both author and reader. Here is one of the points at which Swift accepts the most painful and arduous responsibility of the satirist; it is a human defect which is peculiarly his own which Swift dramatizes and criticizes here; and this is why any sensitive reader must feel the profound ambiguity of the fourth book every time he reads it.

There are yet more ironic traps and inflections to contend with: if Swift allowed us at any time to feel absolutely sure that we had probed to the very bottom of his irony, the irony would lose most of its capability to disturb and distress, and therefore much of its ability to change and enlighten. There is, for instance, the famous diatribe against Pride, which has been taken, rightly, I think, to be central to the whole experience of the *Travels*:

> My Reconcilement to the *Yahoo*-kind in general might not be so difficult, if they would be content with those Vices and Follies only which Nature hath entitled them to. I am not in the least provoked at the sight of a Lawyer, a Pick-pocket, a Colonel, a Fool, a Lord, a Gamester, a Politician, a Whoremunger, a Physician, an Evidence, a Suborner, an Attorney, a Traytor, or the

> like: This is all according to the due Course of Things:
> But, when I behold a Lump of Deformity, and Diseases
> both in Body and Mind, smitten with *Pride*, it im-
> mediately breaks all the Measures of my Patience . . .

The long list of human vocations is masterly in its juxta-
positions, each trade throwing light upon the next one in the
list and the one before. But it is even more pointed in its
irony when one observes who says it: the previous paragraph,
in its embittered revulsion, its utter lack of charity, its insane
withdrawnness, shares pride among several other vices, but
among the Seven Sins *superbia* – Pride – is the most prominent:

> I began last Week to permit my Wife to sit at Dinner
> with me, at the farthest End of a long Table; and to
> answer (but with the utmost Brevity) the few Questions
> I asked her. Yet the smell of a *Yahoo* continuing very
> offensive, I always keep my Nose well stopt with Rue,
> Lavender, or Tobacco-Leaves . . .

There is an extra, especially elegant, flourish to the irony
here when one recalls the prefatory 'Letter from Captain
Gulliver to his Cousin Sympson', which is written in the
persona of Gulliver as he returns to Rotherhithe *after* the
voyage to the Houyhnhnms. Of course, at the same time, it
is an author's preface, and so we are more than usually
conscious of the double face of the man who writes:

> I do in the next Place complain of my own great Want
> of Judgment, in being prevailed upon by the Intreaties
> and false Reasonings of you and some others, very
> much against mine own Opinion, to suffer my Travels to
> be published. Pray bring to your Mind how often I
> desired you to consider, when you insisted on the Motive
> of *publick Good*; that the *Yahoos* were a Species of Animals
> utterly incapable of Amendment by Precepts or
> Examples: And so it hath proved; for instead of seeing
> a full Stop put to all Abuses and Corruptions, at least
> in this little Island, as I had Reason to expect: Behold,
> after above six Months Warning, I cannot learn that

my Book hath produced one single Effect according to
mine Intentions. . . . And, it must be owned, that seven
Months were a sufficient Time to correct every Vice
and Folly to which *Yahoos* are subject; if their Natures
had been capable of the least Disposition to Virtue or
Wisdom . . .

The arrogance of Lemuel Gulliver is so clear here as to
need no comment at all; what makes the passage, and the
whole letter, doubly interesting, is that it is as it were, retro-
flex; it is, in part at least, satire upon the ethical presumption
of the satirist. I have quoted elsewhere from Swift's joyful
letter to Ford: 'I have finished my Travells, and am now
transcribing them; they are admirable Things, and will
wonderfully mend the World.' Satirists commonly defend
their wrath by claiming a reforming zeal; satire 'on the
Motive of publick Good'; but Swift is far too wary even to
let the motives of the satirist pass by without inspection.
Even in satire on Pride there must be an element of vanity;
even this must be dissolved in a further extension to the
satire. So, as a preface to his greatest, and most proud,
satirical work; as a foretaste of his savage energy in lashing
the world, he reveals, with quiet irony, the Pride that lies
in *saeva indignatio* itself.

VII
Swift's Verse

Swift wrote a great deal of verse, and made no great claims for it: 'I have been only a man of rhymes, and that upon trifles, never having written serious couplets in my life, yet never without a moral view.' We should not take Swift's disclaimer too seriously: many 'trifles' survive which we could lose without too much regret; but there is enough really impressive work to justify the claim that Swift is among the best minor poets in the English language.

The odd thing is that some of the most impressive poems Swift wrote are, avowedly, trifles. 'The Humble Petition of Frances Harris', for instance, creates, in seventy-five lines of tumbling, awkward monologue, a character as fully 'alive' as anything in Defoe, Congreve or Sheridan; indeed, its vividness challenges comparison with Chaucer, Shakespeare or Dickens. There is no obvious 'moral view' in it; no apparent intention except to amuse by the dramatic precision with which Mistress Harris's tone of voice, her habit of language, and therefore her whole mode of life is represented. The loose, shambling gait of the irregular fourteeners is ideal for the purpose.

'The Humble Petition' is the poetry of the particular: the most obvious effort of verse in the early eighteenth century was towards the precise and memorable generalization. Pope's verse and Swift's prose are both at their best, perhaps, when there is a calculated tension between the particular and the general; between the immediate satirical observation of detail and the larger statement of general moral truths. Swift, by habit, usually reserved verse for the more immediate observation, though there are moments, as we shall see, when he goes beyond the detail and becomes far more comprehensive in his view of life.

'A Description of the Morning' and 'A Description of a City Shower', for instance, are skilful satirical parodies of the conventions of the pastoral idyll and the heroic mode, but it is not as parodies that they survive to demand our attention; their rapid, compact and vivid pictures of urban life are, as it were, held suspended in the closely organized pattern of the couplet form:

> Now hardly here and there an Hackney-Coach
> Appearing, show'd the Ruddy Morns Approach.
> Now *Betty* from her Masters Bed had flown,
> And softly stole to discompose her own.
> The Slipshod Prentice from his Masters Door,
> Had par'd the Dirt, and Sprinkled round the Floor.
> Now *Moll* had whirl'd her Mop with dext'rous Airs,
> Prepar'd to Scrub the Entry and the Stairs.
> The Youth with Broomy Stumps began to trace
> The Kennel-Edge, where Wheels had worn the Place.
> The Smallcoal-Man was heard with Cadence deep,
> 'Till drown'd in Shriller Notes of Chimney-Sweep,
> Duns at his Lordships Gate began to meet,
> And Brickdust *Moll* had Scream'd through half the Street.
> The Turnkey now his Flock returning sees,
> Duly let out a Nights to Steal for Fees.
> The watchful Bailiffs take their silent Stands,
> And School-Boys lag with Satchels in their Hands.

It is the *clarity* of Swift's account of life that strikes us first here, I think: the action is limited to what one can see and hear, as in an adroitly cut sequence in a film. Each person who appears is vivid and separate, at the same time a representative type; however, the whole adds up to a co-herent account of a street, a city, a way of life. Comparison with a twentieth-century poem may help to bring out my point. Here is T. S. Eliot's early 'observation', 'Morning at the Window':

They are rattling breakfast plates in basement kitchens,
And along the trampled edges of the street
I am aware of the damp souls of housemaids
Sprouting despondently at area gates.

The brown waves of fog toss up to me
Twisted faces from the bottom of the street,
And tear from a passer-by with muddy skirts
An aimless smile that hovers in the air
And vanishes along the level of the roofs.

Eliot's poem happens in the poet's mind (or his *persona*'s);
Swift's is out there in the open street. Eliot's housemaids
(poor things) have no existence except as sensations vaguely
perceived on the outskirts of a reflective consciousness.
Swift's Betty and Moll, though they are meant in the first
place as types, gain some degree of separate life even in the
few lines given to them. It is an *external* kind of life: they are
seen and heard, nothing more; but we do not expect more,
it is not that kind of poem.

Something has happened in between the two poems; and
since it took two centuries to happen it will not be worth
our while to try to describe the change in sensibility fully,
but we can pick out one thing which more than anything
else summarizes what separates the two: the novel happened
in between.

In Swift's day people were beginning to feel a great thirst
for reality: epic and tragedy didn't fulfil this need any more,
though poets and dramatists dreamed of epic and tragedy
still. Comedy was lively still, and throughout the whole
period, from *She Would if She Could* through to *She Stoops to
Conquer* comedy follows a general drift towards realism. But
it was really Defoe who hit on the most effective way to
satisfy his audience's thirst for a precise and detailed
account of actual life: the novel began.

The impulse towards the real lies behind Swift's satire,
even when, as in *Gulliver's Travels*, he employs fantasy to
hook in the reader to his view of things; but in his satire
Swift cultivates the art of seeing things from an extraordinary
point of view. Here, in 'A Description of the Morning' he

challenges the extraordinary point of view which had become conventional in poetry with a catalogue of facts, seen with an eye as ordinary, as little fanciful, as curious for detail as possible.

But it is only the beginning of a process of change which is possibly as important to our whole way of life as the discovery of electricity or of steam. Swift and Eliot plot positions towards each end of the process; let us examine a point somewhere in between the two. This is from Dickens' *The Old Curiosity Shop*, where Nell and her grandfather walk out in the morning:

> All was so still at that early hour, that the few pale people whom they met seemed as much unsuited to the scene, as the sickly lamp which had been here and there left burning, was powerless and faint in the full glory of the sun.
>
> Before they had penetrated very far into the labyrinth of men's abodes which yet lay between them and the outskirts, this aspect began to melt away, and noise and bustle to usurp its place. Some straggling carts and coaches rumbling by, first broke the charm, then others came, then others yet more active, then a crowd. The wonder was, at first, to see a tradesman's room window open, but it was a rare thing to see one closed; then, smoke rose slowly from the chimneys, and sashes were thrown up to let in air, and doors were opened, and servant girls, looking lazily in all directions but their brooms, scattered brown clouds of dust into the eyes of shrinking passengers, or listened disconsolately to milkmen who spoke of country fairs, and told of waggons in the mews, with awnings and all things complete, and gallant swains to boot, which another hour would see upon their journey.

Here Dickens very certainly satisfies our thirst for a detailed account of the real; but the observation is repeatedly coloured and directed by the mind of the observer: 'the few pale people whom they met *seemed* . . .'; 'The wonder was, at first . . .', and so on. But the interchange between the

objective description and the subjective impression leaves
room, as it were, for the servant girls to grow into a rather
fuller life than either Swift or Eliot allow. They are not
entirely seen from the outside; they are not just an incident
in the author's consciousness; they clearly have hopes,
disappointments, grudges, enthusiasms and dreams of their
own.

To return to Swift; the 'moral view' which is in suspension
in 'A Description of the Morning' is closely bound in with
his insistence, felt throughout the prose satires too, that we
should see 'things as they really are'; and yet the poem does
not allow him to describe 'things as they really are' as
completely or comprehensively as, for instance, *Gulliver's
Travels*. There, 'things as they really are' include, not just
the external objects, but the strange complex pattern of
distortions and prejudice, desire and repulsion, belief and
illusion which change man, as they change Gulliver, every
time he experiences a new situation, or rediscovers an old.

'A Description of a City Shower' does something slightly
more complex. To the modern reader the precise detail is
obscured a little by the witty parody of current conventions
in epic simile. But Swift makes the reader distance himself
from the city, encouraging him to see it as a whole; not as a
grand rhetorical unity, but as a fortuitous collection of
accidental facts: cats and coffee-houses; mops and shops;
sedan-chairs and sempstresses; anarchically diverse details
which at last are overwhelmed in the final torrential image
of urban chaos.

> Now from all Parts the swelling Kennels flow
> And bear their Trophies with them, as they go:
> Filths of all Hues and Odours seem to tell
> What Streets they sail'd from, by the Sight and Smell.
> They, as each Torrent drives with rapid Force,
> From *Smithfield*, or *St Pulchre's* shape their Course;
> And in huge Confluent join at *Snow-Hill* Ridge,
> Fall from the *Conduit* prone to Holbourn Bridge.
> Sweepings from Butcher's Stall, Dung, Guts and
>   Blood

> Drown'd Puppies, stinking Sprats, all drench'd in
>   Mud,
> Dead Cats, and Turnip-Tops come tumbling down
>   the Flood.

Oddly, the avowed object of the last three lines misfires.
Swift is parodying the current vogue for the rhyming triplet
with an Alexandrine (twelve-syllable line) to end with; but
the comic stretching both of rhyme and rhythm gives the
verse a welcome irregularity and flexibility of movement. The
tumbling effect produced mimics precisely the flooding
sweep of water and offal and rubbish into the river.

Swift's approach to verse was, for most of his career,
very informal: he wrote poems for his friends, he wrote
poems for himself; he composed broadsides on contemporary
matters which engaged his combative interest, like the
trouble over Wood's Halfpence and the notorious South Sea
Bubble; he wrote lampoons, often of a very dangerous kind,
on political matters. But he always gives the impression (and
perhaps sometimes strives with elaborate energy to give the
impression) that he writes negligently, to amuse himself
and his readers in a spare moment.

Even the most formally designed of his poems, 'Cadenus and Vanessa', plays with the formal mannerisms of
eighteenth-century verse in such a way as to suggest that
nothing should be taken seriously. In fact, behind the brittle
conventional mechanisms there runs the sad and terrible
theme that a true and intelligent relationship between the
sexes is impossible (or very near it). If this were careless
cynicism, a negligent pose of the kind Restoration comic
playwrights were fond of using as a mask, 'Cadenus and
Vanessa' would be a much less painful poem than it is. But
Swift is serious, and has to take pains to hide his seriousness.

He lightens the charge against the human race, and
particularly against women, by arguing it in the chaste and
cold never-never land of a neo-Classic Olympus, and by
importing into that rarefied atmosphere lawyers who speak
in their authentically dusty dialect:

> Which Crimes aforesaid, (*with her Leave*)
> Were (*as he humbly did conceive*)
> Against our Sov'reign Lady's Peace,
> Against the Statute in that Case,
> Against her Dignity and Crown:
> Then pray'd an Answer, and sat down.

The absurd contrast of snuff-coloured legal jargon and the marmoreal neo-Classic idyll of the setting deflects our attention from the passionate argument which goes on beneath the surface. For all his satire upon the amorous illusions of the lover Swift still feels cheated and horrified by the sensuality of women; the body distresses him:

> But Women now feel no such Fire
> And only know the gross Desire.
> Their passions move in lower Spheres,
> Where-e'er Caprice or Folly steers:
> A Dog, a Parrot, or an Ape,
> Or, some worse Brute in human Shape,
> Engross the Fancies of the Fair,
> The few soft Moments they can spare,
> From Visits to receive and pay;
> From Scandal, Politicks, and Play.

Samuel Johnson said of Swift: 'he always understands himself, and his readers always understand him'. Certainly Swift's favourite verse form, the octosyllabic couplet with four stresses, to a line, helps to produce an effect of light-hearted clarity. We are more accustomed to longer rhyming intervals, like those of the heroic couplet, the sonnet, or the ballad stanza, and the rapid succession of rhyme hurries us along from line to line as if we are not expected to pay any great attention to any of them. This is particularly so when Swift allows himself the licence of extending the line by one weak syllable to accommodate a feminine rhyme:

> I find, said he, she wants a Doctor
> Both to adore her and instruct her.

or:

> A Gownman of a diff'rent Make;
> Whom *Pallas*, once *Vanessa*'s Tutor,
> Had fix'd on for her Coadjutor.

In the latter example, particularly, the cheeky boldness of the double (nearly triple) rhyme, and the slight wrench in the proper stress pattern this involves, throws us off balance for a while. Much of the wit lies in a calculated awkwardness of rhyme and rhythm: it is difficult to take it entirely seriously, as Dryden and Pope demanded to be taken seriously, even when they were being humorous. One could say that in 'Cadenus and Vanessa' this deliberately careless manner helps to absolve him from full responsibility for the passionate intensities of hate and fear which constantly creep into the verse only to be partially concealed by the negligent manner. It also helps to compensate for the chilly neutrality of the Houyhnhnm-ish virtue he recommends in place of the sexual passions which make him flinch away:

> But Friendship in its greatest Height,
> A constant, rational Delight,
> On Virtue's Basis fix'd to last,
> When Love's Allurements long are past;
> Which gently warms, but cannot burn;
> He gladly offers in return:
> His want of Passion will redeem,
> With Gratitude, Respect, Esteem:
> With that Devotion we bestow,
> When Goddesses appear below.

However, 'Cadenus and Vanessa' is far from being Swift's most typical poem; in it he is using verse as a shield against too close a personal involvement. More often his verse is the medium for most personal communication with friends rather than defence against the dangers of intimacy. Whereas 'Cadenus and Vanessa' dilutes emotion by witty elaboration, the birthday poems to Stella, for instance, convey the warmth and genuineness of that relationship with directness, honesty and sensitivity.

Swift is capable of expressing less intimate relationships, too, with a delicate truthfulness; sometimes, it seems, verse is the only way in which he can convey exactly what he wishes to say. 'An Apology to Lady Carteret' is addressed to the wife of the Viceroy of Ireland with whom Swift had recently been in vigorous combat over the affair of Wood's coinage. The Carterets were able to overcome the bitterness of political strife and strike up a friendship with the turbulent Dean, but Swift's shyness and diffidence at first proved to be an obstacle; Swift didn't turn up to honour Lady Carteret's first invitation:

> The Message told, he gapes, and stares,
> And scarce believes his Eyes, or Ears.
> Could not conceive what it should mean,
> And fain would hear it told again.
> But then the 'Squire so trim and nice
> 'Twere rude to make him tell it twice,
> So bow'd, was thankful for the Honour;
> And wou'd not fail to wait upon her.
> His Beaver brush'd, his Shoes, and Gown,
> Away he trudges into Town;
> Passes the Lower Castle Yard,
> And now advancing to the Guard,
> He trembles at the Thoughts of State;
> For, conscious of his sheepish Gait,
> His Spirits of a sudden fail'd him,
> He stop'd, and could not tell what ail'd him.
> What was the Message I receiv'd?
> Why certainly the Captain rav'd?
> To dine with her! and come at Three!
> Impossible! it can't be me.
> Or may be, I mistook the Word;
> My Lady – it must be my Lord.

Here, the rapid informality of the short couplet is used to quite different purpose than in 'Cadenus and Vanessa'. The tight rhythm and the chiming rhyme of the verse contrast with the plain simplicity of the words, each one in its true conversational order: the rhythms of speech win over the spare metrical patterns, not by breaking them down, but by absorbing them. This oddly achieved power of ease gives the verse both dramatic directness and the sense of a great firmness of control beneath the careless sequence of the surface. Thus he is able to achieve a certain dignity of pathos when he explains his awkward diffidence to the Lady Carteret:

> If you, who long have breath'd the Fumes
> Of City Fogs and crowded Rooms,
> Do now solicitously shun
> The cooler Air, and dazzling Sun;
> If his Majestick Eye you flee,
> Learn hence t'excuse and pity me.
> Consider what it is to bear
> The powder'd Courtier's witty Sneer;
> To see th'important Man of Dress
> Scoffing my College Aukwardness,
> To see the strutting Cornet's Sport,
> To run the Gauntlet of the Court,
> Winning my Way by slow Approaches,
> Through Crowds of Coxcombs and of Coaches,
> From the first fierce cockaded Sentry,
> Quite thro' the Tribe of waiting Gentry;
> To pass so many crowded Stages,
> And stand the Staring of your Pages;
> And after all, to crown my Spleen
> Be told – *You are not to be seen.*

If this were a public poem in the sense that, for instance, most of Pope's poems were public, we might decide there is an unwelcome note of self-pity here; but the whole tone of the poem works against our taking it that way. The poem is part of the easy commerce of friendship; the potential self pity is dissolved away by the lightness with which Swift admits his vulnerability and loneliness.

Things tend to be different in Swift's political poems; personal animus takes over far too often, and Swift frequently allows himself to indulge in character assassination of the meanest kind, giving the lie to his claim in 'Verses on his Own Death', that 'He lash'd the Vice, but spar'd the Name'.

In 'Directions for Making a Birthday Song', for instance, there is the elaborately sly hint that George II is a bastard:

> Why, then, appoint him son of Jove,
> Who met his mother in a grove:
> To this we freely shall consent,
> Well knowing what the poets meant;
> And in their sense, 'twixt me and you
> It may be literally true.

The standards of ordinary courtesy may not all apply in satire, but it is, surely, gratuitously ungallant to make so much sport of Queen Caroline's age as Swift does, and it is noticeable that Swift, in an effort to keep the satirical pressure high, begins to do to death some of the devices, like comic double rhyme, which elsewhere serve him so well:

> Next call him Neptune: With his trident
> He rules the sea; you see him ride in't
> And, if provok'd, he soundly ferks his
> Rebellious waves with rods, like Xerxes.

Swift's political satire is far more often effective in poems like 'Mad Mullinix and Timothy', in which the dialogue form enables him to use his consummate skill in marrying the spirited rhythms of colloquial speech with the sharp-paced octosyllabic metre. However, the two most successful political satires are two late products; 'On Poetry, a Rapsody' and 'The Legion Club'.

'The Legion Club' gains much of its energy from Swift's own fearful sense of the nearness of insanity, not only in his personal life but also in society as a whole, lying just below the surface of the world's conventional patterns of behaviour. The poem takes its title from the fifth chapter of the Gospel of St Mark, in which Christ exorcises the unclean spirits which have possessed the Gadarene madman, and transfers them to swine. Christ asks the spirit for a name, and he replies 'My name is Legion, for we are many'. The name, the 'Legion Club' is given to the Irish Parliament, but in the end this, and the various petty politicians who are named, matter little. The satire takes on the character of a tragi-

comic descent into hell; partly this is enforced by the insistent reference to the fifth book of the *Aeneid*, where Virgil's
hero descends into Hades. But, over and above this, there is
the black wit of the language, which, in its vivid pictorial
quality, reminds one forcibly of Hogarth, and anticipates
Shelley's 'Mask of Anarchy' and 'Peter Bell the Third' in its
emphatic terseness.

It's an unpleasant poem, a poem which is itself very
close to hell and madness, and its diabolical intensity is
made even greater, paradoxically, by the off-hand raciness
of its metrical structure: the couplets are in seven-syllabled
lines (except where the feminine endings stretch the line to
eight syllables), with four stresses crowding into the very
short line. The effect is even more wry and abrupt than the
true octosyllabic couplet, and the tricky feminine lines tie
up each couplet with an even bolder-faced air of challenge:

> As I strole the City, oft I
> Spy a building large and lofty
> Not a Bow-shot from the College,
> Half the Globe from Sense and Knowledge.

The line proves to be an ideal vehicle for vehement
denunciation, as might be expected; what is, perhaps, less
to be expected is the way in which it moves so easily into
the epic mode (not mock epic, but farcical epic) of the descent
into hell. Here one has a near equivalent to the odd blend
of fantastic farce and profound solemnity which Aristophanes
exploited:

> Near the Door an Entrance gapes
> Crouded round with antic Shapes;
> *Poverty*, and *Grief* and *Care*,
> Causeless *Joy*, and true *Despair*;
> *Discord* periwigged with Snakes
> See the dreadful Strides she takes.
> By this odious Crew beset,
> I begin to rage and fret,
> And resolv'd to break their Pates,
> 'Ere we enter'd at the Gates;

> Had not *Clio* in the Nick,
> Whisper'd me, let down your Stick;
> What, said I, is this the Mad-house?
> These, she answered, are but Shadows,
> Phantoms bodiless and vain
> Empty visions of the Brain.

Clio's answer adds an odd new dimension, putting the reader into some confusion as to the true relationship between fantasy and reality in the satire. In the more obvious sense it can be taken to mean that the inmates of the parliament or madhouse, are unreal and meaningless; in another, penumbral sense, it casts doubt upon the sanity of the *persona* who sees them. The ambiguity hides in the shadows of the satire; the *persona* is involved in a curious way with the chaos; a chaos which drains him of his spirit and energy just as the careless visitor seeking amusement in Bedlam may be more deeply involved in the madness than he would care to admit. I take it that this is what lies behind the *persona*'s curiously hasty withdrawal at the end of the poem; a deliberately weak ending in which all the vehement animus dissolves in a tame oath and the taking of snuff; an ending in weary dismissal rather than violence and hatred:

> Keeper, I must now retire,
> You have done what I desire:
> But I feel my Spirits spent,
> With the Noise, the Sight, the Scent.
>
> Pray be patient, you shall find
> Half the best are still behind;
> You have hardly seen a Score,
> I can shew two hundred more.
>
> Keeper, I have seen enough
> Taking then a Pinch of Snuff;
> I concluded, looking round 'em
> May their God, the Devil confound 'em.

The tone of the poem is rough and embittered, even at times coarsely violent, but there is a genuinely powerful pressure of emotion which drives the verse on, and justifies the impassioned emphasis. One is reminded forcibly of 'The Mask of Anarchy' in such a passage as:

> Who is that Hell-featured Brawler,
> Is it Satan? No, 'tis *W*[*aller*]
> In what figure can a Bard dress,
> *Jack*, the Grandson of *Sir Hardress*?
> Honest Keeper, drive him further,
> In his looks are Hell and Murther;
> See the scowling Visage drop
> Just as when he murther'd *T*[*hrop*]

Swift's freedom, one might almost say recklessness, is the freedom of an old man with nothing to lose. 'On Poetry: A Rapsody', written in 1733, three years earlier than 'The Legion Club', is more circumspect. As in 'Directions for Making a Birthday Song' Swift ironically assumes the guise of adviser to the aspirant poet as a cover for political satire. But the satire is not narrowly limited to political and court personalities, as it is in the 'Directions'. Swift satirizes Grub Street poets, pamphleteers and critics with energy and wit; indeed he goes further still, probing to discover the innate perversity of the human race:

> *Brutes* find out where their Talents lie:
> A *Bear* will not attempt to fly:
> A founder'd *Horse* will oft debate,
> Before he tries a five-barr'd Gate:
> A Dog by Instinct turns aside,
> Who sees the Ditch too deep and wide,
> But Man we find the only Creature,
> Who, led by *Folly*, combats *Nature*:
> Who, when *she* loudly cries, *Forbear*,
> With Obstinacy fixes there;
> And, where his Genius least inclines,
> Absurdly bends his whole Designs.

The theme is a familiar one for a reader of Swift: not only is it the basis of an earlier poem 'The Beast's Confession'; it is implicit in the fourth book of *Gulliver's Travels*, where

Gulliver, being typical of man, attempts to be what man cannot be. The word 'Nature' crystallizes certain complex and deeply felt assumptions about man and his place within an ordered universe: man was the only animal who dared to challenge its harmony. But – the paradoxes of the age are innumerable – it was conceded that Nature necessarily involved conflict. The chaos of the Civil War was still remembered; the time when Hobbes, the most important philosopher of the generation of regicides, declared that the life of man was nasty, poor, brutish and short. For Swift, who had seen the Irish peasants starving and soldiers returning maimed and blinded from Whig wars, Hobbes was still right: 'Hobbes clearly proves that ev'ry Creature/ Lives in a State of War by Nature'. The sinister implications of this are dissolved into laughter, but a bitter laughter, using a microscope borrowed from Leeuwenhoek via Lemuel Gulliver to place the feeble squabbles of Grub Street in perspective:

> So, Nat'ralists observe, a Flea
> Hath smaller Fleas that on him prey,
> And these have smaller yet to bite 'em
> And so proceed *ad infinitum*.

The wry, perverse satirical manner, the briskly contemptuous tone, conceal a greater and more anxious concern for the dangers of man's condition than would at first appear. Swift chooses advice to a poet as a vehicle for this general satire, and shows infinite contempt for the inadequate poet, but at the same time he makes the highest possible claims for poetry in his paradoxical way; the following must be taken as a double irony:

> Not Beggar's Brat on Bulk begot;
> Not Bastard of a Pedlar *Scot*;
> Not Boy brought up to cleaning Shoes;
> The Spawn of *Bridewell*, or the Stews;
> Not Infants dropt, the spurious Pledges
> Of *Gypsies* litt'ring under Hedges,
> Are so disqualify'd by Fate

> To rise in *Church*, or *Law*, or *State*,
> As he, whom *Phoebus* in his Ire
> Hath *blasted* with Poetick Fire.

One can interpret the expletive, alliterative energy of this either way, as further insult to the inadequate Grub Street hack or as a genuine protest at the way the world treats its great men. The ambiguity is key to the ironic strategy of the poem. The 'old experienc'd Sinner' who gives his advice to the young aspirant to poetry is wise in the ways of the world, and follows them; pretending to shape poetry and Wit to the world rather than to shape the world by poetry, which is, it is implied, the proper way.

So Swift maps out the Poet's Progress: the first stage, to attempt to write as a real Wit and poet should, following the impulse of his own Genius; the second stage, when this fails, to try and fail again. The third stage, try once more, taking into account all the critics' comments, and when this too fails, write for a party or for a political figure. If the failed poet can't stomach this, he can always be a critic. Whether he ends up a party hack or a coffee-house pundit the poet has travelled, like one of Hogarth's heroes, through the whole range of truth and falsehood; from aspiring to be the true artist who tries to mend the world to becoming, at last, a servant of the world's vices, shaped by the world's changeable whims.

The failure is a failure of Wit; and here, as elsewhere in Swift, this means not simply a lack of invention, but also an inadequately developed sense of the fitting, the harmonious, the relevant, the 'Natural'. Swift evokes this kind of failure in the following passage; like so many other passages in which Swift's inventive genius is most fully engaged, it oddly resembles the wit of the Metaphysical poets:

> Or oft when Epithets you link,
> In gaping Lines to fill a Chink;
> Like Stepping-stones to save a Stride,
> In Streets where Kennels are too wide:
> Or like a Heel-piece to support

A Cripple with one Foot too short:
Or like a Bridge that joins a Marish
To Moorlands of a diff'rent Parish.
So, have I seen ill-coupled Hounds,
Drag diff'rent Ways in miry Grounds.
So Geographers in *Afric* Maps
With Savage Pictures fill their Gaps;
An o'er uninhabitable Downs
Place Elephants for want of Towns.

The resemblance to the Metaphysical poets is doubly ironical; it is the late Metaphysical habit of the decorative conceit, the kind of thing which Samuel Johnson attacks in his *Life of Cowley*, which Swift is pillorying here. And yet Swift contrives to give us some of the delight we feel in the deliberately outrageous metaphor while at the same time putting those who cultivate it to hide their poverty of Wit in their proper places.

Swift is above all an author who insists on the Greek maxim 'Know thyself'; again and again his satires return to this fundamental theme. Johnson, who, though he knew that there were virtues which preceded lucidity, was all his life deeply concerned with self understanding and precision and clarity of expression, praised Swift for his straightness: 'he always understands himself, and his readers always understand him'. Johnson's words might be interpreted as expressing some limitation as well as achievement, particularly in the present age, when certain kinds of obscurity are prized for their own sake, but there is no doubt what were the qualities Johnson admired in Swift: 'all his verses exemplify his own definition of a good style – they consist of "proper words in proper places".'

One would expect an Apologia like 'Verses on the Death of Dr Swift, D.S.P.D., Written by Himself, November 1731' to be unusually detached and honest in its self-criticism, coming as it does from an author who saw the vices of others so clearly, and strove so hard to be truthful about his own. Pope, who was one of Swift's closest friends (though not especially distinguished for truthfulness or lack of vanity) wrote to Orrery that the Verses were 'too vain in some respects, and in one or two particulars not true'. Dr King, to whom Swift had entrusted the publication of the poem, mauled and cut it drastically, excising whatever he, Pope, or other friends of Swift thought to be self-congratulatory, self-centred or simply untrue. The poem remains full of the note of anxious and indignant self-defence, even of self-pity.

And yet the poem would have been far less interesting if it had shown more real composure, more inner peace. Moreover, it would have been inconsistent with all we know of Swift and his writings: a personality so troubled with self-contradiction and so driven by inner paradox; a body of written work which takes its origin from the personal conflicts and always, even in the most completely successful work, remains profoundly ambiguous in motive and meaning. It would have been far less moving if Swift had really shown he 'knew himself', far less of a complement to the complex and shifting ironies of that magnificent assault on pride, *Gulliver's Travels*; if Swift had not permitted himself the authentic accent of pride:

> He never thought an Honour done him
> Because a Duke was proud to own him:
> Would rather slip aside, and chuse
> To talk with Wits in dirty Shoes:
> Despis'd the Fools with Stars and Garters,
> So often seen caressing *Chartres*:
> He never courted Men in Station,
> *Nor Persons had in Admiration*;
> Of no Man's Greatness was afraid,
> Because he sought for no Man's Aid.
> Though trusted long in great Affairs,
> He gave himself no haughty Airs:
> Without regarding private Ends,
> Spent all his Credit for his Friends:
> And only chose the Wise and Good;
> No Flatt'rers; no Allies in Blood;
> But succour'd Virtue in Distress,
> And seldom fail'd of good Success;

As Numbers in their Hearts must own,
Who, but for him, had been unknown.

Pride comes in many forms, and can, after all, be justified; as much of Swift's pride is here; but it is the kind of Apologia in which pride, justified with a certain insistent clamour, shows itself at last insecure, and slips over into a cry of pathos:

Poor POPE will grieve a Month; and GAY
A Week; and ARBUTHNOTT a Day.
ST JOHN himself will scarce forbear,
To bite his Pen and drop a Tear.
The rest will give a Shrug and cry,
I'm sorry; but we all must dye.
Indifference clad in Wisdom's Guise,
All Fortitude of Mind supplies:
For how can stony Bowels melt,
In those who never Pity felt;
When *We* are lash'd, *They* kiss the Rod;
Resigning to the Will of God.

How strange it is that the Swift who created the Struldbrugs in order to draw the very human reader into an admission of the absurdity of fearing death, longing for immortality, grieving over the death of others, should write like this. If, in Luggnagg, Fortitude is a virtue which springs, not from indifference, but from intelligent realism, why should things be otherwise at the death of this one, old, quarrelsome, sick and angry man, on whom nobody depends and who has outlived his generation?

But there is a sense in which entire consistency and purity of motive is the last thing one should look for in a srtirist of Swift's peculiar kind. A man who feels no fear of death, no vainglory or violent irrational impulses, no sense of grievance or injustice at the neglect of others is not a man equipped to satirize mankind for fear of death, pride, irrationality, or self-importance. Swift's satire is not consistent with the kind of self-knowledge that has enabled a man to come to rest, entirely at peace with himself. It is the product of a continuing and strenuous internal struggle, and the violence of conflict shows in every feature and contour of his work, often raw and unassimilated; sometimes crude and distasteful, never entirely serene or assured. The word 'mature', with all its evasive and uncertain implications, so useful to the modern critic seeking for a broad gesture of approval which will not commit him too deeply to a precise meaning, is not an easy word to use of Swift, though T. S. Eliot uses it in his essay on Tourneur in a way which begs all sorts of unexpected questions about maturity: 'Tourneur's "suffering, cynicism and despair" . . . are static; they might be prior to experience, or be the fruit of but little; Swift's is the progressive cynicism of the mature and disappointed man of the world'. But, in a way, the only coherence about the world in Swift's view *is* his disappointment; and his cynicism is the defeat of a trusting child, whose trust reveals itself each time he asks, in ever more shockingly innocent ways, whether there is anything left in humanity to trust. If the stout armour of his satire, secreted as a defence for this, the most vulnerable of all men, against all the world's offences, makes Swift a 'mature . . . man of the world', then to be a man of the world involves far more suffering and instability of emotion than the poise, assurance and ability to manipulate one's surroundings that 'man of the world' usually implies.

Swift never achieves or expresses an emotionally or intellectually coherent view of the world. On the other hand, his restless questioning, which grows from his own intensity of suffering, remains capable of upsetting the poise of every new generation, setting each reader the problem of himself.

Saintsbury remarks that Swift is 'the most interesting study of literary character that we have'. I have argued that the most important thing which Swift does is to make each of us, his readers, more interesting, by forcing us into strange, compelling and challenging situations and letting us fight our own way out. The two ideas have something in common: Swift offers more internal contradictions; more opportunity for speculation and argument about the relationship between the artist and his work and the reader and his work than artists commonly do. For all his use of diverse satirical *personae* Swift never creates a character that is not partly the reader, and is not, in a queerly persistent way, partly Swift himself.

We can, and perhaps should, reverse this equation for the 'Verses on his own Death'. The 'Verses' are as much about himself, and no more about himself than is 'A Modest Proposal'; Dr Swift is as much truth and as much convenient fiction as any of the several 'Gullivers' of the *Travels*. The 'Verses' are a moving fiction; a last self-justification of a dramatic character who was a little more weak, violent, worthy, pugnacious, brilliant, proud, intelligent, witty and stupid than any of us. The brilliant use of the colloquial idiom matched perfectly with the pert, abrupt couplet makes the fiction sharp and clear, not just as a comment upon a man but as an abrasive comment on his society:

> My female Friends, whose tender Hearts
> Have better learn'd to act their Parts,
> Receive the News in *doleful Dumps*,
> 'The Dean is dead (*and what is Trumps?*)
> 'Then Lord have Mercy on his Soul
> '(Ladies I'll venture for the *Vole*)'

There is less dignity in the poem than in other, more directly truthful poems, like some of the birthday poems to Stella. But we do not value Swift firstly either for dignity or for truth: except as far as truth is the sting of pain that warns us of the coming of sickness, danger and disease.

Select Bibliography

BIBLIOGRAPHIES

LOUIS A. LANDA AND J. E. TOBIN, *Jonathan Swift. A List of Critical Studies published from 1895 to 1945* (New York: Cosmopolitan Science and Art Service, 1945)

J. J. STATHIS, *A Bibliography of Swift Studies, 1945–65* (Nashville: Vanderbilt University Press, 1967)

HERMAN TEERINCK, *A Bibliography of the Writings of Jonathan Swift* (2nd ed., revised by A. H. Scouten, Philadelphia: University of Philadelphia Press, 1963)

EDITIONS

HERBERT DAVIS *et al.*, *The Prose Works of Jonathan Swift*, 14 vols. (Oxford: Blackwell, 1939–68)

HAROLD WILLIAMS, *Poems*, 3 vols (2nd ed., Oxford: Clarendon Press, 1958)

JOSEPH HORRELL, *Collected Poems*, 2 vols. (London: Routledge and Kegan Paul, 1958)

HAROLD WILLIAMS, *Correspondence*, 5 vols. (Oxford: Clarendon Press, 1963–5)

HERBERT DAVIS, *Drapier's Letters* (Oxford: Clarendon Press, 1935)

HAROLD WILLIAMS, *Journal to Stella*, 2 vols (Oxford: Clarendon Press, 1948)

A. C. GUTHKELCH AND D. NICOL SMITH, *A Tale of a Tub* (2nd ed., Oxford: Clarendon Press, 1958)

ERIC PARTRIDGE, *Swift's Polite Conversation* (London: Deutsch, 1963)

SELECTIONS

JOHN HAYWARD, *Selected Prose Works of Jonathan Swift* (London: Cresset Press, 1950)

RICARDO QUINTANA, *Gulliver's Travels and other Writings* (New York: Random House, 1958)

EDWARD ROSENHEIM JR., *Selected Prose and Poetry* (New York: Holt, Rinehart and Winston, 1959)

LOUIS A. LANDA, *Gulliver's Travels and other Writings* (Cambridge, Mass: Riverside Editions, 1960)

HERBERT DAVIS, *Jonathan Swift: Poetry and Prose* (Oxford: Clarendon Press, 1964)

PHILIP PINKUS, *Jonathan Swift: A Selection of his Works* (London: Macmillan, 1965)

BOOKS ON SWIFT

J. M. BULLITT, *Jonathan Swift and the Anatomy of Satire: A Study of Satiric Technique* (Cambridge, Mass: Harvard University Press, 1953)

A. E. CASE, *Four Essays on Gulliver's Travels* (Princeton: Princeton University Press, 1945)

HENRY CRAIK, *The Life of Jonathan Swift* (2nd ed., London: Macmillan, 1894)

HERBERT DAVIS, *Jonathan Swift: Essays on his Satire and Other Studies* (New York and London: Oxford University Press, 1964)

NIGEL DENNIS, *Jonathan Swift* (London: Weidenfeld and Nicolson, 1964)

DENIS DONOGHUE, *Jonathan Swift, A Critical Introduction* (Cambridge: Cambridge University Press, 1969)

W. A. EDDY, *Gulliver's Travels, A Critical Study* (Princeton: Princeton University Press, 1923)

IRVIN EHRENPREIS, *The Personality of Jonathan Swift* (London: Methuen, 1958)

IRVIN EHRENPREIS, *Swift: The man, his works and the age* (London: Methuen)
  Vol. I *Mr Swift and his Contemporaries* (1962)
  Vol. II *Dr Swift* (1967)
  Vol. III in progress

ROBERT C. ELLIOTT, *The Power of Satire: Magic, Ritual, Art* (Princeton: Princeton University Press, 1960)

W. B. EWALD, JR., *The Masks of Jonathan Swift* (Oxford: Blackwell, 1954)

OLIVER W. FERGUSON, *Jonathan Swift and Ireland* (Urbana: University of Illinois Press, 1962)

MICHAEL FOOT, *The Pen and the Sword* (London: MacGibbon & Kee, 1957)

PHILIP HARTH, *Swift and Anglican Rationalism: the religious background of A Tale of a Tub* (Chicago and London: University of Chicago Press, 1961)

MAURICE JOHNSON, *The Sin of Wit: Jonathan Swift as a Poet* (Syracuse: Syracuse University Press, 1950)

LOUIS A. LANDA, *Swift and the Church of Ireland* (Oxford: Clarendon Press, 1954)

RONALD PAULSON, *Theme and Structure in Swift's Tale of a Tub* (New Haven: Yale University Press, 1960)

EMILE PONS, *Swift: Les Années de Jeunesse et le 'Conte du Tonneau'* (Strasbourg: Istra, 1925)

MARTIN PRICE, *Swift's Rhetorical Art, A Study in Structure and Meaning* (New Haven: Yale University Press, 1953)

RICARDO QUINTANA, *The Mind and Art of Jonathan Swift* (2nd ed., London: Methuen, 1953)

RICARDO QUINTANA, *Swift, An Introduction* (Oxford: Clarendon Press, 1955)

C. J. RAWSON, *Gulliver and the Gentle Reader: Studies in Swift and Our Time* (London: Routledge and Kegan Paul, 1973)

E. W. ROSENHEIM, JR., *Swift and the Satirist's Art* (Chicago: University of Chicago Press, 1963)

MIRIAM K. STARKMAN, *Swift's Satire on Learning in A Tale of a Tub* (Princeton: Princeton University Press, 1950)

MILTON VOIGT, *Swift and the Twentieth Century* (Detroit: Wayne State University Press, 1964)

KATHLEEN WILLIAMS, *Jonathan Swift and the Age of Compromise* (Lawrence: University of Kansas Press, 1958)

COLLECTIONS OF ESSAYS ON SWIFT

FRANK BRADY (ed.) *Twentieth Century Interpretations of Gulliver's Travels* (Englewood Cliffs: Prentice Hall, 1968)

DENIS DONOGHUE (ed.) *Jonathan Swift: A Critical Anthology* (Harmondsworth: Penguin, 1971)

MILTON P. FOSTER (ed.) *A Casebook on Gulliver among the Houyhnhmms* (New York: T. Y. Crowell, 1961)

NORMAN A. JEFFARES (ed.) *Fair Liberty Was All his Cry. A Tercentenary Tribute* (London: Macmillan, 1967)

NORMAN A. JEFFARES (ed.) *Swift, Modern Judgments* (London: Macmillan, 1968)

C. J. RAWSON (ed.) *Focus: Swift* (London: Sphere Books, 1971)

JOHN TRAUGOTT (ed.) *Discussions of Jonathan Swift* (Boston: Heath, 1962)

ERNEST TUVESON (ed.) *Swift, a Collection of Critical Essays* (Englewood Cliffs: Prentice Hall, 1964)

BRIAN VICKERS (ed.) *The World of Jonathan Swift* (Oxford: Blackwell, 1968)

KATHLEEN WILLIAMS (ed.) *Swift: The Critical Heritage* (London: Routledge and Kegan Paul, 1970)

Background Reading

HISTORY AND BIOGRAPHY

J. C. BECKETT, *The Making of Modern Ireland, 1603–1923* (London: Faber, 1966)

J. C. BECKETT, *A Short History of Ireland* (London: Hutchinson, 1966)

W. S. CHURCHILL, *Marlborough, His Life and Times*, 2 vols. (London: Harrap, 1933–8)

EDMUND CURTIS, *A History of Ireland* (London: Methuen, 1950)

H. T. DICKINSON, *Bolingbroke* (London: Constable, 1970)

K. G. FEILING, *History of the Tory Party, 1640–1714* (Oxford: Clarendon Press, 1924)

J. A. FROUDE, *The English in Ireland in the Eighteenth Century*, 3 vols. (London: Longmans Green, 1881)

W. E. H. LECKY, *A History of Ireland in the Eighteenth Century*, 5 vols. (London: Longmans, 1892)

ANGUS MACINNES, *Robert Harley, Puritan Politician* (London: Gollancz, 1970)

GEORGE O'BRIEN, *Economic History of Ireland in the Eighteenth Century* (Dublin and London: Maunsel, 1918)

GEORGE O'BRIEN, *Economic History of Ireland in the Seventeenth Century* (Dublin and London: Maunsel, 1919)

J. H. PLUMB, *Sir Robert Walpole: The Making of a Statesman* (London: Cresset Press, 1956)

J. H. PLUMB, *Sir Robert Walpole: The King's Minister* (London: Cresset Press, 1960)

G. M. TREVELYAN, *England under Queen Anne*, 3 vols. (London: Longmans, 1931–4)

SOCIAL AND CULTURAL

ALEXANDRE BELJAME, *Men of Letters and the English Public in the Eighteenth Century, 1660–1744*, tr. E. O. Lorimer, ed. Bonamy Dobrée (London: Kegan Paul, Trench, 1948)

M. D. GEORGE, *England in Transition, Life and Work in the Eighteenth Century* (London: Routledge, 1931)

M. D. GEORGE, *London Life in the Eighteenth Century* (Harmondsworth: Penguin, 1966)

A. R. HUMPHREYS, *The Augustan World, Life and Letters in Eighteenth Century England* (London: Methuen, 1954)

PAT ROGERS, *Grub Street: Studies in a Subculture* (London: Methuen, 1972)

LESLIE STEPHEN, *English Literature and Society in the Eighteenth Century* (London: Duckworth, 1904)

J. R. SUTHERLAND, *Background for Queen Anne* (London: Methuen, 1939)

A. S. TURBERVILLE, *English Men and Manners in the Eighteenth Century, An Illustrated Narrative* (2nd ed., reprinted New York: Oxford University Press, 1957)

SCIENTIFIC AND INTELLECTUAL

HERBERT BUTTERFIELD, *The Origins of Modern Science* (London: Bell, 1957)

JOHN CRAIG, *Newton at the Mint* (Cambridge: Cambridge University Press, 1946)

R. J. FORBES AND E. J. DIJKSTERHUIS, *A History of Science and Technology*, 2 vols. (Harmondsworth: Penguin, 1963)

D. G. JAMES, *The Life of Reason: Hobbes, Locke, Bolingbroke* (London: Longmans, 1949)

R. F. JONES, *Ancients and Moderns: A Study of the Rise of the Scientific Movement in Seventeenth Century England* (2nd ed., St Louis: Washington University Press, 1961)

R. F. JONES et al., *The Seventeenth Century, Studies in the History of English Thought and Literature from Bacon to Pope* (Stanford: Stanford University Press, 1951)

A. O. LOVEJOY, *Essays in the History of Ideas* (Baltimore: Johns Hopkins Press, 1948)

HENRY LYONS, *The Royal Society, 1660–1940: A History of its Administration under its Charters* (Cambridge: Cambridge University Press, 1944)

KENNETH MACLEAN, *John Locke and English Literature of the Eighteenth Century* (New York: Russell and Russell, 1962)

M. H. NICOLSON, *The Microscope and the English Imagination* (Northampton, Mass: Smith College, 1935)

M. H. NICOLSON, *Newton Demands the Muse* (Princeton: Princeton University Press, 1946)

M. H. NICOLSON, *Science and Imagination* (New York: Cornell University Press, 1956)

THOMAS SPRAT, *The History of the Royal Society* (2nd ed., London, 1702)

LESLIE STEPHEN, *History of English Thought in the Eighteenth Century*, 2 vols. (3rd ed., London: Smith, Elder, 1902)

DOROTHY STIMSON, *Scientists and Amateurs: A History of the Royal Society* (New York: Schumann, 1948)

WILLIAM TEMPLE, *Five Miscellaneous Essays*, ed. S. H. Monk (Ann Arbor: University of Michigan Press, 1963)

FRANÇOIS MARIE AROUET DE VOLTAIRE, *Lettres Philosophiques, ou Lettres Anglaises*, ed. R. Naves (Paris: Garnier, 1951)

A. N. WHITEHEAD, *Science and the Modern World* (Cambridge: Cambridge University Press, 1926)

BASIL WILLEY, *The English Moralists* (London: Chatto & Windus, 1964)

BASIL WILLEY, *The Eighteenth Century Background* (London: Chatto & Windus, 1940)

BASIL WILLEY, *The Seventeenth Century Background* (London: Chatto & Windus, 1934)

WILLIAM WOTTON, *Reflections upon Ancient and Modern Learning, with a Dissertation upon the Epistles of Phalaris by Dr Bentley* (London: 1697)

Index of Swift's Works

General Index